PRAISE FOR

A $500 HOUSE IN DETROIT

"In this impassioned memoir, a young man finds a community flourishing in a city so depopulated that houses are worth less than a used Chevy. . . . Philp ably captures the frontier feel of Detroit as he laboriously rehabs his ruined house from foundation to roof. His homebuilding narrative is engrossing. . . . The book shines [in its depiction of] the 'radical neighborliness' of ordinary people in desperate circumstances."

—*Publishers Weekly*

"An important and powerful memoir that looks at the struggles and great efforts being spent on breathing life into a decayed city, and delves into the complicated and diverse people trying to carve out better futures."

—*New York Journal of Books*

"Experiences like Philp's . . . have rarely been told in such detail, or with as much awareness of their inherent cultural worldview."

—*The Architect's Newspaper*

"A fascinating inside look . . . Philp writes with exuberance and sincerity. . . . Inspiring."

—*Minneapolis Star Tribune*

"[Philp] quickly becomes an involved resident, using creativity, resourcefulness, ingenuity, and positive thinking to create a place for himself in a depressed city. . . . Highly recommended for general readers interested in the history and resurgence of Detroit and other U.S. cities."

—*Library Journal*

"Engrossing . . . Philp is a great storyteller, and he has done a good job of documenting his struggles to carve out a home. It's also easy to see why he intends to stay."

—*Booklist*

"[A] deeply felt, sharply observed personal quest to create meaning and community out of the fallen city's 'cinders of racism and consumerism and escape.' Philp ably outlines the broad issues of race and class in the city, but it is the warmth and liveliness of his storytelling that will win many readers. A standout in the Detroit rehab genre."

—*Kirkus Reviews* (starred review)

"Philp, the twenty-three-year-old recent college graduate, begins with a carcass, and over time constructs a house that becomes the prism through which he determines not only his place in the world but also what he wants out of life. A reader can't help but finish the book and begin asking themselves the same questions."

—*Los Angeles Review of Books*

"Philp's book gives us a glimpse of a world saved not by trying to do the right thing. But of doing the right thing because we have worked to transcend our differences and to know and care for each other across all the lines—including the lines between our backyards."
—Colin Beavan, *YES! Magazine*

"Lots of young bohemian types are fascinated by Detroit—land of the fabled $500 house!—but few take the plunge as headily as Drew Philp did, not only buying his own place but renovating it from the inside out, getting to know the neighbors, and learning about one of America's most fascinating cities as only a true resident can. Philp writes about his experience with sensitivity, humility, and humor, and his voice is a necessary addition to the literature of the Motor City."
—Mark Binelli, author of *Detroit City Is the Place to Be*

"Downright eloquent and deeply moving. Beyond the sheer, compelling force of Philp's writing, his account is insistently honest and full of insight. No shortcuts. No unrealistic fantasies. No pretenses of the sort that made my nerves twitch before I gave up on the literature of Nightmare Detroit. Philp the twenty-three-year-old kid comes alive convincingly, in all of his confused but determined effort to rebuild a house and sink roots. He captures the city in all of its horrors and hopes, contradictions and blind faith."
—Frank Viviano, eight-time Pulitzer Prize nominee
and *National Geographic* writer since 2001

REBUILDING an ABANDONED HOME

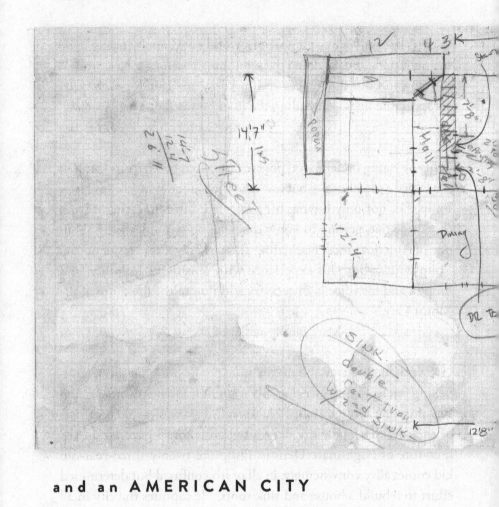

and an AMERICAN CITY

A $500 HOUSE
in DETROIT

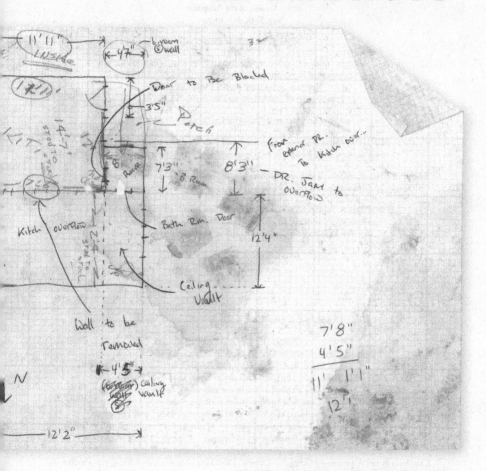

DREW PHILP

SCRIBNER

New York London Toronto Sydney New Delhi

SCRIBNER
An Imprint of Simon & Schuster, Inc.
1230 Avenue of the Americas
New York, NY 10020

First Scribner trade paperback edition April 2018

SCRIBNER and design are registered trademarks of The Gale Group, Inc.,
used under license by Simon & Schuster, Inc., the publisher of this work.

For information about special discounts for bulk purchases, please contact
Simon & Schuster Special Sales at 1-866-506-1949 or business@simonandschuster.com.

The Simon & Schuster Speakers Bureau can bring authors to your live event.
For more information or to book an event, contact the Simon & Schuster Speakers Bureau
at 1-866-248-3049 or visit our website at www.simonspeakers.com.

Interior design by Kyle Kabel

3   5   7   9   10   8   6   4

Library of Congress Cataloging-in-Publication Data

Names: Philp, Drew, author.
Title: A $500 house in Detroit : rebuilding an abandoned home
and an American city / by Drew Philp.
Other titles: Five hundred dollar house in Detroit |
Rebuilding an abandoned home and an American city
Description: New York : Scribner, [2017]
Identifiers: LCCN 2016046283| ISBN 9781476797984 | ISBN 9781476797991
Subjects: LCSH: Philp, Drew—Homes and haunts—Michigan—Detroit. | Detroit (Mich.)—
Biography. | Dwellings—Remodeling—Michigan—Detroit. | Urban renewal—
Michigan—Detroit—Citizen participation. | Subculture—Michigan—Detroit. |
Community development—Michigan—Detroit. | Working class whites—Michigan—Detroit—
Biography. | African Americans—Michigan—Detroit—Social conditions—21st century. |
Detroit (Mich.)—Race relations. | Generation Y—Biography.
Classification: LCC F574.D453 P55 2017 | DDC 307.3/4160977434—
dc23 LC record available at https://lccn.loc.gov/2016046283

ISBN 978-1-4767-9798-4
ISBN 978-1-4767-9799-1 (pbk)
ISBN 978-1-4767-9801-1 (ebook)

Portions of this book originally appeared in slightly different form on BuzzFeed.com.

For my family

"All right, then, I'll go to hell."

—Huck Finn

Contents

Contents

Author's Note

When I moved to Detroit I never intended to write a book. As such, many of the conversations and scenes depicted herein are reconstituted from memory or detailed journal entries. Each person in this book is real, and in their own private way attempting to build a castle from ashes. Names—unless indicated by surname—identifying details, and occasional places have been changed out of respect for this work, often best performed in quiet anonymity. In addition, burning down houses is a pastime in Detroit, and I wish no more danger on my community than I've already brought.

Best Bid

Starting bid: $500

I had one chance. We all did.

"Does anyone want anything else on page 267? Nothing on 267? 268? Anyone for page 268?"

The auctioneer read aridly from an enormous book in front of a crowd of murmuring people. I had come to a hotel downtown for a live auction of properties in Detroit. Starting bid was $500, less than the price of a decent television.

I looked like I'd come straight from the farm. My jeans had holes in them, my sweater was ripped, and I had on a woolen hat for the cold. I had purchased a brand-new Carhartt for the coming winter and it was still stiff. There was no heat in the house on the east side where I was living.

Aside from some Greeks bidding on numerous commercial properties and some mansions in the ritzy areas, my neighbor Jake and I were the only white people there. Jake had moved to Detroit from San Francisco two years before and was trying to buy the land next to his newly purchased, and formerly abandoned, home.

The structure I wanted had run wild, open and unclaimed for at least a decade.

"Page 271?"

A hand shot up from the audience.

"All right, 466 Franklin. Going once, going twice. 466 Franklin. 564 Franklin. Anyone for 564? Going once, going twice. 783—"

A group of three hands shot up in the middle of the bidding floor. One held an orange card with a number written on it. They stood, obviously a family, probably trying to buy back their house from foreclosure, or that of a relative, or to purchase the abandoned lots next to where they'd lived, maybe for decades. The county was auctioning off tens of thousands of properties that day, most abandoned and in Detroit.

"I see you guys. Keep calm. The starting bid is five hundred dollars for 783 Franklin, Detroit, Michigan. The gentleman standing in the back has the opening bid at five hundred. Any counteroffers? Five hundred dollars. Going once, going twice, three times, sold! To bidder 6579! Please stay in your seat. We'll come to you."

A generation earlier 783 Franklin would have been desirable property. Only a few people cared for Detroit now. This was October 2009 and the city's average home price hadn't even dropped to its lowest. Detroit certainly wasn't yet fashionable, and naïvely I thought it never would be.

It seemed almost everyone was moving out, a city of 2 million people down to fewer than 800,000. In the ten years between 2000 and 2010, 25 percent of the city's remaining population left. Half of the elementary-age children left. Since the 1940s more than 90 percent of manufacturing jobs had left. No longer was the talk about "white flight," but of "middle-class flight." The city that put the world on wheels drove away in the cars they no longer made.

I had three cashier's checks each for $500 in my pocket. It was just about every cent I had in the world. I was going to attempt to buy a quaint little Queen Anne I had recently boarded up as well as the two lots next to it. If someone were to bid against me on even one of the properties, my plan would fall apart. The auctioneer was now working through one of Detroit's oldest and wealthiest neighborhoods, and I waited, nervous.

When the auctioneer arrived at a property on Boston Street a young man in a United States Army uniform stood to bid. The houses in Boston-Edison are mansions that used to hold Henry Ford, members of the Motown stable, Detroit Tigers, politicians. Almost all of the houses still stood, but many were abandoned.

The soldier was sitting directly behind me and had brought his family, his sons and daughters, his aging and dignified parents, their hopeful eyes looking on at their father and son as he stood to attention and raised his orange bidding card.

"Going once . . ."

Someone had begun to bid against him. It was one of the Greeks, wearing blue jeans and a denim shirt, who had already purchased multiple properties that day. He obviously had deep pockets and was buying for an investment company against a man who wanted a place for his family.

The restless room became alert. The price climbed and the young soldier raised his sign higher with each increasing bid, now standing on his tiptoes at $15,000, beginning to bounce at eighteen, the room cheering him on, their hopes projected momentarily onto this one kid who had done good, who had escaped Detroit the only way he knew how, made something of himself, and come back.

At $20,000 the room audibly sighed. There were a smattering of boos at the Greek as the young man's money ran out, beaten by the speculator and the dozens of properties he had already purchased to make money for someone else, someone already wealthy. Instead of a family moving into that house, it would likely lie empty until the neighborhood was "stabilized" by others, perhaps that young soldier himself if he was lucky. Then, as plucky young people like me came tumbling in during Detroit's second gold rush, the house would be sold at a profit to someone almost certainly unaware of its provenance. I felt a little bitter for the young man and his family. They were probably bidding with every cent they had in the world, too.

I'd been in the stuffy room all day without lunch, and as the hours passed, My House—what I had begun to think of as my house—had not yet been called. I'd been running my finger over the page so often that the cheap printer ink had begun to smear. I was growing sweaty from my farm clothes and the pressure.

Just before they called the day over, the auctioneer read my page number. I slowly stood with my sign, number 3116. Another group of people stood with theirs.

There were almost twenty properties per page, but could they want the one I wanted, too?

The auctioneer began to go down the list. I was more than half-way to the bottom.

Could those people be bidding on *my* house? Could they have seen it boarded up and decided it was a good investment?

The auctioneer droned on. One property closer. Another.

I didn't have the money to spend more than $500 for the house. Potentially I could try to spend $1,500 for just the structure and forget the lots, but I wasn't sure I wanted it if someone else owned the land next door. There were only two other families on the entire block. It once held more than a dozen.

Then my number. I raised my sign.

"Going once."

This was it.

"Going twice."

No going back now.

"Sold! To the young man in the back."

I bought the two adjacent lots as well, and it was over that quickly. I let out a whoop and began to climb over people toward the aisle. All of a sudden other participants were wishing me luck, touching me, shaking my hand. I felt a remarkable amount of approval from the people around me in the audience, almost all black. Truth was, I wasn't sure how a city more than 80 percent African American would accept a strange white kid in a place whites had almost completely abandoned in the latter half of the twentieth century.

"Young man! In the back. Please stay in your seat. We'll come to you. Please stay seated and a representative will be with you momentarily."

I waved my apology and within a few seconds a woman showed up with a clipboard to take my money. I signed some papers and I was a homeowner in Detroit.

Those next years as I lived in the city a massive change began, Detroit growing, shifting, molting. Old grudges clashed with new ideas and nowhere was America's fight for its soul clearer than in what was the Motor City. Eventually, Detroit would become the Lower East Side of the '80s, the Berkeley of the '60s, the Greenwich Village of the '50s, but up to that time it had only been understood as an open and active wound on the American body that we had been ignoring for decades. The greatest sea change in American culture since the 1960s was about to happen in Detroit, and it contained the seed of something brand-new and revolutionary for urban areas across the United States and Western Europe.

The age of irony is rapidly coming to a close. Irony can't build anything, can't be used to create a new world. And nowhere did we need the tools to imagine a new world more than in this broken city. I know now that Detroit has ruined me for living anywhere else and I won't be able to take back the ideas that have grown from what I've seen. The Millennials, as they would begin calling us, had our victory and elected our man. He had let us down. There isn't a person on the planet who wouldn't have, because no one man could undo what we had collectively done to ourselves over decades. It was just too big. Politics wasn't going to fix things any longer. We'd have to do it ourselves.

During the nine years I've lived in Detroit the banks stole the money of average folks and no one went to jail.

The richest sixty-two people in the world owned half of the planet's wealth, and the top twenty-five hedge fund managers in the United States made more money than every kindergarten teacher in America combined.

Scores of black men were killed by police, and those who pulled the trigger were largely acquitted.

Students got beaten on college campuses, the people of Ferguson rose up, and the kids of Occupy Wall Street sat down.

Lots of foreign children were killed by flying robots made in America.

The United States tortured people.

For nearly the entirety of my life my country has sent young Americans to die in foreign lands. It has spent trillions of dollars on war that could have been desperately used in places like Detroit, with little to show for it aside from wealthy businessmen, craven politicians, and flag-draped coffins.

During that decade it was no different in Detroit, except.

Except for a swelling of hope, of naïveté, that we hadn't yet ruined what had been ruined before us. We thought maybe, just maybe, we could succeed where our hippie baby-boomer parents couldn't: creating the world anew. We knew they had failed—Detroit was the proof—but maybe they had failed so spectacularly we'd get another go at it. During those ten years I found something I didn't know I was looking for, what a lot of us were looking for.

We were a long way from "Yes we can." But there was one place people did. One place of *except*.

That was Detroit.

CHAPTER 1

Raw Material

Poletown, an urban prairie

I moved to Detroit with no friends, no job, and no money. I just came, blind. Nearly anyone I told I was moving to the city thought it was a terrible idea, that I was throwing my life away. I was close to graduating from the University of Michigan, one of the best universities in the world, and I was a bit of an anomaly there, too. Aside from an uncle, I'm the oldest male member of my family with all of my fingers intact, and the first in at least three generations never to have worked in front of a lathe. Growing up, I thought blue collar still meant middle class. No longer. At the university I met only one other student whose father worked with his hands.

On a sweltering day my pops and his truck helped move my few possessions into the Cass Corridor, which had been recently renamed "Midtown" by developers in an attempt to obscure the past. It was the red-light district, containing a few bars, artists, and at one time the most murders in murder city. Detroit's major university was just up the street, skid row down the block. An ex-girlfriend who had spent time in rehab for a small heroin addiction helped me find the place. She was the only person I knew who lived in Detroit, and she left for Portland the day I moved in.

Both my father and I nervously carried what little I had into my efficiency apartment: a single pot, a bed to lay on the floor, a futon frame I'd fished from the trash and fixed with a bit of chain-link fence. My father didn't always have the money to buy me new things, so he taught me how to fix old ones. School nights growing up were spent hunched under the sink with the plumbing, summers reroofing the garage, always right next to my father and his gentle guidance. The futon frame was a first attempt to fix something by myself. Sitting on the thing was terribly uncomfortable.

So was the move-in. If I was out of place at school, I was way out of place here. I was in one of two apartments occupied by white people in the building, which was filled with folks whom society has deemed undesirable: drug dealers, gutter punks covered in stick-and-poke tattoos, petty thieves, a thin and ancient prostitute who covered the plastic hole in her neck with her finger when she smoked. She once told me, "You'll pawn your clothes for your nose, cuz horse is the boss of your house," referring to heroin.

My dad locked the truck between each trip up the three flights of dirty vinyl stairs. I could sense he was uneasy—I was, too—but he never said anything aside from smiling and helping me lift my cheap necessities. Year to year, Detroit was still the most violent city in the United States, with the highest murder rate in the nation, higher than most countries in South America. My walk-up (nobody could remember the last time the elevator worked) was less than $300 a month and didn't come with a kitchen sink. The landlord waived the security deposit if I agreed to clean the place myself.

I wasn't quite through with school, but the wealth of Ann Arbor had become stifling. Compared with many Detroiters I was wildly privileged, but at the university I was feeling increasingly distant. I had great friends who were generous, and I felt lucky to get the education I did, but I wanted to use that for something meaningful at home. At the time more than half of UMich students were leaving the state upon graduation, and I didn't want to be one of them.

I thought I might be able to use my schooling to help somehow. I naïvely thought, with all the zeal of a well-read twenty-one-year-old white kid, that I could marry my education with my general knowledge of repairing things and fix the biggest project, the ailing city that had loomed over my childhood, as if it were a sink or a roof. I thought I'd just be there for one summer.

The giant man across the hall from my apartment was moving out as I was moving in. He wore a green sweatshirt printed with the name of a Greektown bar where by his size I figured he must have been a bouncer. He asked if I wanted his dresser and television. I decided I could use the former. He must have sensed my unease, because as we clumsily carried the furniture into my apartment he looked me dead in the eye. He had these big beady bloodshot eyes. He whispered, "You're welcome here," like an incantation.

I wasn't sure what to make of that. No stranger had ever thought to tell me I was going to be safe when moving into a new apartment.

If I was going to stay in Michigan, Detroit seemed natural. It was the most important city in the state by any measure, and in some ways it was the most important city in the Midwest. In symbolic terms, it's maybe the most important in America. Henry Ford and Detroit had invented the modern age along with the assembly line. Then, when it was convenient, that line had turned into a conveyor belt dumping Detroit straight into the junkyard of American dreams.

At the time, I didn't realize Detroit was just America with the volume turned all the way up, that what was about to happen would have repercussions for the rest of the Western world. Detroit was the most interesting city on the planet because when you scratched the surface you found only a mirror.

After wishing me luck my father left, and I spent that first night looking out my third-floor window. My parents were hardworking people who had followed the rules of the boomer generation, and it in turn had treated them well. They went to work faithfully, saved their money, and in the waning years of their employment had achieved a measure of middle-class comfort that was the envy of the world. What they didn't understand was that the rules had changed and their prosperity had been mortgaged against the future. Their children would be the first American generation with less material wealth than their parents. Some of that complacent bliss they had enjoyed had been stolen, and the wars, wealth inequality, and environmental exhaustion they had allowed to go unchallenged would someday need to be repaid.

I imagined my father spent the same evening having a drink with my mother, hoping they wouldn't be burying their son and that I'd figure out what I could do with the general studies degree I was about to be awarded, along with a steaming pile of student loan debt, about equal to the national average. Although they loved me fiercely and had given me every advantage they could afford, they couldn't understand what I was doing in Detroit.

I spent most of those early days sitting on the stoop watching the neighborhood pass by, hoping to find a job. It seemed like everyone who could, and wanted to, had left. I wasn't eager to begin the meaningless corporate work to pay off the tens of thousands in debt I'd accumulated, on the student loans I'd signed at seventeen before I could buy a pack of cigarettes or drink in a bar, so I stayed. At the time, moving to Detroit meant "dropping out," in the Timothy Leary sense, to remove myself as one bolt in the proverbial machine—not as a *sabot* to throw in the cogs—but to get out of America by going into its deepest regions.

A few days after I'd arrived, one of the few other white kids in the building asked me to help move a television to the Dumpster. I walked into his apartment as he was shooting up.

"You want some? I have clean needles."

I declined, but asked him if I could watch.

"Sure."

He had just begun to tie off around his biceps, and the shot was in a syringe that he held between his teeth. I watched as he put the tip of the needle slowly into his vein at an oblique angle, his knuckles resting on his forearm. He pulled back the plunger, his blood clouding the heroin like a drop of red food coloring in a vial of vinegar. He pushed the shot into his circulatory system, like the colored acid kissing the baking soda in a science fair volcano. A great bubbling calm washed over him as he lit a cigarette. This, apparently, was going to be my new life. I rolled one myself and we smoked in silence, until he broke it.

"So you want to move that TV?"

In a scene that would repeat itself as I got deeper into the city, those kids soon left, too. In this case, they hopped trains to California and the marijuana harvest. I was the only white face left in the building.

I would get offered drugs or sex, on the street, almost daily. Buying drugs was then almost the only reason a white kid would be in the city. With nothing to do I wandered the neighborhood in boredom and was mistaken for a customer.

"No thanks, ma'am, I stick with the amateurs."

"I'm all right, I just quit."

"Nah, man, crack isn't my style."

Drinking, however, was. On Mondays the bar behind me would brew beer and the whole neighborhood would smell like baking bread. I'd never been to a bar or even a film alone, but started going there to drink by myself all night, occasionally chatting with the bartenders or the barflies, semigenius immigrants from Africa, artists working in strange materials such as pigskin, labor historians and Communists, Mexican poets, Iranian gear heads, Korean illustrators, an entire drunk UN. It made me realize there might just be more to Detroit than the death and poverty that was all I saw on the news.

The staff would often take pity on me, too, serving me free drinks or letting me stay after they switched off the neon OPEN sign. One friendly bartender drove me to the grocery store in nearby Dearborn to show me where to buy food. Until the Whole Foods showed up in 2013 there wasn't a single grocery store chain in the city.

———

On my stoop I met a man named Zeno who was a crack dealer. We had little in common, but became friends out of habit and proximity, our floating schedules aligned. He had a difficult time understanding what I was doing in a place like that. So did I. But I'd learned something by facilitating poetry workshops in prisons over the previous couple of years: when you have little in common with someone and you are forced to interact, you talk about what you do have, big stuff, God and Man and War and Love. Things get deep pretty quickly and it often creates bonds not easily broken.

"Are you a cop?" Zeno said.

"What?"

"Are you a cop? Are you wearing a wire, motherfucker?" He

grabbed the front of my shirt in his fist and pressed his face close to mine.

We'd been drinking pretty heavy one night and had gone into his apartment to roll a joint. He had repainted his three rooms himself, and paid the super extra to add carpet to the living room. The floors were spotless and the furniture made of dark wood. A saltwater fish tank had a pleasant blue glow and sat at the end of the small hallway, and he'd installed a chandelier over the glass kitchen table. He had created a little oasis inside the tenement. He had once told me, "Your home is your refuge. When the world outside is so fucked up, you have to have somewhere nice to come back to. Your own castle."

"A wire? What are you talking about?"

He stared silently at me, his brow hard and aggressive.

"Take off your shirt." He flicked the front of my T-shirt with his thumb. "If you aren't wearing a wire take that shit off."

"Dude, how long have you known me? What the fuck."

I reached to get a cigarette from a pack on the table. He got to it first. He picked the pack up slightly and dropped them, his eyes never breaking contact with mine.

"Not long enough. Take it off."

I wasn't sure what to do next. So I took off my shirt. If there is a cool way to put your shirt back on after having been ordered to take it off by your only friend in a new town, I haven't found it.

After that he made it his business to show me around. He took me on crack deals and to his sister's house for dinner, introduced me to the projects, and when I said I didn't know what Belle Isle was— our version of Central Park on an island in the Detroit River—he made me get in his car and go, right then.

As we drank forties out of plastic cups sitting on his hood, watching the sun set over the skyscrapers downtown, he told me about his life. Kicked out of school at fourteen, mother an addict, father nonexistent. To him, selling dope was more honorable than the food line. There was little to no honest work for a high school dropout, and what he'd tried—the docks, for example, were controlled by the Mob, racial hierarchy, and bored animosity—never seemed to make ends meet. So he did his work, and was good at it. He sold just enough to eat and keep a roof over his head. He never touched anything harder than marijuana and had never been in any serious trouble. He was a unicorn in his line of work.

After months of looking I managed to find a job in the most unlikely of places: the classified section of a newspaper. I met my new boss for the first time in a bar with Formica tables and moody waitresses because I was too wary to bring him to my apartment. He was a large man with an enormous voice and a black SUV just as big. He had grown up in the city, but had since moved to the suburbs to raise his kids.

He explained his company was an "all-black construction company" and he needed a "clean-cut white boy" to sell his jobs in the suburbs—people wouldn't hire him when his address read Detroit and the first person they saw was black. I grew up in a small rural town far outside Detroit's suburban sprawl, and knew little about the animosity between the city and the ring of municipalities that surrounded it. I didn't know that Detroit is the most racially segregated metropolitan area in the nation.

The semester before, nearly all my classes had concerned race and were mostly filled with white people. Our discussions would tiptoe around the subject, students performing incredible verbal yoga, twisting themselves into absurdity to avoid mentioning anything that might offend anyone. I was happy to be my boss's white face. At work we talked frankly about race. When a call would come in, we would discuss whether she *sounded* white or black. If she sounded white, I would bid the job. If she sounded black, my boss would.

I would also work alongside everyone else sanding floors for $8.50

an hour, plus commission if I sold a job. When I came home and blew my nose the snot would be black from sawdust and polyurethane. I worked out the summer there, hunched over a thirty-pound disk sander, a long way from the university.

In August we had a job for one of my boss's relatives, also kin to my coworker Jimmy, a kind man with whom I worked closest and who taught me everything I know about hardwood floors. The relative's flat was on the second story, so we had to carry the machines upstairs and the sawdust down. The homeowner had worked thirty years on the line at Ford and had lived in what he called the ghetto for most of his life, but he was proud and comfortable, in his finances and with who he was. After shaking hands and looking me over suspiciously, he showed me each gun he had hidden around his home.

"Whoa! There's another one," he said as he pulled something long from under the couch.

"Bam!" He mimed shooting an invisible intruder, then winked at me.

I got the sense everyone respected him, but he didn't trust me because I was white. While we sanded and scrubbed, he apparently felt the need to work as well, and stood outside with a chain saw, cutting down tiny invasive trees that had grown into his yard, none thicker than his wrist. His adult son followed him, admonishing him to take it easy.

"Boy, I take shits bigger than you. You're slowing me down." He reared the saw in his son's direction. "Now get on the other side of that tree there and look out."

At midday, he offered to buy us lunch.

"Do you guys eat chicken?"

The crew, all black aside from me, sat bone-tired on his back steps, shrugging at the question and pulling at bottles of Gatorade. I could have passed an anatomy test on the muscles in my back.

"Now, I said I'm going to buy you lunch. Do you guys eat fried chicken?"

Jimmy answered, "Of course we eat chicken, we're black."

The record stopped with a scratch. Everyone looked at me. I was a vegetarian, something I had picked up at the university, as a challenge to myself. I hadn't had any flesh of any kind in more than two years, but I hadn't told any of my coworkers for fear of ridicule.

"I, um . . ." I was a little too stunned to come up with what to say. I'd be breaking a pact I had made with myself. Then again, maybe I'd be exchanging it for a new one.

"He lives right around the corner. He's black," Jimmy said, saving me.

"I, um . . ."

"Well, do you eat chicken?"

They all looked back at me.

"I eat chicken."

———

Sanding floors showed me many areas of the city outside my bubble in Midtown and got me thinking. Maybe I could make a go of it here. Maybe I could buy a house, live in it while I was fixing it, and flip it or rent it when I moved elsewhere. They were practically giving them away. The problem was I had no idea how to buy a house, let alone fix one up. It was just a vague idea. I thought I might start with something in the vast and relatively dense residential ghettos of the city where crime ruled second only to abandonment. Or maybe in a nice historic district where proud people still raised families and mostly kept to themselves.

But first, I had to finish school, at my parents' behest. I wouldn't leave Detroit, not yet. I blocked my classes on two days a week so I could still work at the floor place, but $8.50 an hour doesn't buy much gas when it's four dollars a gallon, as it was then, so I would often hitchhike between the two cities. One time a professional gambler picked me up, going to one of the new casinos in Detroit. The houses of gambling were the latest in a long line of economic silver bullets that never seemed to make the city any less broke.

The gambler had holes in his jeans and hollow eyes. I asked him what game to play in a casino if I wanted to win. What were my best odds? He, too, looked me dead in the eye. He said, "Don't ever walk into a casino."

Commuting between the desperate poverty of Detroit and the cosmic wealth of the university had made me sick, gave me economic jet lag of the conscience. The explosive inequality was eating me from the inside. Detroit was among the poorest cities in the United States and located only forty-five minutes away from Ann Arbor, one of the richest. The University of Michigan, a public school, costs more to attend for an out-of-state student than the average American makes in a year. I'd begun to think of them as different worlds, and having a foot in each was taxing on my view of the country that placed them so close together, and disrupting for my love of the university that had seemed to insulate itself from the desperation just down the street.

I'd known, too, just a little bit about what it feels like to be hungry and watch someone eat. I was dangerously broke and in Detroit unsupported by the orbit of wealth at the university, where I could casually walk into a dining hall past the bored attendant for a free, stolen meal or rely on my wealthier friends to pick up the tab at the bar. I began to question if I could go back at all, sanctimony about my new home working as an antidote to my sickness of dissonance. Living in Detroit wasn't exactly easy, but it seemed more noble somehow, and honest.

Amid the glass chandeliers and ivy of the university I had been selected to teach a class concerning race to other undergraduates, overseen by a kindly older professor named Charles. As I was getting a firsthand look at scratching out a living working near-minimum-wage jobs and the drug trade, other student teachers in the class were taking internships at places like Goldman Sachs and questionably capitalistic nonprofits in India. I thought this was bullshit and told them so. I told my teachers, including Charles, I thought academia was bullshit, too, sequestered from the real conflict. It didn't win me many new friends. I drifted farther away from the place that four years earlier had sent me an acceptance letter that had made my father cry in front of me for the first time in either of our lives.

But Charles would often insist on taking me out to lunch. He would listen patiently to my complaints and fury as I told him of my gestating plans to buy a house. I had formulated a vague notion I would start some kind of folk school, buy a big place or a duplex and use half for instruction, half for my home. Charles, knowingly and gracefully, nodded and smiled as I laid out my dreams for changing the world. Maybe, I thought, it would start with a house. That naïve dream came one step closer when I dressed as an organ grinder for Halloween.

Just down the street from my apartment in Detroit sat a contemporary art museum that threw wild dance parties. I had concealed some cheap liquor inside the organ and set it down in the corner to dance more freely. When I took a break to retrieve an illicit swig of Old Grand-Dad, by chance, sitting next to the liquor-cabinet-cum-music-box was a white guy dressed as an organ grinder's monkey. Something seemed meant to be.

He said he was a carpenter and his name was Will and he hated crowds, and people in general. He had just moved back to Detroit after ten years or so of traveling the States by freight train and thumb, typical methods of crusty-punk locomotion. Now he had become something different. We were both, somewhat desperately, looking for friends, both cynical about finding them.

"I kind of want to buy a house," I told him outside the party, smoking. The crowd spilled out into the street and ignored us.

"I just did," he said. "It's probably burning down right now. With my dog in it."

I called him the next week, nervous and wretched, like asking for a platonic date. He invited me over.

His house stood in a neighborhood on the near east side called Poletown. It looked like the apocalypse had descended, that the world and this life was but an afternoon performance that had reached its uneasy conclusion, the players having washed their hands and left for home, the crowd disappointed. This didn't look like a city at all. In my tiny car I crossed a set of disused train tracks and the houses all but disappeared. Poletown seemed prairie land, a huge open expanse of gently waving grass, the sightlines broken only by what appeared as crippled and abandoned houses twisting in on themselves. Aside from the grid of roads scarring the expanse, it must have looked close to how the land had appeared when it had been stolen from the Native Americans. One of the biblical meanings of apocalypse is "New World."

What structures remained looked like cardboard boxes left in the rain. Ominous two-story monstrosities with wide-open shells and melted porches lurched in bondage like tortured Greek gods of the underworld. Forgotten rosebushes ran over palsied fences, and the houses seemed to watch with yellowed eyes, like two-story Goya paintings, naked and ragged and proud. Trash seeped from the orifices where windows used to be. Abandoned dreams, abandoned lives, facades contorted into abandoned smiles.

Most of the houses had been deserted while still functioning. They had died by the elements, harvested clean of valuables by scrappers working as scavengers. Slow-moving nature had done the rest, reclaiming what it had lost a century ago. One of the original areas of white flight, Poletown had also been abandoned by all levels of government, the people who stayed left to fend for themselves. The average police response time was about an hour, if they came at all. Aside from some brave and stubborn holdouts and their solitary immaculate homes, the neighborhood was dead. Or so I thought.

Will's house stood on the edge of all this, just across the tracks. His street, named for the saint of the abandoned cathedral four blocks down, was pimpled with manhole covers spewing great columns of steam from the trash incinerator looming on the horizon. In the evening the exhaling bowels of the city created an opaque curtain of fog. The only other house on the block was a hideous cinder-block project house built by an architecture student from Cranbrook, the same private college Mitt Romney attended as a teenager. Whoever built the structure apparently didn't want to live in it either, and it, too, was abandoned, the water pipes burst from freezing long ago.

As I drove into the alley where Will parked his truck, I noticed behind his place lay a paradise of forest land abutting the Dequindre Cut, a long-abandoned railroad trench. Any homes and buildings had been torn or fallen down, and nature reigned once again. Thirty-year-old trees grew up between dumped boats and hot tubs and railroad ties and piles of rubble. A sextuple of abandoned grain silos presided over the blooming expanse of forgotten land. Scrappers would burn the jackets off copper wires at the bottom, as they were doing the first night I visited.

"The fire department will show up soon," Will said contemplatively as I got out of my car. He sipped a can of beer and his eyes never left the silos until I walked through the fence gate made from a pallet. His yard was filled with things he'd found on walks through his neighborhood, shingles, scraps of wood, pieces of sheet metal, halves of garden tools, sad lawn ornaments. Will appeared part of the cast-off junk as well, the tired leader of a lonely circus. I got a good look at him in the light, without his monkey costume, and he was a dead ringer for Hank Williams, the same goofy resting grin, the slim ghostly figure. Had he not been moving the cigarette between his mouth and ashing on the scrubby ground, he would have looked like a mannequin, frozen in time with the forgotten things he'd collected and given a home to.

He noticed me side-eyeing at some blue 55-gallon barrels.

"Oh, I'm going to make a rain barrel system with those," he said. He moved the pouch of tobacco from his lap. "I'll catch the rain coming from the roof and use it to water the garden. The water bills here are outrageous." In fact, they were. In spitting distance of the planet's largest source of fresh water, the Great Lakes, the water bills were almost twice the national average.

Will had dragged the barrels from the market across the tracks, which was still full of working slaughterhouses. He'd squirreled them away one by one when they would appear next to Dumpsters and scrubbed some out with bleach.

"I'll let the rain clean the others," he said, and stood, opening his back door. The security gate was padlocked near the bottom and a cinder block served as the step up to the threshold.

"This is like a tree house, you can do whatever you want," I said, stepping into his home.

Will demurred.

"This is great."

"It's not bad," he said, his hands in his pockets.

"*This* is freedom," I said.

He didn't look so sure.

He gave me the short tour: an entryway where he kept his garden tools, to a room that held the furnace and the kitchen sink that was not the kitchen, into his kitchen piled with houseplants and mail and knickknacks. The living room was a cacophony of found objects, art he'd made by himself or presents from friends, a piano covered in trinkets and records, a rack of mixtapes he had saved over the years. His house was as full as the outside was empty.

He wound an ancient child's toy on the piano. A tin horse and carriage ran in a circle around a saloon. The tinkly music glistened, but one of the bars was broken, rendering a sour note with each revolution.

"I found that last week out back," he said. "This is my tool room."

He walked across the hardwood floors and opened a creaking door. A table saw stood in the center on a platform made from logs with the bark still attached. The rest of the room was filled with dusty tools and half-finished birdhouses.

"These are cool," I said, picking up one with an irregular shape and a tin roof. "What's this?" I thumbed the perch, a fat nail with the number "66" stamped into the oversized head.

"It's a date nail. You find them walking along the train tracks. It tells the year they were put in." He took the birdhouse from my hands. "This one's from '66. That was a good year."

The half dozen birdhouses in various stages of completion had all been made from junk—lath, pieces of half-burned pine, tiny sheets of metal picked from the dirt, forgotten pipe. He was making delicate houses for the free birds of the air at the same time he was building his own, nearly out of the same materials.

"I just do that for fun," he said, shutting the door to the shop. Years later the mayor's wife would buy one priced in the hundreds of dollars.

The house was as much Will as he was it. Walking inside was like hiking through his cluttered and brilliant mind. I would come to call this aesthetic "junk punk," common in Detroit and rusting cities like it where the predominant vernacular was of objects cast off then repurposed and reloved by people who had been cast off themselves. The old was new again, and you needed a good eye to recognize value among chintz.

"I moved to Detroit right after high school," Will said as I sat in a sagging armchair in the living room. He had graduated about a decade earlier than I had. "I lived downtown in a building across the hall from Kid Rock before he was famous, but never really talked to him. I moved out a couple years later to travel the country, riding the trains and hitchhiking, lived in a few cities. But I would always come home and drive the streets."

He stroked his pit bull named Meatballs as he talked. "It was Armageddon, man! It was crazy!" His voice became excited for the first time in the evening, his sinewy frame inching closer to the edge of the seat. "I'd drive around for hours and I always noticed this house surrounded by nothing. I looked it up and it was for sale for three thousand dollars but for years, nobody had purchased it. I'd always drive by here to see if anyone had bought it. One time I drove past after I'd just broken up with my girlfriend in North Carolina and I told my roommate at the time, 'Man, if I had three thousand dollars I would buy that house right now.'"

His roommate happened to have received a windfall while he was gone and lent him the money that day. He purchased the house, in cash, from a Detroit police officer, the son of the former owner, and had spent the better part of the summer camping there, without much electricity or any plumbing. He bought bottled water and mopped with rainwater, planted a garden, and attempted to learn all the trades he needed to get normalcy to the house. At the beginning he didn't even have a door, just a sheet of plywood, and would let himself into and out of his own home with a screwgun.

I pulled open a yellow window shutter behind the chair and watched: one lonely house, a lonely empty street, a lonely stoplight doing its duty for no one but us.

"This is the coolest thing I've ever seen," I told him.

"Can you go with me to the hospital today?" With no warning, Zeno had called when I was in my socks making eggs.

"Of course. What's wrong? Are you hurt? Do you need an ambulance?"

"I'm fine. I'll tell you on the way."

He picked me up in his blue Ford Escort, with his girlfriend, Amy, sitting shotgun. She was about half the size of Zeno, and looked shrunken that day. The hospital was only a block from my house, and we could have walked, but he picked me up and stopped in the parking garage. There was something about the formality of it all.

The three of us signed in at the desk and received "visitor" name tags to stick on our chests. We walked a short distance to a small one-room chapel in the center of the building, a dark chamber with two rows of pews and a stained-glass window behind an altar that was backlit with electric light. I sat a few rows behind and in the other aisle from Zeno in the front, who put his arm around Amy. I wasn't exactly sure what was about to happen.

After a few moments, a fat white preacher wheeled in a small plastic gurney and parked it before the stained-glass window. I scratched at the oak grain in the pew. I wasn't sure what I was doing here.

On the gurney lay a tiny bundle, swaddled from head to toe in a blue blanket. The child Amy had been carrying, Zeno's unborn son, was dead, stillborn.

Zeno and I had discussed the child months ago. He told me he had gotten Amy pregnant, and although neither of the parents had the type of lifestyle that might be considered best to raise a child, they wanted to keep it. Zeno explained that living such a dangerous life, in such a dangerous place, he wanted the chance for his lineage to carry on. He might not have another opportunity for his seed to be planted, even if the soil wasn't as fertile as to be hoped. Why wait for better days when you don't believe there will be better days, and you don't think you'll live to see them anyway?

The preacher folded his hands and opened his sermon with one of the Psalms. He spoke about God and Man and Love and read from other religious books and holy works, background noise to the tiny speck of life, extinguished, lying before the altar. I don't remember exactly what he said, but I remember Amy crying softly, and Zeno holding her, silent tears streaming down his face. Eventually Amy asked the preacher to stop.

"I want to see him."

Oh my God.

"All right," the preacher answered. "We usually advise against—"

"I want to see him."

The preacher, with trembling and careful hands, removed the blue blanket from the child. Inside, wrapped in a white shroud and no bigger than half a baguette, was their son. From the back of the small chapel I could make out his tiny head and little arms and legs inside the blanket, the clear shape of a body. A dead little Moses in a plastic basket.

"I want to see his face."

The preacher hesitated.

"I want to see him for the last time."

I'd only been in Detroit for a few months, and this was what it was going to be like?

The preacher removed the final blanket.

The child had a stomach and delicate fingers, chubby legs. He was still and stiff and I cannot remember if he had hair, but I remember his eyes. Tiny, black, and open.

I tried to leave, meditate, anything. I imagined myself far away, outside the hospital, beyond that the city for miles and then the suburbs, the nice places and the places of peace and silences and waves and amniotic rocking and quiet. This world is a sphere, and if you go straight long enough you'll end up right back where you were. Try as I might, I couldn't escape those black eyes pulling me back into a reality I wanted to ignore.

The preacher covered the child.

As long as I live I will never forget the image of those black eyes.

Afterward, on the ride home, some stereo or other piece of equipment had to be sold to pay the rent. Zeno drove us to the place, and when he went inside I sat in the back of the car smoking while Amy wept softly, her head resting against the passenger-side window.

I think Zeno was trying to show me something, to warn me. Maybe it was because I didn't know what to say, that with all my education I didn't know how to fix it. That I couldn't bring the baby back was a given. That I couldn't make things feel any better, for Zeno or myself or everybody in this city and places like it, was a heartbreak. Maybe I'm projecting. Maybe I'm not supposed to say anything at all. Maybe all the tragedy of this place represented by one dead child isn't for me, a white kid, to try to explain, that I should bow out gracefully, that this world isn't for me and I should admit that my mistake was coming in the first place and never come back. Maybe I should have never come at all.

But I was there. I saw it. And I cannot unsee it, and I don't know what it means, if anything. Now it's yours, too. Welcome to Detroit.

———

A couple of weeks later I went alone to an art show held in a repurposed factory. I was still trying to shake off those few moments in the hospital chapel, and school was only making it worse. I knew I couldn't go back, but now I was unsure if I could stay here either. I tried to keep busy while I decided what to do.

Past stalls filled with BDSM art and Day-Glo paintings of dead rock stars, I stopped at a booth containing dozens of bales of hay. A couple of people who seemed to shine as if they had been scrubbed with a brush for the first time in a long time chatted with pedestrians or made roses from painter's tape.

I introduced myself to a white guy, naked under his overalls, who said his name was Garrett and the hay in their booth had been grown in Detroit. After some pleasantries, he invited me to an art show that just happened to be in Poletown, half a mile or so from Will's. Everyone in the booth lived on a strange and special block tended by a wild and virtuous farmer who had been in the neighborhood for decades. Farm animals roamed freely and the farmer had figured out how to make hundreds of bales of hay each year in a neighborhood fifteen minutes by bicycle from downtown. The street was named Forestdale. The building holding the art show, which they were rehabbing, was named the YES FARM.

He handed me a hand-typed business card:

```
the yes farm will help
  you with your dandru
ff, make your skin sme
ll shiney, make your
feet white and crisp,
like lettuce, and we

 will help you with th
at thing you never wan

t to talk about
```

I thanked him and asked if I could bring a friend.

On the day of the show Will and I pulled up to the block in his little white truck. It was located within the shadow of the Packard plant, an Albert Kahn–designed factory that had come to a comfortable end as a toxic trash heap. At one time steel, sand, and rubber went in one end, and a car came out the other. Now trees grew out of the roof. It was often on fire, and people talked about it like the weather. Aside from the abandoned train station, it was the best ruin porn in the city. People hadn't started to take high-fashion pictures of nude models in it yet, though, and there was still a notable piece of graffiti placed in the windows of the plant's bridge, spanning Grand Boulevard.

It read, "Arbeit macht frei."

On this block, though, all the houses seemed to be standing and well maintained, an incredible feat for a neighborhood with enough space to grow hay. Even without the fires and demolitions, gravity was inescapable. Someone had taken care of this place for a long time.

A community garden with neat little rows and a brightly painted sign sat across the street. On the corner was the YES FARM, brick, brightly painted and unmistakable. A former apothecary, the front had been painted in stencils and sunshine and brilliant waves of blue. Plywood cutouts of exotic animals had been screwed into the crumbling brick. A hole was blown into the back of the second story, which I later found out was made when a house across the street exploded, its gas line illegally hooked up with a garden hose. A wire, with what looked like an extension cord zip-tied to it, was strung between the YES FARM and a window in the house next door.

As I got out of Will's truck, a fat brown-and-white dog sniffed at me and wagged his tail. He had a collar and nobody seemed concerned that he was just wandering around, so I shooed him away and he went to sniff in the garden. I knocked on the side door to the YES FARM, which appeared to be made from two-by-fours stacked on top of one another, old and new. I could hear music from inside and voices. I pounded again and still no answer. Will shrugged and pushed the door open.

The room was filled with construction materials and tools. The extension cord leading from the house next door was powering a few caged work lights strung across the room like blue-collar Chinese lanterns. Someone had just finished painting the room with a city scene, black buildings on a red background, primitive style. There were doors lying around and stacked against the wall, but none of them hung in the doorways. It appeared there was no heat, but there was energy. People were working on the place and it seemed this show was part of its renovation.

I stepped over a ladder and some boxes containing papers and bolts into a room filled with televisions. The first piece in the show comprised a diorama of them that had been shot with a gun, Elvis-style. The title card explained that each set was carefully se-lected from a mass inventory of TVs found dumped around the city and pistol-shot in the basement of the building. Another project was signed "Molly Motor" and consisted of a television that held a live rooster with straw and food, a TV terrarium. Inside was also a set of what looked to be hairy cigars, tied in a bouquet.

"What the hell is that?"

"Those are my dreadlocks. I just cut them off," said an enormous voice from behind me. It definitely wasn't Will.

I turned to see a woman wearing rubber boots and a Carhartt, on which someone had spray-painted a spider stencil. She reminded me of Ma Joad from Steinbeck's *Grapes of Wrath*, a woman you would never want to fuck with and who might throttle you if backed into a corner, but with a fierce love and mothering instinct to match. She introduced herself warmly as Molly and said she lived across the street. She mentioned I could use her toilet if I needed to, and walked through the anteroom, parting a curtain into a whole new world, common in many cultures, but new to me, that of the dissatisfied and creative, the artists whose medium was society itself, those attempt-ing, however naïvely, to make the world anew, and better this time.

I followed her in. The room was warm and neighborhood children were performing a puppet show called *Patrick's Weird Beard* inside a huge cardboard television that had been constructed onstage. A half dozen kids in homemade costumes were giggling and stumbling through the show of their own creation. The small room was packed and the lights had been dimmed. The fire in the wood-burning stove was raging and you could hear its roar in the silences. I found Garrett in the crowd and slid in silently next to him. He whispered that earlier in the night they had hosted a City Council candidate who gave a speech inside the TV. He was a dark horse, and had just gotten out of prison, but seemed to make a big impression. Garrett also mentioned I could use his toilet if I needed, because the one in here had frozen.

After the play the lights were turned up and everyone milled around in conversation. There were about thirty people in the room, most of them in different states of dirty, but none of them filthy—it was like the healthy glow and smell you get after taking a run, not the kind of funk when you're lazy and haven't showered in a week. This dirt was from work.

The children scurried among all manner of art made from TVs, grabbing food off the tables, continuing their puppet show offstage, laughing. Garrett pointed out the farmer, Paul, in a pair of coveralls, who had grown the hay. He was skinny with a neatly trimmed gray beard, and was drinking a can of beer, talking with a red-headed black boy. He had a wiry, electrical energy, and scurried away before I could introduce myself. He seemed important, revered even, someone with an entire spinning globe of knowledge inside his hyperactive head, a leader of a leaderless tribe. Who was this man with a tractor and hay and a block of diverse people in East Detroit?

I asked about the TVs. Garrett said this show was called the *TV Show*, and the irony of it was that almost no one in the room owned a working one. He said everyone from the block had been pitching in to get the building functioning just enough for the evening.

He pointed out a new mural that had just been painted, a mother-earth green figure growing too big for the wall and onto the ceiling with doleful eyes and huge feet. The artist who had painted it sat beneath the picture on a reclaimed church pew with his wife. She was intensely pregnant.

"That's his unborn son he painted," Garrett said. "He's about ready to burst from Erin's stomach. He'll get raised in Detroit, right here on the block."

I realized the room and this block were the incarnate vision of a philosopher I had read in college, then living just a few blocks away and more than ninety years old. Grace Lee Boggs was Detroit's patron saint of transformation, the spiritual center of almost anything truly innovative in the city. Although difficult to pinpoint exactly, her fingerprints touched many communities like this, striving for a new image of possibility. I had found an idea made manifest.

Busy introducing me to everyone, Garrett forgot to tell me about himself. When I asked, he said he had moved around some, but had come from an art colony in San Francisco that had just been gentrified out of the Mission. Originally from Boston, he was trying to decide if he was going to make a go of it in Detroit or just keep wandering the polluted and harried cities of America's urban wasteland. Not liking to talk about himself, he quickly introduced me to more people whose names I immediately forgot, but stopped at a slight woman who had painted a picture of two hands stretching a tape measure that hung over the doorway. Garrett introduced us and we shook hands. Her daughters had been two of the children performing the play.

"Hi! I'm Kinga!"

We were interrupted by a ghoulish guitar chord from the stage. A tall and tattooed man sat behind the drums, and a redhead I recognized from the last art show manned the guitar. It appeared the final order of business was a jam involving anyone who wanted to play.

"That's Andy, Kinga's husband, behind the drums," Garrett shouted into my ear.

"Do you play?" Kinga yelled to me on her way to the piano.

"Sure."

I grabbed a guitar, and much of the neighborhood was onstage, more than a dozen people, adding their little sounds, working on one more thing as a community before the night was through. The rest sat in the audience, clapping and hollering and drinking. Andy sang into a microphone:

> Nobody can unplug my drums
> That's why I'm beatin' 'em
> And no one can unplug the sun . . .

———

I sold my car and bought a truck for $1,000, a rusted F-150 built when I was still in elementary school. That birthday, my twenty-second, I asked my parents for a power tool set that included a reciprocating saw, circular saw, drill, and flashlight. I thought leaving would be turning my back on everything that dead baby boy represented, and I needed something to keep me in Detroit, keep me from running away. I was going to try to buy a house and I was hoping Forestdale could show me how to build it into a home.

My father was excited that I wanted to do something befitting a man. While he and the rest of my family had been building things, I had been writing poetry. This was something he could understand. Wisely, he had bought me a single tool each Christmas since I was a toddler, so I already had many of the basics, screwdrivers, wrenches, and such. He was happy to oblige with more of the same.

Will said I could live for free at his house that summer, but no longer. He was a private man.

Aside from a single paper, all that was left of school was to graduate. The essay was for Charles, the kind professor who would take me to lunch. It concerned that dead baby. I was angry and hurt, both at myself and my peers, who I thought were leaving their posts at the most crucial point. The paper was dramatic and not particularly self-aware. I was slashing with a knife of self-righteousness at anything near me, including potential allies. Maybe I needed to do it to leave both behind, Zeno's raw world of the drug trade and tenements, and Charles stifling, pretentious world of circular and hopeless discussions at the university. I was looking for something far more meaningful than either, something closer to the American heart. In lieu of a grade for my paper, Charles gave me this response:

> My guess, based again on my own struggle (projection?), is that you feel empathy and horror for the pain you see in Detroit, and that you feel revulsion at the comfort you see in Ann Arbor. That you may also feel drawn to Detroit as a way not only to support the people there, but also to work out your own personal anger. That your anger sometimes frightens you, because you do not want to lose the love and acceptance of the people you are angry with. That you feel panic sometimes because, despite your good intentions, you feel helpless to do anything about the social conditions that you see . . . That you deeply, desperately want to create change, and that you do not really know how to take effective action. That "dropping out" seems the only alternative, but an ineffective one. That you feel deep confusion about who you are and what your identity is in all this mess. That you feel excited by possibility, and deeply sad and lonely. That what you really want in an ally is someone who can see not only your courage and ideals but also your fear, loneliness, and shame.

CHAPTER 2

Clapboard Siding

The YES FARM door

Two statues, located downtown and mere steps from each other, represent the dual nature of the city. The first and perhaps most famous is called *The Spirit of Detroit*. Located in front of City Hall, it's twenty-six feet tall and in patinated bronze depicts a cross-legged man with his arms spread apart, his breast open to the city. In his hand he holds a gilt sphere like the sun, representing God, and in the other he holds a golden family representing the people of Detroit. It was commissioned in 1955 at the height of Detroit's worldwide economic dominance, when everyone had two cars in the garage. It cost more than half a million dollars in today's money. The inscription reads, "NOW THE LORD IS THAT SPIRIT / AND WHERE THE SPIRIT OF THE LORD IS, THERE IS LIBERTY," from the second book of Paul's letters to the Corinthians.

Steps away, and within sight, is a twenty-four-foot-long black fist suspended from a pyramid. It represents the forearm of Joe Louis, the Brown Bomber, champion boxer from Detroit. It was dedicated in 1986, the year of my birth, and one of the toughest times in Detroit's history. It represents both Louis's strength in the ring as a prizefighter, and outside it as a combatant against segregation. It's a huge Black Power fist set at Detroit's most prominent intersection.

Two statues for two Detroits, one white and the other black; two statues for two Americas. Both were painted on the red steel door I stood before, the threshold to a house calmly sitting at the end of Forestdale. The depictions had been modified, though, by the artists inside. Like a Hindi god, *The Spirit of Detroit* had arms emanating from its back, each resembling Louis's fist. Each hand held a shovel. I was hoping this door would open up to a path to my own house, and hopefully the strength and generosity built of hard work represented by the painting. I knocked.

"Hey, Drew, come on inside."

Andy Kemp, the singing poet from the show at the YES FARM, opened the door and turned back toward what he was cooking. Garlic hung upside down in the hallway, swaying as we walked by, and trays made of window screen built into the walls dried herbs from the vast garden outside. I took a peek out the rear window and saw the garden built in a circle, cobbled-together woodsheds, a greenhouse, and a little pond so quaint it struck me immediately and crushingly as sad, like an unexpected and forgotten children's doll found by chance in an attic.

The kitchen was tiled with broken pieces of porcelain and a wood-burning stove sat in the middle, radiating tender heat. The cabinets and trim were reclaimed and mismatched, but the room hung together somehow, like a calico cat. I could see into a pantry that now contained musical instruments, and a porch swing dangled in the parlor. Their home, on the whole, gave the feeling of being inside a cabin at a friendly sleepaway camp on a rainy day. A cat sat on a bar stool and swished its tail like a gambler.

"Here, sit down," Andy said.

He put a plate of homemade tortilla chips and guacamole in front of me, and I ate.

"Try these, too."

He set down a bowl of what looked like marbles wrapped in a husk.

"What are they?"

"Ground cherries, you eat them like this." He popped the fruit out of the rind and into his mouth all in one motion.

His house was once a squatted crack house. With his wife, Kinga, also from the show at the YES FARM, they entirely rebuilt it, down to the studs. I aspired to their artistry, and thought I might accomplish something similar myself in a couple of years' time. Andy and Kinga had been working on theirs, together, for more than a decade. It was the second they'd accomplished; the other, on the west side of town, was rented to a young cellist and activist. I wanted not only for my future home to look like theirs someday, but for my life to resemble theirs as well. The answer they were about to give me would help determine that.

Andy threw the natural wrapper of the ground cherry into a pullout compost bucket built into his countertop. He was six foot two and built like a bicycle racer. His legs were covered in tattoos that he did himself, and his wedding ring was tattooed on his fourth finger. He had used a needle and a bottle of India ink. It must have hurt something awful, all that shading with a sewing needle, probably sterilized with a lighter.

I popped a ground cherry into my mouth.

"That's like candy," I said. "Did you grow these?"

"You know it." He turned back from the pot to look at me. "So what's up, man?"

"I was hearing from Garrett that you might need someone to stay in your brother's house over the winter." The house was on the opposite end of the block and vacant. Andy's brother had purchased it from an old Polish couple most of the neighborhood called "Betty and Sweaty," although some people found the nickname unkind.

"Well, yeah. Are you looking for a place to stay?"

"I'm thinking about buying a house in the neighborhood and Garrett said you might be willing to trade work for rent."

"We could be. It's pretty hit in there, though."

"I have a place to stay for the summer," I said. "But I need to be out by fall. I figured I'd have enough time to get your brother's place ready before the winter, while I'm looking for a permanent one."

"Have you found a house yet?" Andy asked.

"Not yet, but I'm looking. I need to be sure I have somewhere to live while I'm working on it before I really jump in."

"Nice. All right. I'll have to talk to Kinga, but it sounds like that might work out, we can help you get your start. There's probably enough time to get it ready," he said. "Hey, Kinga!"

Andy stirred what he was cooking on his Detroit Jewel stove, made in the 1930s. Before Detroit was the Motor City and manufactured automobiles, it was the heart of stove making in the United States. That had moved elsewhere, too.

"We already have the house demoed, all the plaster and lath is sitting in the yard," Andy said, attending to a cast-iron pan. "We'll need to finish the electricity and get it insulated. Trying to get you in might light a fire under us to get going over there."

"Hey, Drew," Kinga said as she walked into the kitchen. "Mmm. That smells good."

She wrapped her arms around her husband and kissed him on the back of the neck.

"Here, try this." He put the wooden spoon in her mouth.

"That's wonderful," she said.

He dipped the spoon back into the pot and brought it my way, blowing on it as he held his free hand underneath to catch drips.

It was a fantastic curry.

"So Drew here wants to live in Bunk's house for the winter," Andy said, looking at his wife.

"I thought Jesse had already claimed that one."

"I think he found somewhere else."

"You know there's not going to be any heat," Kinga said, looking at me.

"I can take it."

I popped another ground cherry into my mouth. At least for a little while I'd be a resident of this magical place. I hoped I could take it.

———

Will and I rode our bikes around Poletown, ducking into wide-open shells, not even plywood covering the doors, stepping over broken glass and broken tile and broken dreams. Occasionally neighbors would peer from behind steel-barred security doors, and sometimes they would ask what we were doing. I would explain that I wasn't a scrapper or a speculator, but I was going to fix one of these up and live in it. They would laugh, or appear skeptical. To the best of my knowledge no one ever called the cops.

"What about that one over there?" Will said, riding his bike with no hands and pointing to a duplex that looked smushed in like a pug dog's face.

I had three goals: I wanted a big kitchen, a chimney for a wood-burning stove like the Kemps, and a large front porch. Having some land around the house for a garden and to insulate myself from any trouble would also be essential. Will hated vinyl siding and what it represented, and his view had rubbed off on me. We would pass by any of those. Condition didn't matter. The duplex Will had pointed to didn't have a porch or space for one.

Next.

I imagined life in my yet-unfound house to be pastoral and wonderful, a life in which I could make most of what I needed, grow a bunch of my own food, and live in a manner I thought responsible. I'd spend my free time woodworking and inventing little contraptions to make life easier. One of my goals was to have nothing plastic in the house, nothing cheap and disposable and made by the hands of children in Asia, nothing with built-in obsolescence. I'd be self-contained, and warm and content. I'd read books by soft desk-light and go to work and come home honest and tired. I'd eat a lot of peaches, ones that I grew myself.

There was one house we looked at a couple of times. A piece of plywood barely covered the door, and Will peeled it back as I stepped inside. It had a sloped gambrel roof and robin's-egg-blue paint over clapboard. It was dirty and broken, but seemed friendly, like a cheery home-bum contented with a mellow drunk in the sun.

Although this house was just a simple wood-frame, like most of the other places in the neighborhood it was well built. It was also in fair condition for an abandoned house, but each time we would return more and more of it would have been stolen. First it was the wiring, then it was the plumbing in the bathroom—the

tile was pink and hideous, but the pipes and fixtures were still intact, a rarity in the neighborhood. The tile had been smashed out
battering-ram-style, and the copper pipes and brass fixtures taken.
It could have been workable, but was directly next to an occupied
house, the only other on the block.

"What do you think?" I asked Will.

"It's your house," he said, picking up a shard of tile from the
ground. He spat on it and wiped it clean with his thumb like an
urban geologist. "Seems like you could do better. Makes me nervous,
someone keeps picking it clean. You might have trouble."

There were more abandoned options to explore. Next.

I didn't think I wanted to buy a house right on Forestdale, although I'd been spending more time there. What was going on was
special but, I thought, insulated. I wanted to see what life was like
for the vast majority of Detroiters who didn't live downtown or
anyplace special, who lived in the sprawling wilderness of the city.
There were other places like Forestdale, and I thought I might be
able to start something similar, fix up other abandoned houses and
spread the idea. Or join something just as tight, if not as colorful
and easy to spot.

"It's kind of like living in a fishbowl," Will said. "Everyone knows
your business. On the other hand, it's safe and fun. You gotta decide
what's more important."

I also looked into some move-in-ready foreclosures, pert brick
homes in Detroit's stable and well-populated areas. I could have
purchased many of these for less than $3,000. I just couldn't bring
myself to profit from someone else's misery. All I could think of
were the families once living in these homes and the day the banks
and sheriff put them on the street. Just between 2005 and 2007,
67,000 houses went into foreclosure in Detroit. Not only did the
forced sales leave many homeless, they further decimated Detroit's
tax base, one of the crucial factors in a municipal bankruptcy that

people had begun to whisper about but no one thought could actually happen.

I decided I wanted a house nobody wanted, a house that was *impossible*. The city was filled with these structures. It would be only one house out of thousands, but I wanted to prove it could be done, that this American vision of torment could be built back into a home. Fixing it would be a protest of sorts.

Will and I laid our bikes in the grass outside a tiny yellow house. It only had a half dozen rooms total and was so small the city had no record of it, the property classified as an empty lot. Likely it had been a mother-in-law house, a kind of satellite behind a larger one. It gave me the creeps, for no reason in particular. Some of the houses we went into had an eerie feeling, more than the normal unease of stepping into an abandoned home in Detroit, as if some past crime marred the vigor of the place and hadn't yet been washed away by rain and carried into the atmosphere by wind. I felt that way with this one.

"This is what I'm *talking* about," Will said. "It's so itty-bitty. If you don't buy it I might get it myself. You could have this fixed up in two years."

I told myself it wasn't the one because it was on a fairly main street, near a bus stop. If lots of people could see progress, it would be incentive to steal the tools that made that progress, and opportunity for the city or police or government in general to poke around. The goal was to be anonymous. Will suggested I could plant pine trees in front of it to obscure the view from the road, but this posed its own problems. You still wanted your neighbors, and only your neighbors, to be able to watch over it. They were unlikely to steal or call the cops, less so for someone passing through. Really, though, it just gave me a bad feeling. I figured I could do better. Next.

It was during that time I decided I was going to do this the old-fashioned way, without grants or loans or the foundation money beginning to pour into the city. I would work for everything that went into the house, because not everyone has access to loans or foundational grants. I could have called the house "art" and people would have thrown money at me. It would have been comparatively easy, and I likely would have been able to get more done. But I wanted to prove one man could take a house and make it into a home without someone subsidizing it, like the baseball stadium downtown. If it needed to be done that way, what was the point? What could you prove?

It seemed wrong, too, to come into a place, especially one so poor, and suck up all the money. There were people who had been around much longer who could use a roof that didn't leak or plumbing that didn't either. I didn't want any part of that. It would separate me from my neighbors.

In the northern part of the city there is a six-foot-high concrete wall that runs along 8 Mile Road. It was built to keep black people out of the suburbs. 8 Mile is the historic dividing line between black and white—also the dividing line between suburbs and the city—the same road made famous by Eminem in his titular film. The wall was built in 1940 by a white neighborhood developer, supported by the federal and city governments.

When the soldiers returned from World War II, President Franklin Roosevelt, along with Congress, instituted the GI bill that we generally think of as a law paying for the college education of soldiers. But the bill also built infrastructure and widely expanded federal home-loan programs. Coupled with other federal and state initiatives and subsidies, it spurred a house-building boom, the suburban living of the '50s, and ensured the United States would be a nation of homeowners. This all happened in the lifetime of your grandparents, and maybe even your parents or you.

Those home loans were not available to blacks in Detroit. The same soldiers who fought under the American flag across the world against fascism, Japanese imperialism, and Nazi racism did not qualify for U.S. federal home loans because of the color of their skin.

In fact, blacks were only allowed to live in a few crowded neighborhoods in Detroit, houses and apartments that were widely considered substandard. A typical black dwelling cost three times what a comparable place in a white neighborhood would—for half of the amenities. Many didn't have running water, and rat bites on babies were a common problem.

That concrete wall was built by a real estate developer attempting to turn virgin land into a subdivision with federal money. Not only were the loans not available to blacks, but they were also not available for development in black neighborhoods; they weren't available for white neighborhoods either if they contained even one black person; and finally, they were also not available for all-white neighborhoods *bordering* black neighborhoods.

This process is called "redlining" because of the color used on maps to denote areas where loans would not be made in any case. Its explicit use has now been made illegal, but the practice continues in many ways.

The neighborhood south of 8 Mile was a black neighborhood, one in which the professional-class residents were allowed to purchase land and were building homes without the help of federal loans. The suburban developer was initially turned down for funding because of the proximity to the black neighborhood. His solution was to build the wall, appeasing the civic government managing the federal loans. It ensured blacks would not even be able to see into the neighborhood he built.

The wall is still there today.

This is the "once great city" the newspapers pine for.

I figured free money might put me proverbially on the other side of that wall. Anyone who controlled that money, really controlled it anyway, lived on the other side. It wasn't just a demarcation of area and governance but of wealth and consequently of character. White folks in Detroit had gotten enough free money in the past through subsidies and uneven dealings, so I felt I could leave that for someone else. I wanted, as much as possible, a clean break from the past.

Neither was I going to make the banks and bankers any more money by paying their usury on a mortgage. One piece at a time would cut out the middleman and his gleaning of profit for nothing, for being wealthy already. I was going to do this the old-fashioned way, through sweat and labor. Work it was and work I was going to do.

Will and I rode past a monstrous white Queen Anne with a wraparound porch. We didn't go in, but I took note.

———

Six-foot-tall piles of kitsch. Hundreds of plastic Santa Claus decorations. Ceramic ducks, elephants, geese. Strings of lights. A lawn mower that looked like it didn't work. Andy Kemp wasn't kidding about the demo on his brother's place. I stood in the yard.

Plastic houseplants. Piles of plaster, concrete, lumber. Flower vases filled with nails. Upsetting paper dolls crumbling in the rain. Indeterminate jugs. A coffeemaker.

There was a drizzle and I tried the door. Locked. I sat on the topless bookshelves that doubled as a bench and smoked. I needed to get a good start here before I had to leave Will's at the end of the summer. I was grateful to the Kemps for letting me stay for free in exchange for a bit of upkeep and looking after the place. Any money I made could go into my own future home, and I was about to learn how desperately I was going to need it.

I noticed a two-foot-tall aluminum sculpture of a knight holding a sword hanging on one of the brand-new posts holding up the porch roof. I touched its foot and the whole thing crashed to the ground, making a hellish noise. I stood and returned him to his perch, watching sentinel over what was to be my new home.

The property consisted of two lots, and in the back was a dripping garage. It was rumored that the porch I sat on had cost Betty and Sweaty their home: they paid for its construction then couldn't afford the taxes. So they left for Florida—and left behind all these trinkets and a ten-grand water bill. The state of the place wasn't uncommon for Detroit. Houses in the neighborhood didn't last long without someone living in them. They would succumb to fire, get stripped of their valuable metals at night, fall to the relentless rollback of nature. Less likely is that someone would begin squatting one and turn it into a crack house, but stranger things had happened and it was a real concern.

I wandered into the backyard and stared into the pond, a shallow hole about as big as a cafeteria dining table. It was bordered by rocks and plants that had been dug up from around the neighborhood, and odd bricks and chunks of concrete that could be found anywhere. At one time there had been a pump, but it wasn't running now and the water was stagnant and beginning to go to algae. A mottled carp surfaced and ate a water bug. Looking closer, I found the pond was filled with these fish, white, gold and orange and black-spotted, and variations between the two.

I looked at the house. There were holes in the roof and water would drip inside when it rained. One of the first projects would be to string a tarp across and patch the holes as best we could—

I heard a mutinous racket and walked back out front. Andy and Kinga pushed a giant box with a broken wheel down the road in the rain, laughing at their folly and achingly in love a dozen years after marriage. One corner would scrape on the ground and careen in a circle like a race car losing a tire, and they would laugh and when they got back on track it would happen all over again. The drizzle had become harder, and Kinga wore a yellow rain slicker three sizes too big. She kept sweeping the hood back out of her eyes while pushing and laughing and shouting at Andy to get the box back on track. They looked like puppies in a mud puddle, a big mess of joy.

It was a scene I never would have imagined coming out of Detroit.

"What's this?" I asked when they wheeled the ornate box into the yard.

"Obviously we can't work without music, man. What are we, animals?" said Andy.

We lifted it up the porch steps. The stereo was old, a piece of furniture really, and had been found in an abandoned house. Nearly the size of a Harley-Davidson motorcycle, it had provided the working music for at least a half dozen project homes around Detroit so far. It would move again with me to my own place, when I found one.

Andy and Kinga were both soaking wet and gorgeous. Kinga removed the hood from the yellow slicker and Andy shook himself dry like a dog. Their smooth muscles and homemade tattoos, come by honestly, were devoid of any pretense or irony.

"Hey, Drew." Kinga waved.

"Have you been inside here yet? You ready for this?" Andy said.

He opened the door. The house, stripped down to the studs and bare like a cabin, consisted of three rooms in the front, a bathroom, kitchen, and living space. There was a chimney in the center, crumbling. The rear of the house contained more rooms but would be shut off from the rest and were filled with junk and construction materials. The upstairs was one large room. During the winter as I lived there I could have sworn I heard strange and unexplainable noises coming from the second floor, but when I went up to check I found nothing. Andy told me later that the son of a previous tenant had committed suicide up there. He was found hanging from the rafters.

"So what do you think? You think you can make it here over the winter?"

I looked around. I had slightly exaggerated to the Kemps my experience with tools. I didn't doubt for a minute I could do it, but when I looked at all the work, it seemed like an absurd amount. I was eager to get my hands dirty—when something was done it would be done, either the lights would turn on or not. Water would come out of the faucet or not. Things would look square and plumb or they wouldn't. Still, what would my parents say? Would I ever be able to bring a girl here?

"Of course. I'm excited."

"Let's plug this bad boy in and see what we got."

The radio turned on to Bob Seger, Michigan's blue-collar poet laureate.

"You and Kinga can finish putting in the switches and outlets and I'm going to run to the hardware store for lumber. Does anyone need anything?"

"I don't think so."

I had replaced switches before but never installed them new. Kinga gave me a crash course and we set to work. She had brought a plastic kitchen timer, one of those with the large dial in the center, and set it for an hour.

"What's that for?"

"It's so I remember to pick up my kids from school. Sometimes I get working and I get so into it I forget about anything else. I started doing it when Andy and I did our house."

"When was that?"

She told me the story as we stripped wires and threaded them through the small plastic outlets we take for granted.

They met one summer when Andy was a camp counselor and

Kinga a camper on holiday from Hungary. She had grown up in the Eastern Bloc just after the fall of communism and her father was a brilliant mathematician, his career stunted by fascism. She had lived in a typical Communist apartment block, gray, concrete, and with few creature comforts. After the fall of the Wall she discovered punk music and fell in love with it. She still had tapes from Eastern Bloc hard-core and punk bands in the pre-Wall era that she lent generously.

She bonded with Andy over music at camp, and when Kinga went home they wrote to each other across the ocean. "We fell in love through letters," she said.

The next summer Andy went to Hungary to visit her. They had wedding rings tattooed on their fingers soon after. Andy found a job as an English teacher at Catherine Ferguson Academy, the same school for pregnant and parenting mothers where he would meet Farmer Paul. Paul would eventually convince the two, plus their two daughters, to move to Forestdale. At the time the place was still a crack house.

Paul had turned the dealers out with an ingenious solution. One day when they were gone he began stacking hay bales inside, filling the house and blocking entry. "From a crack house to a hay house," he told me, grinning. Soon after, Andy and Kinga purchased it legally and turned it from an empty shell into the envy of the east side.

By the time we had finished with the wiring the sun was out. We helped Andy load the lumber into the house, and Kinga had to pick up her children from school, so Andy and I began to sister the second-floor rafters with strips of plywood. I asked Andy about the pond outside and told him about the one we had just made at Will's.

In the forest behind his house we had found a dumped hot tub, and after some fiberglass patching from my grandfather, we sank it into the ground behind his garden. Will had piled rocks and concrete and rubble around the edges and created a little waterfall from a red beverage cooler. We installed the pump that he had found and I had repaired, and finally Will had bought water lilies and other plants, and filled the pond with a handful of tiny goldfish.

"Do you think he wants some of our fish, from the pond?" Andy asked.

"Yeah, sure, I think he'd like that."

We stopped what we were doing and Andy found a five-gallon bucket that he filled with water. He straddled the edges of the pond, finding a foothold on the rocks, his long and tattooed legs ropy with muscle. He was attempting to catch the fish with his hands, stumbling into the pond more than once, wetting his enormous tennis shoes. He'd dart in and the fish would flick away with little thought, his probing fingers only a minor annoyance. Without losing hope he found a milk crate and was stabbing at them with it like a net and having some more luck.

"Aw, yeah! Let's get this one with the spots."

I stood aside, dumbstruck at the man's energy and enthusiasm.

Back in he shot with the makeshift net, sliding the fish into the bucket.

"You said Will has some fish in there already? Don't tell him you put these in there. Let's see how long it takes for him to notice."

"The fish in the pond got huge! Like overnight!" Will said three days later. "They grew, like, ten inches!"

I wanted to play along but couldn't hold in my laughter. Living with Will was great. I had traded my construction job for one at a bar downtown—better money and less taxing on the body. If I wasn't serving customers from the suburbs attending baseball games or the opera, I'd chat into the night with Will. We played instruments or read or I might sew a pair of pants that had ripped during the day. Will would work on a birdhouse or drink canned beer, or we'd just sit and talk.

The conversation would inevitably turn to Detroit, and how to live responsibly but successfully as a white kid coming in from somewhere else. Even though we were both punks at heart, we knew there was an imbalance, and it wouldn't make a pleasant or noble life to take advantage of the neighbors and the situation and become some slumlord or be driven by economic profit. There was no point to dreaming of a better world if you couldn't sleep with yourself at night.

At the same time, you had to be able to come home in the evenings with your head held high. You couldn't spend your life getting kicked around. You needed to be able to look yourself in the mirror and see a man without getting trapped up in any of the petty ghetto bullshit. Aside from work in the drug trade, protecting your manhood was the number one reason people got shot.

To live in Detroit was to live not just in a city but in a concept. And it's strange to live in a concept. We had to make up the rules as we went, because there weren't yet a whole lot, not many we knew of anyway. Other American cities could only hint at the devastation and uniqueness of Detroit.

Is it right to live in an opulent house and have nice things amid so much poverty?

"Not if you buy it," Will said. "But you can have anything you want if you make it yourself. If you built it with your own hands you don't have to be ashamed of anything."

Is the world getting better or worse?

"Hell no, the world's garbage," Will said. I disagreed. I thought at least we have history to build upon.

Is it okay to steal materials from an abandoned house to build your own?

Under certain circumstances. You had to watch the house for a reasonable amount of time to make sure no one owned or was squatting it, and the stuff you took could only be used to build your own place, keeping history alive in the neighborhood. Selling or melting it down made you a scavenger, the material carrion.

What do you do if someone tries to kick down your door?

Will had stashed blunt objects around the house, but didn't own a gun.

And how do you get the electricity turned on in an abandoned house?

We lived simply.

We were separate from the world aside from the radio we only occasionally used. The house didn't contain a television or computer and neither of us had smartphones. Will instinctually avoided mainstream culture and the warping of the truth that comes with it. Long live King Ludd. Most entertainment we made ourselves, and we listened to music without regard to what was popular. Will reintroduced me to country music and played the clawhammer banjo. I could pick a little bit on my guitar. We traded stories about hitchhiking and riding trains, Will telling me about his nights spent in a Mexican jail or driving into Lubbock as dawn was breaking.

I never, ever went to the suburbs. It felt to me like a place a crime had been committed long ago and going there made me feel complicit. A lot of the things I hated about modernity were present in the most tasteless way, as well, just driving around: endless traffic and big box stores selling the cheap wares of near-slavery, impersonal subdivisions, and a lack of community or feeling, years of racial animosity that not only didn't I want a part of, I was actively attempting to work against it by building my place in Detroit.

While over the last sixty years or so Detroit itself lost more than half its population, the population of the suburbs has grown exponentially. In fact, the population of the Detroit *metro area* has grown since the '70s. The narrative goes that people left Detroit. That is correct but not complete. What isn't included is that those people didn't go far. Mostly they just went to the 'burbs, and all of us paid for the infrastructure to get and keep them out there while the core of the city deteriorated.

Occasionally Will and I would climb the ruined grain towers behind his house and look out over the city, smoking cigarettes and drinking 40s. Most of the fire escape had been scrapped away, and lifting oneself overhead onto the rusted stairs was a feat of gymnastics. I hated heights but I liked the view more. I'd try not to fall through the crumbling roof, and we'd point out landmarks, churches, schools, empty factories, trying to figure our place in it all.

"It's like the pilgrims," Will told me, looking out over the city. "They came to America for religious freedom and got along with the Native Americans pretty well. It wasn't perfect, but they ate Thanksgiving together, you know. It was the people who came after. They said, 'I can make money from this.' They were the ones with the smallpox blankets, not the pilgrims."

"That sounds like a total bastardization of history."

"It may be. But it rings true."

The cut abutting the silos was pulsing with all kinds of flora and fauna: pheasants, rabbits, the odd sapling, little red foxes, waist-high grass, chicory, cattails, burdock. Will swore he saw a deer down there once, staring at him with glistening eyes before bounding off. After dinner, cooked from what we grew in his garden and beans from a can, we would take walks down there with his dog, during what

Will called the "golden hour," quietly picking our way among the roaring yet silent nature. We could walk for forty-five minutes and not see a soul. Some evenings we would stumble on a stray spray-can artist or a gentleman making his home amid the rubble, but never anyone other than that.

There was one guy down there that we called "the Oracle," maybe cruelly. He lived in an igloo made from Vitamin Water and Gatorade bottles filled with chicken bones and other detritus, sometimes urine. We'd quietly walk by his home and occasionally he would stick his head out from the pile, his hair long and wispy, bleeding into his Fu Manchu mustache. He would never wave, but would recognize us, nod, and flit back inside his abode. There were other makeshift shelters that we treaded around carefully, not wanting to disturb the peace of the owners. Most were friendly but wanted to keep to themselves, and we respected that.

Mostly we were alone. We would meander through the grass and industrial waste and climb out of the cut into Eastern Market, Detroit's central open-air marketplace, all but abandoned at that time on weekday evenings. As we walked past the stout brick buildings with the sunlight peering down, the emptiness made it feel as if we could have been the only people left on earth.

This was the first time I saw a pack of wild dogs. There were a half dozen hiding and romping in the bushes a hundred yards ahead of us. Will never left home without rocks or a chunk of steel in his pockets, to throw at the dogs if they looked like they might attack. He had to do so once, and I would find out soon enough how terrifying that was. We stopped for a moment to watch them play, wild and glistening and free like stallions, fierce and terrible and killers like wolves.

Bloomberg News once put the number of wild dogs in Detroit as high as 50,000, one for every sixteen people in the city, which is an exaggeration. But the threat is real nonetheless. Dogs are generally cowards, and turning your back on one is never a good decision. It's the only thing in the city I'm really scared of. You can't reason with a dog. A mugger wants your money, a dog wants your flesh. This poses a problem for children. Imagine walking your daughter home from school with the threat of packs of wild dogs hanging over you.

———

I had a pile of logs to split, stacked in the backyard on Forestdale. While looking for houses and on other business in the neighborhood, we'd look for downed trees for firewood. Jake the redhead and I bought a chain saw, splitting the price. Along with Will, we would drive around the neighborhood after the summer storms, cutting up the dead or fallen trees that had collected in the empty lots and in some cases across the road. It would take the city days, and often weeks, to clear the trees blocking streets, and never if they had fallen in a lot. One of us would cut slices in a log lying on the ground, and all three of us would roll it over to finish the cuts on the backside.

We didn't really know what we were doing. We had very little knowledge of forestry and what was good for burning or how to identify trees, but the best teacher was experience. Sometimes we would cut down dead and standing trees, ones the city should have taken care of. Someone would climb the tree with a rope, tie it at the top, and then, back on the ground, pull as it was being cut to make sure it toppled in the right direction. I built a small woodshed at the Forestdale house, and thought I had enough with my pile stored up for the winter.

"If you want to heat your house with wood, you need to be able to fill up the space you're going to heat with split logs," Molly told me, stopping by to check on my progress. A tile setter by trade, she was wearing the same rubber boots and Carhartt with the spider stencil she appeared in at the YES FARM.

Filling the house with logs seemed impossible.

"You might consider buying some," she said.

That seemed like throwing money away.

"I guess I can cut some more in the neighborhood," I told her.

She launched into a story about Farmer Paul. He was a few blocks from Forestdale cutting firewood with a crew of his sons and neighbors. He had an enormous chain saw, with a bar longer than a man's arm, which he was using. A smaller saw sat in the back of the truck. Someone walking by snatched it from the truck bed and ran. Paul chased him, still holding his. As Paul caught up, the thief turned on him, wielding the ultrasharp chain like a two-handed sword. Paul stopped, and they squared up like Wild West duelers at ten paces.

"You want to go, old man!" the thief shouted.

Paul started his chain saw.

When the police arrived all the thief would say was "This man is crazy! He tried to attack me!" The cops knew what was up and took him away.

A Detroit farmer who wasn't afraid of a chain-saw fight?

I still hadn't been able to corner Paul, and he'd slipped away numerous times. I got the sense he wouldn't give up what he knew to just anyone, who might leave and take it with them. He didn't have time. Like a lot of people in the city, it seemed he wanted some sure investment, not empty promises. It wasn't really that cold. I would be fine.

The search for houses went on. Will and I again rode past that two-story Queen Anne. It was on a quiet corner on a street named after a dead slave owner and located halfway between Forestdale and Will's. Next to it sat two empty lots, about a quarter of an acre in all, plenty of space for a dog and a garden, a shed and a pond. The neighbors on the block to the south were friendly and kept their homes well maintained, but there were four other naked abandoned houses on the block with the Queen Anne. A red one sat as open as the ocean right next door, not three feet away. If it burned, the house I had my eye on would go, too.

The neighbors said the Queen Anne had been abandoned for at least a decade, simply left behind, anything of value stolen long ago. They described the last owner as a "slumlord," and "maybe he was a racist." He had been attempting to fix the house to rent as a business proposition. When the neighbors offered to help watch it so it wouldn't get scrapped, he was rude. One day he came to check on the progress and all the brand-new windows he had put in had been stolen, frames and all. The neighbors were almost glad he was gone. I couldn't blame them for being skeptical of me.

The house had a mangy wraparound porch and a big kitchen, but no chimney—I could build one of those—and had been gorgeous at one point. You could still make out its beauty, like a ninety-year-old starlet from the golden age of Hollywood. It had good bones.

But it was filled with trash and had lived a hard life: two monstrous stories of no doors or windows, plumbing, or electricity—nothing. There was a pornographic hole in the roof. The backyard was a literal jungle, and it was going to take years to clear out with a machete and a rake. The porch needed to be ripped off and done again, the front yard looked like it wanted to be cut with a scythe. The piles of trash inside reached as high as my chest. The house was just a white-and-gray clapboard shell on a crumbling brick foundation, filled with junk. The first time I cautiously walked inside, I knew it would be my home.

When I told the neighbors I wanted to buy it, they looked at me like I was insane. A young white kid stuck out like a snowball in Texas, and I was self-conscious and very aware of my color, stumbling over my replies. When I was moving in, most other people, white and black, were moving out.

I found the neighbor to the south, a big guy, walking into his house. It was essential to speak to the neighbors at least for a moment. If you were going to live close to one another, you wanted to make sure nobody was against what you were doing, as it could make everything crumble. With no police protection and little security, the only safety was in the people around you and what you could do for yourself.

"Just looking at it, it's a lot of work," he said, figuring I would give up after a year or two.

But it was the one. I had heard rumors about a massive tax auction where houses were sold for $500. But first I had to find out who owned this place, the city or the county or a private individual. There wasn't even an address, so figuring out whose it was was going to be difficult. There was also an orange square painted on the front. At the time, lots of houses in the city had these, some with a slash inside, others with an *X* like in New Orleans after the hurricane. We thought it signified how close the house was to demolition. I knew stories about people buying a place only to have it torn down by the city a month later.

To find the address I went to Detroit's property mapping department. I had been instructed by the gentleman working at the counter to fill in on my sheet that I was a college student doing a project and the printout would be done right away, for free, instead of going through layers of bureaucracy. I went in with my hand-drawn map of the cross streets and walked out with a computer-generated one of the parcels and their addresses. Next, I needed to look up the tax records on the Internet through the county's website. It appeared the Queen Anne was owned by the county, also a good sign.

I then went to the demolition department and asked if it was slated to be torn down. They explained it wasn't, and the orange squares signified to the fire department how dangerous the houses were to enter. An orange box meant unsafe, if it had one slash inside it meant greater danger, and two slashes meant more dangerous still. The house I wanted wasn't the most hazardous, and they weren't going to tear it down, but it was a treacherous structure.

Next, I had to go to the water department and find out if there would be an enormous debt from the previous owner. Water bills stick with the property in Detroit, not the homeowner, and it was possible that the bill could be in the thousands of dollars, even tens of thousands. For example, if the pipes had been stolen but not the water meter and the water had been pumping into the basement—possibly for years—it could be astronomical. I checked the bill in a separate building. Only ten dollars. Another good sign.

The last thing to do was check the auction. This was not online at the time, as it is now, and each year the county would publish a book containing tens of thousands of properties for sale.

The line to purchase one of these golden books was nonexistent and I bought it for a few dollars. Armed with my map, address, and clean water bill, I sat down in the marbled hallway inside City Hall, the Spirit of Detroit and Joe Louis fist statues standing proudly outside the window. I opened it and scanned for my page and then my house, my hands sweaty.

There it was. For sale. The two lots next door were available also.

I've just described in a few paragraphs the process of buying an abandoned house. In reality it took months. Nothing was streamlined and no information was available aside from hearsay about how to go about it, what to look for, and whom to speak to. It took trips back and forth between different municipal buildings, ending up in the wrong office or with the incorrect paperwork, asking security guards where departments could be found, questioning neighbors about which offices I needed to go to in what order in the first place. It was a scavenger hunt spanning downtown and the Internet. You'd think they'd make it easy for people to buy abandoned houses.

———

Will and I had gone back to the Queen Anne and measured the window openings, and I marked the sizes on a diagram of the house I had drawn. Friends at a community art gallery had donated some reused OSB plywood, the kind made from glued wood chips. I worked to cut the donated boards to size in Will's backyard as he built a chicken coop using some little pieces of glass, hardwood flooring, and tin roofing he had found. Thrifty to the fasteners, he pounded secondhand nails straight on the concrete as I created what was to be the first separation between the inside and the elements that the Queen Anne had seen in a decade.

We wanted to be able to do this as quickly as possible. It's illegal to enter abandoned homes owned by the government, and I hadn't bought it yet. If we were caught inside with tools, just a crowbar even, we could be taken to jail for breaking and entering. It had happened:

Norman moved to town about a year after I did. He's an MIT graduate and his mission was to start "maker spaces" for children to learn STEM trades. He spends his time visiting schools, teaching kids about magnets, electricity, and batteries, with readily available materials like copper nails and ten-cent lights. He set up one of his maker spaces in a church basement on Detroit's east side, working with the pastor, who's a special and fabled man himself (bursting out of caskets on Easter, waving around a pistol at service to decry gun violence, and having live donkeys present for the Christmas procession). By all accounts Norman's an upstanding gentleman, an asset to the community.

One day, he and some of his compatriots boarded up an abandoned building that was being stripped of valuables, the future site of a school that he would be working in. They had secured the building as best they could and from time to time would check on it. One day Norman was driving by and some of the boards had been ripped off, so he stopped to investigate. He chased away the scrappers inside, and was eventually able to flag down a police car. He told them the deal.

"Were you just in there?" the cops asked him.

"Well, yeah, I boarded it up. I just ran some people off who were inside scrapping it. If we hurry we can probably catch them."

He spent thirty-six hours in jail. He was lucky that was all. The police took him in, and since it was a weekend, he couldn't be arraigned until Monday. He was finally able to get hold of one of the preachers he knew, who gathered up a posse of other religious men and community leaders and let the police know, in no uncertain terms, that Norman was to be released.

I didn't know any pastors who could spring me from jail. Will gave me an unused steel door for the front so I could enter and exit easily, and I would lock it with a padlock from the outside. Garrett agreed to help, along with Jake. Will and I loaded everything into my truck and headed over and inside.

The house became darker as we added boards to the window openings, and we had to labor to keep from stepping in the piles of human shit the scrappers had left in the middle of rooms, the uncapped needles, and the crack vials. We all wore leather boots with thick soles.

While Jake and Will worked together downstairs, Garrett and I took the second story. We nailed two-by-fours into window openings with a cordless framing nailer that Jake had brought and attached plywood to these makeshift brackets. The master bedroom, a shallow room that spanned the width of the house, looked like it had once been two bedrooms and a hallway. The previous owner had removed the walls and vaulted the ceiling, removing part of the floor in the attic to do so. He'd begun to drywall but had failed to put any insulation in first. All that work would have to come out, and much of the framing would need to be redone.

"The piles of shit are the worst," Garrett said, grabbing another board.

"I can deal with the shit, it's the needles I hate," I told him. "AIDS is real, man. Hepatitis."

"The worst is when the needles are sticking out of the shit," Will chimed in. He was wandering around taking pictures with his digital camera because I didn't own one. He had found a raccoon living in the house and had taken photos of his muddy little paw prints exiting the windows.

I was finally seeing what this would entail. The house was huge, bigger than I needed. I had probably chosen—on the spectrum of abandoned houses that were feasibly repairable—one of the worst. Everything needed to be redone. I could see daylight through the hole in the roof, and I would have to string a tarp up there first thing after I bought it. The trash was overwhelming. Even just the windows would cost a fortune, if I had someone else do them. The only way I got comparatively lucky was there were only a few holes in the floor and the risks of falling through a story was minimal.

As we finished there was a spectacle in the neighborhood, caused by our presence. Will busied himself hanging the steel door in the front while I told the neighbors about my plans. They looked at me as if they didn't know whether to laugh or call the authorities. The only other two occupied houses on my block were inhabited by single women. Behind the Queen Anne was only one house, holding a friendly elderly family and their children, the rest of their block recently cut grass. I recognized some of the people to the south and got the sense everyone knew one another, and many of the people were family. Nobody called the police.

Will was just finishing up the door and Jake was nearby, cheering him on. As I went to the truck to get the lock, Jake spray-painted on the door, "Drew's house, WATCHED," and "Protected by Smith and Wesson." I thought this gave the wrong message so I spray-painted over it, the gray door turning blue. I fitted the padlock into the door and for the first time in ten years the house was no longer open to the world.

————

After I purchased the house with my orange bidder card, I was shuffled into another room to sign papers concerning the deed. I took photos of everything I signed, knowing the City of Detroit was notoriously bad at the details. When the deed came a month later, they had spelled my name wrong.

When Jake and I returned to Forestdale from the auction, neighbors were waiting for us in Paul's house. Two other people on the block had purchased houses or lots that day and there was a celebration going on. Paul had killed and cooked one of his chickens, and as I walked into the house Molly threw me a can of beer.

"You got a new Carhartt and an old house!" she said.

Paul gave me a hug and shook my hand. It was the first time he'd done so. "They call it real estate because it's real," he said, his eyes twinkling.

That night all of my new friends piled into cars with six-packs and went over to my new house. We smoked a joint on the porch, and I looked upon the dream and the nightmare of the best years of my life.

There was a grumpy quality to the neighborhood, and the city, but it eased open with familiarity. Detroit wasn't a blank canvas.

There were people already making their lives there, and I hadn't "discovered" anything. As it turned out I would need their help.

Detroit stayed the same. It was I who had changed. I'd lived there less than two years, but I was learning. Detroit ceased to be a black stone monolith and became a garden of variety. It had always been that way, but my ignorance had hidden it from me. The city wasn't a playground, and I had a responsibility if I was going to do this. I wanted to add my voice, not overwrite what was already happening. There was a community already here, not a grotesque one that needed changing as I had been told, but a powerful and innovative one I wanted to assimilate into.

I would be staying in Detroit no matter what. I was a home-owner, I paid taxes, and in time I would be a true Detroiter. I was twenty-three years old.

CHAPTER 3

Someone Else's Trash

A nearby house burns down

The Forestdale house was looking less like a shell and, while not exactly like home, maybe a dusky cottage. I had gotten as far as I could before winter. I had insulated the walls and ceiling, but wouldn't put drywall or any covering over it. For the kitchen and the bathroom I had made makeshift sink basins from pieces of plywood and scrap lumber. There was an empty stud wall between the two rooms, but nothing facing it. You could see right through. Entertaining was going to be a problem.

Kinga and I had finished all the electricity, so the lights worked, but still the only plumbing I had was cold water. I had a cookstove and arranged my workbench in the kitchen as best I could to make a food prep space. My family had donated some rugs, so they added some cheer to the room, and I did what I could to hang up any art that I had or had been given to me by the block. This is key: cheer, in the form of wall hangings and trinkets of joy, is essential for making it in a formerly abandoned house.

An ex-girlfriend had given me a wood-burning stove, which really wasn't a stove but a porous and thin fireplace insert, that I hooked into the crumbling chimney and surrounded the best I could with bricks so as to not burn the house down. I placed two chairs in front of it, both plucked from the city dump.

When the house was clean it wasn't bad. The new place got plenty of light with new windows installed, and I used bedsheets for some makeshift curtains. There was a claw-foot bathtub, but it wasn't hooked up, and the last item I had was a bookshelf I had found in the trash. I had no idea how cold the winter would get, no idea what brutal, unending cold can do to a person. This was my first stab at building a habitation. Everyone starts somewhere. It was time to start thinking seriously about my own house.

I understood how brave the Detroit firefighters were when I saw a three-story home in my neighborhood on fire, smoke and flames spewing from the windows. As the fire trucks surrounded the blaze and firemen in yellow-and-brown suits rushed around connecting hoses, shouting into radios and spraying water into the void, there was someone on the roof. Straddling the ridgeline was a firefighter. As the house burned he *chopped at the roof with an axe.* He's not only sitting on a flaming house, he's cutting away at the very thing supporting him. Furiously he chopped, finally making a hole that began to gush thick black smoke.

A few weeks later I saw a group of firemen at a local diner and asked them about it. They said they needed to open a hole in the roof to let out the smoke, like a chimney, so they could go inside and make sure nobody was still in there. I tried to buy their lunch but they refused.

Detroit is the most flammable city in America. We even have an image of the city burning on our flag, and a quote in Latin, "We hope for better things. It will rise from the ashes." There are a dozen "suspicious" fires a day on average, marked thus because the city has only seven arson investigators, total. The fire department itself says it responds to 9,000 structure fires a year, at least 5,000 of them suspicious. That's one fire for every eighty people in the city. Conservatively. If each of the arson investigators worked every day of the year, seven days a week including holidays, and investigated one fire a day each, they wouldn't even get to half of them. Realistically, they are able to investigate only one in every five "suspicious" fires a year.

People, I've learned in Detroit, burn down houses for all kinds of reasons. Sometimes it's a firebug who does it for the spectacle or because they are mentally ill; some houses are burned down for insurance profit or to get rid of a structure being used as a dope house or brothel; some fires are set for revenge or out of anger; some to make the scrapping of the house easier. People in places like Detroit witness so much change but have little control over it, and burning things down can be their chance to take that control back.

I myself have seen too many fires in my neighborhood to count. We used to chase them, follow the black smoke in our trucks to see what was burning. It was exciting, something fun to do. I don't do that anymore, having realized how grotesque and morbid that is. With enough time I didn't even need to go far. In total I have watched two houses and an abandoned store burn to the ground from my back porch. That's three fires within one block of my house.

One of the first I saw up close was just a block away from Forestdale. I watched it burn, and the closest I could get was thirty yards away. These houses don't just smolder, they *blaze*. The houses are old and balloon-framed, and the wood is incredibly dry. They go up spectacularly. You can feel the heat from hundreds of yards away, watch the rising black smoke for miles. Entire two-story houses wrapped in roaring flames. They actually roar.

Some days are worse than others. In 2014 there was a day with thirty-six fires. Some weekends are bad as well. There were a hundred fires over July 4 weekend that same year. But the king of them all is Devil's Night, the annual orgy of arson and destruction on Halloween weekend. At its peak in 1984, there were eight hundred fires over a three-day period. The words "Devil's Night" still bring chills to longtime Detroiters and the understaffed and underfunded fire department—sometimes using stacked pop cans and a fax machine for an alarm—their ladders and hoses critically unmaintained for lack of money.

Devil's Night occurred two weeks after I bought my house. I decided this should be the first time I stayed in it, to make sure it didn't burn. I gathered my supplies: a fire extinguisher and smoke detector I bought earlier that day; an axe for protection; a climbing rope borrowed from a friend; various lanterns and flashlights; a battery-powered radio for company; and some blankets, beer, a book. I also included the deed in case the cops or firefighters wondered what I was doing in this abandoned house. The last thing I brought was a snow shovel, because I would still need to clean out a bedroom.

None of the entryways into the house had stairs yet, and the rear door was just a piece of plywood screwed to the frame, so I pulled my truck bed against the front porch and hopped up. A family of pheasants flew from the backyard and startled me. I watched their halting glide for a moment, glad for the presence of another living being.

I opened the door for the first time, unlatched the padlock with a click, and threw open the steel: piles of trash, darkness, the stairway leading up. I turned on the flashlight, grabbed my bag, and headed to the second floor. It began to drizzle, and the evening was cold. It was barely still daylight, and I needed to get to work.

I selected a bedroom in the front corner, figuring this would give me the most visibility. The walls had been painted pink by whoever owned it before me, but because of the scrappers ripping out electrical wires and the leaking roof, there were great holes in the ceiling. The lath jutting out was ragged, hanging this way and that, angry, like a poisonous plant. The floors were buckled from the water and littered with piles of plaster. There was a stack of rotting drywall in the corner. Home sweet home.

I took the plywood off the windows to let in what light I still had left, and I set lanterns in each signaling "someone is here." I tied the rope around a sturdy stud in the bathroom and uncoiled it near the window, so in an emergency I could throw it out and climb down. I set the radio, axe, and fire extinguisher in the cleanest corner and got to work with the shovel on the plaster, piling it in the bathroom.

In one of the piles of garbage downstairs I found a mop with a yellow handle and missing only half its bristles. I captured some rainwater from the roof in a bucket, also found in the house, and mopped the bedroom as best I could to at least wet the plaster dust down. It's deathly toxic. I brought the blankets from the truck, made a pallet, turned on the radio to the oldies station, and surveyed my home. That's when it began to drip in the room. I moved my blankets to escape the water. That's also when the cops showed up.

I first heard them shouting outside, but when I looked out the window I could see only the car, no officers. I fished the purchase documents from my bag and headed downstairs. I opened the door and saw three pistols pointed in my direction.

Reflexively I put my hands up. I explained that I owned the house and was watching over it for the night. I told the lead officer I had the documents in my hand and they put their weapons down. The first officer holstered his and I handed him the papers and he smiled.

"You're making our job easy tonight."

I told them how much I'd spent, and they smiled and shook their heads as they left. I was alone in my house for the first night.

I walked through the filthy rooms with a lantern, looking for treasures, planning. It was laid out with a double parlor in the front, and a kitchen, bathroom, bedroom, and dining room in the rear. I figured I would have to carve out a small space, just a couple of rooms, to start. Basically I would need to fashion an efficiency apartment within the house. I would only heat this small section and everything else would run wild for the time being, a common practice in rehabbing Detroit homes without using loans.

The backside of the house was the most suited for this outpost. I could remove the walls separating the kitchen, bedroom, and dining room, creating one large space. The cramped bathroom could be enlarged to fit a shower. Getting clean was crucial if I wanted to work and make money. In the winters it would be the warmest fifteen minutes of my day.

The kitchen would have to be totally redone, the plaster demolished, the basement door moved to provide more space for countertops, and a new, bigger window put in to provide light, a back door added, plumbing, sink, stove, gas, everything. In the coming weeks Eric, a kid from New York in for an artist residency, would help me measure the space and draw a crude picture of what I hoped it to be. I would take this picture and measurements to my grandfather, a master draftsman and carpenter, and he would teach me to make a scale drawing using an architect's scale. He'd never received any formal training as an architect, but he was a damn good one, his teacher being experience building houses. He had tiny cardboard cutouts of toilets, refrigerators, and stoves that I could move around within the drawing and get a sense of where I wanted appliances placed.

For now I was left with the night. Some ratty cabinets lay spilled across the floor along with some bags of leaves and garden clippings. One of the bags had broken open and leaves crunched beneath my feet.

Looking closer in one of the cabinets, I found children's toys: a pink-and-yellow carousel that appeared to be in ideal shape, some grungy-looking crayons, an action figure missing the head. As I explored further I found more children's things, a tiny Superman onesie, marbles, squirt guns. On the inside of the closet door in the first-floor bedroom someone had scrawled "Colby's closet" in childlike lettering. This made me sad.

It was raining hard now, the wind gusting. I was in for a cold night. Through the roof, through the second-floor ceiling, through the second floor and first-floor ceiling into a frank little puddle, the water had begun to drip into the kitchen now as well. The rain crept toward an upside-down photograph, which I picked up. A smiling family, a boy, maybe Colby, his hand in excitement in the air, his teeth straight and white and distinct like Chiclets.

I returned upstairs. Both of my lanterns had been knocked off the windowsill and the rain was whipping inside. The puddles from the dripping ceiling had begun to run. It was going to be a wet night, too. I replaced the lanterns and opened one of the beers and began to read from the complete Shakespeare that I had brought.

I tried my best to creep into the corner, away from the wet, but it was going to be impossible if the rain kept up like this. I should have considered bringing a book that was maybe a little easier, because try as I might, the Shakespeare wasn't keeping my attention. This wasn't going to be like a camping trip. It's hard to have any fun when your jeans are soaked to the knees and the hems of your shirtsleeves play about your wrists with the tickling and stinging cold of wet.

But this was my duty. This wasn't always going to be fun. This was work, my cross to bear—

Someone outside was yelling, and I figured it was the cops again so I grabbed my deed and headed downstairs. What I saw instead made me happy and interrupted my sanctimony.

Sunny had moved to Detroit at about the same time I had. He had just come from living in a Buddhist monastery and had the soft and jolly countenance of a monk—not the silent kind, the beer-making kind. He had a hearty clucking laugh and was quick with it. People called him Sunny for a reason, and he could instantly change a room with his goodwill and joviality. His real name is Patrick, from Irish stock, and the Buddhist name he received was Sun-Chim. Sunny made more sense.

As I hopped off the porch he was untying a sleeping bag from his bicycle, one of those touring rigs people ride across the country, as he had done the year before. I had told him I would be defending my house from fire this night but must have forgotten, and he had come through at the last minute. I was hoping the sleeping bag meant he was in for the long haul, too. Maybe this journey wasn't going to be as lonely as I thought.

"Sunny!" I approached him to shake his hand, but he gave me a hug instead. He was soaking wet.

"Thanks for coming by, buddy." All of my other friends were looking after their own houses.

"I wasn't going to leave you alone on a night like this. I brought beer, too." Sunny was studying to be a brewer and once let me make a batch with him. After we bottled it for storage, he found a couple of mice among our additional grain. We called it Two Mouse Porter.

He clapped me on the back one more time after looking me in the eye and headed into the house.

"It's drippy in here!" he said, laughing. "It's like a sewer, like the Teenage Mutant Ninja Turtles."

"Yeah, I guess."

"I get to be Donatello."

"Wh—"

"You can be Michelangelo. This is a bitchin' pad. You're going to have so much fun in here. Where can I put my stuff?"

I showed him the room we were sleeping in and he laughed, rubbing his hands together. "Rustic." He clapped. "I like it. Yeah, yeah, yeah. Real manly like."

He grabbed me on the shoulder and shook me, hard enough to chatter my teeth, smiling. He laughed again. "Well, let's get down to business." He opened a beer and sat against his sleeping bag. "So what are you going to do first?"

We chatted into the night, and Sunny told me stories from his past and his travels, his shadow playing against the wall as he stood and gestured, pacing around the room, inhabiting the characters and using different voices. He fiddled with the radio, explored the house, made little dioramas with the trash, wrote his name on the wall—on the inside—so "you can remember who slept with you on Devil's Night," and generally made the time pass quickly. Before we went to bed he asked me, "So, you really think you'll be able to make it here?"

"There's no other way than to find out."

"Let me know when you need any help."

"I will, bud. I'm sure I'll need a lot."

"I hope you're all right here, man. I don't think I'd be able to do this."

I didn't have anything to say to that.

We slept fitfully in the cold.

I awoke to daylight and Sunny shouting "Victory" to the morning. He was awake before me and was bare chested, looking out the window with his hands at his sides, hooked into his belt. He crowed like a rooster and observed me with a devilish grin. "Victory," he whispered. "Victory!" He shouted that time.

"We made it through Devil's Night!"

"Roll up your victory sleeping bag so you can buy me victory breakfast," he said.

He crowed and strutted around a bit more, gathering his things, happily talking to himself. "And these are my victory shoes, and now I'll roll up my victory sleeping bag . . ."

"Hold on, wait, what? I just. Why don't you have a shirt on? It's freezing."

"You better hurry up because we need to stop at my house first so I can take a victory shit."

———

I had an impossible number of things to do to get ready to live in this bad boy.

I was going to have to accomplish all this mostly on my own with whatever help I could rustle up from friends and family. The first thing to do was to clean the trash out, which I did with a pitchfork and a snow shovel. I'm talking small mountains of clothing, yard waste, empty tin cans, toys, diapers, those white foam trays that raw meat comes in, used auto parts, construction debris, liquor store plastic bags and bottles, rolls of old carpeting, broken furniture and glass, literal piles of human shit, uncapped needles.

I found the better part of a Dodge Caravan inside, cut into chunks with a reciprocating saw. From what folks who grew up in Detroit told me, it was an "insurance job." Someone had needed the money, so they reported the van stolen and paid a couple of guys to cut it apart and deposit it around the city. Most of it made it into my house. The amount of garbage that had found its way inside was amazing. The initial cleanout took three months. Including plaster, I removed more than ten thousand pounds of trash, five tons, from my house.

TO DO:

Start Garden!
Collect scraps
& compost

- Patch the Roof, tarp the rest

- Move Trash to incinerator

- Remove oak trim from Doors
  Windows & Baseboards - carefully

- bust & haul out Plaster

- remove lath & make neat piles outside

- Brick up holes in Basement (RATS)

- 7 windows to Frame & install.
  Black Window for Shower

- rear door - Find | Install now |

- Build Porch to reach Door

- Sister Broken Floor Joists

- Jack up house to compensate for
  Missing Posts. Add Bracing.

- move Basement door out of Kitchen
  to Crawl Corner

- Two walls to tear out

- | Header to load bearing |
  -Get from collapsed building
  down street

- Tear out Bathroom - add space for
  built in Shower with basin

- Install Plumbing to Kitchen, bathroom
  & H₂O heater. 2 Sinks, 2 toilets, Shower.
  Make Plan for installation w/o freezing

- Vent Plumbing: Replace Broken Soil Stalk
  Vent whole system through Roof

- Build Shower: Pour basin, tile, grout

- Set up Lectrical Box in basement
  run Service wire to top of house
  Wire All outlets Before Sheetrock
  | Pass inspection |

- Install H₂O Heater - Buy | Insulate |

- Install Furnace - Buy

- Install Black iron gas PIPE to stove
  Plus Stove

- DUCTS enough for winter | Keep fingers SAFE ✓ |

- Install Wood Stove & Hearth

- Install temporary metal chimney - Buy

- Machete through Backyard

- build Fence for future dog (!)

- Firewood: Find, cut, split | Build Shed |

- Install interior Doors - Seal rooms for
  (gaps - install trim)   Winter

- Hang Sheetrock: MUD 4x Sand, Paint

- Gather Supplies - Sinks, Furnace
  Stove, H₂O Heater, electrical, Tools

I would back my truck up to the porch and push everything into the bed. I carried what I could from upstairs in trash cans I had found in the neighborhood, slipping, lifting, falling down the stairs, spilling the contents of the cans on myself. It was a filthy job, and I was scared of being pricked with a needle, of which I found many. I shoveled the feces, picked out the metal to scrap, and attempted to save anything else useful or possessing artistic merit for souvenirs.

I removed the existing trim carefully. It was truly beautiful, not something that would be stocked in any big box home-improvement store anywhere, ever. Made from old-growth oak, the baseboards were almost a foot tall, door casings six inches wide with intricate bevels. Header casings over windows were oak nearly an inch thick, eight inches tall with mitered corners and painstaking flowing ornate detail. For a reason I can't understand, it had all been painted. Likely the slumlord before me had been in a rush and covered up the natural beauty to save a few pennies.

They don't make material like that anymore. It was in thousands of houses around the city, houses the politicians were calling blight. That old-growth oak, pine, maple would be pushed into the ground with the backhoe like everything else, gone forever. It could have been harvested, WPA-style, and provided quite a few jobs. But you needed imagination to see the wealth amid the danger. For now it was simply destroyed in what amounted to a stunning waste of resources.

All the plaster in my main three rooms needed to go. It was a shame, because plaster is better-looking and blocks sound better than cheap drywall, but this was too far gone to save. It had crumbled in many places, and I wanted to get utilities like wiring and ducts in quickly anyway. I'd be able to use roll insulation instead of having to blow it in, too. I wanted to start, at least in these first rooms, with a clean slate.

The plaster was original to the house, and made with real horsehair. A lost art, it consisted of a layer of lath, thin rough strips of wood nailed with quarter-inch gaps horizontally across the studs. This would hold a rough cement layer, reinforced with horsehair and smeared on quickly to flatten the wall and create a base. This rough undercoat would support a final smooth top layer of plaster that could be painted. I learned to smash it out in reverse. Beat out the layers of plaster without disturbing the lath and it could be scooped up with a snow shovel and dumped into buckets. The lath could then be removed on its own and stacked for future use, kindling, decorative wall cover, spacers.

Wearing a respirator, I worked one room at a time, miniature sledge in one hand, crowbar in the other. It was like Mordor in there. Because there was no electricity I worked by the light of a battery-powered fluorescent and whatever I could get from the windows. The dust swirled with each shovelful, the plastic of the respirator sticking to my face with sweat, swing after swing. The rooms would become filled with plaster smoke and get darker as I worked, the open windows like a bright hole in ice viewed from underwater. When I couldn't take any more I'd head outside and tear the mask from my face, drinking the clean air. I'd let the dust settle for a moment, then head back inside.

I would come home with black soot covering any exposed part of my body. When I rinsed off in the shower the water would pool darkly about my feet. Jeans and T-shirts used for demolition had to be washed all by themselves. It was repellent, but I'd come home to Forestdale closer to my goal by one day.

I removed the wall between the dining and living rooms. It was non-load-bearing and came out pretty easily. The wall running east and west separating the kitchen from this space was going to be a bit more tricky. It held the weight of the house and would have to be replaced with a giant header. The studs on each end needed to be reinforced underneath, and temporary walls had to be built on either side to hold the house up while this was happening. A chimney had once run along this wall and had been removed, leaving a dangerous hole in the floor and sagging main beams in the basement that appeared to have once rested on corbels in the chimney. The beam now sagged, lacking support. The whole house would need to be jacked up. I patched the hole in the floor and left the rest for later.

In the wall separating my main three rooms from the parlors hung a pocket door, five feet wide, two inches solid, made of oak. It was likely worth more than I'd bought the house for. There had been others in the parlor, but they had been stolen. This one had jammed unmovable in the wall, saved because it wasn't functioning. When I broke out the plaster, I was able to pry the door up and onto its track. I greased the bearings and the slab slid in and out like magic, closing off my three little rooms from the rest of the house. Good as new, aside from the hideous lime-green-and-silver paint job the landlord had done. The door would need to be stripped eventually, but for now sliding it into place was good enough.

I saved all the materials I could for future use. I also saved pictures I found, including one of a woman with an enormous rear in lacy panties posing suggestively. I found a half dozen doors in the pile, saved those, some errant trim, saved that, too. The rest went to the incinerator. I must have looked strange as hell to the neighbors, pulling this horrid shit from this house that no one wanted, struggling by myself to get it in my truck and come back for more.

At the incinerator, located down the street, they would take only one load a day, maximum one thousand pounds. Occasionally I would recruit Will or someone on Forestdale to come with me for the second go-round, use their ID so I could make two trips before the sun went down. The guy at the entrance was the same each time, a white guy with a walrus mustache who could be friendly on the right day. He'd take your address at a little kiosk as the garbage trucks whizzed past. If I was overweight he would let me go back and pick up some of what I'd left instead of paying the forty-dollar fee.

"I remember you," he said one slow afternoon. "You're the only white guy that comes here."

Past the gate, an enormous shed, as long as a football field and just as deep, held a trash pile almost three stories tall. You'd dump your garbage on the ground in front and a bulldozer would scrape it onto Trash Mountain, the dozer climbing the pile itself, listing backward like a caterpillar on a heap of horseshit. Seagulls fought in the yard and the smell was gut-wrenching, sour and poignant. You could taste it.

The "world's largest municipal incinerator" was heavily subsidized. Detroit has an asthma hospitalization rate three times the national average, and the highest rate of asthma in children among large cities in the United States. Nearly one in six residents suffers from the disease. The incinerator releases almost five tons of toxins—about what I removed from my trash-packed house—into the air each *day*. It's inconceivable they would place something like that in a neighborhood that wasn't poor and black.

Because of hideous deal after hideous deal the city worked out with various businesses (including at one time Philip Morris the tobacco giant, in some kind of perverse joke about air quality), suburban communities pay less to burn their trash in the incinerator than Detroit does. Some cities in the suburbs not only bring their trash to be burned in my neighborhood, for me and my neighbors to breathe, they pay less to do so than we do.

In 2010 the incinerator contract, despite one of the largest community outcries in Detroit's history, was renewed until 2021. In an amazing bit of Orwellian language the new owners are now calling the literal garbage fire "green energy," because of some steam heat and electricity it generates for downtown. More suspect tax credits for the incinerator were passed that year, with two city council members switching their votes at the last minute without explanation.

If you would like an inside look at Detroit's continuing third-world level of corruption, a good place to start is the incinerator.

"The only difference between Detroit and third world nations—where corruption is concerned—is goats in the streets."

Sam Riddle said that, and he would know. In 2010 he was convicted of corruption, extortion, bribery, fraud, etc., along with Monica Conyers, then president pro tem of the city council and wife of the storied U.S. representative John Conyers. Riddle and Monica Conyers both spent time in prison, Conyers while her husband was seated in the House.

You can safely say there is a culture of corruption in your city when the top two politicians, including a former mayor, have been, or are currently, in prison for corruption, racketeering, and the like. One former city councilwoman allegedly requested a bribe including seventeen pounds of sausages. The former police chief was indicted for theft totaling $2.6 million. The former school board president resigned from office only after masturbating in front of the female superintendent. Former Detroit city council president Charles Pugh just pled guilty to having sex with a fourteen-year-old boy and received five and a half to fifteen years in prison. The former city treasurer was just locked up. One Detroit high school principal used to drive a Maserati, purchased with crooked dollars.

The list of corruption, just over the last few decades, is too exhaustive to publish here. It could be its own book. And these are just the ones that got caught, just in Detroit. In its latest national study, the Center for Public Integrity listed Michigan dead last in laws and safeguards for ethics and transparency.

Soon after I bought my house the incinerator was sold again, and the private company started charging forty dollars a half ton to bring debris. Not only did I have to breathe its air, I couldn't take my junk—which was really someone else's—there anymore either.

The danger of sorting through someone else's trash, *breathing* someone else's trash, is that it can make you misanthropic. You can begin to hate the petty little modern conveniences such as plastic bags that never disappear, and with it begin to loathe not only the people that dropped them there, but the society that allowed them to. When the wind is right I smell not just the vomitus stench of a pile of burning trash, but years of corruption and neglect, not just in Detroit but of a society itself that refuses to come to terms with the waste of our rabid consumption.

But who am I to talk? I smoke cigarettes and sometimes throw the butts on the ground. I give part of the money I earn to a giant corporation whose profits are built solely upon addicting people and keeping them hooked until they die. What can I say, they got me early. As much as I hate it, I plunk my seven dollars on the counter for a pouch of tobacco and I roll it up and I smoke it. It might make me a hypocrite, but does it make me less worthy of clean air in general? The kids on Forestdale? Does what I do as an individual prevent me from criticizing a moneymaking entity from poisoning a city? Do I have to be perfect, beyond reproach, to criticize anything? Is the truth less the truth from the mouth of a sinner?

Just this year the owners of the incinerator notified some Poletown residents, including many on Forestdale, of a class-action lawsuit settlement they can take advantage of. They're offering about $7,000 in exchange for waiving all rights to take future legal action against the owners of the plant spewing the smog that's killing them.

———

There wasn't much more I could get done at my place before the winter snowed everything in. I'd gotten most of the trash out, but had accomplished little else, not that I'd planned to. It was getting too cold. Shivering without heat at my house on Forestdale didn't exactly provide the energy for dirty construction work. At least on Forestdale I could sit by the fire. The winter was for planning, and getting through it. I took as many shifts at the bar as I could to build up some money for the spring, not that there was much money anyway. Working just above minimum wage doesn't allow one to get ahead. Any money I did gather was spent immediately on storing materials for the spring so I didn't spend it on something stupid in the meantime.

The first weekend in November had come, and so time for the Harvest Party, Forestdale's annual celebration of the bounty of the summer. The farmer's carnival includes hayrides, bonfires, and homemade apple cider and cherry wine, pressed from fruit grown right on the block. On unlucky years it'll snow. It marks both a relief from the work of the summer and a push through the frigid and lonely winter, a promise spring will return.

Paul drives the tractor, a blue Ford diesel from the '40s, good-looking in the sinewy-horse sort of way of mechanical vehicles built just after World War II. He reserves a couple of dozen bales of hay each year to fill the wagon to give the children hayrides. The adults love them, too. They get faster and wilder as Paul becomes increasingly drunk. He's hit parked cars in the past.

The ride begins by snaking first through what we call the Back 40: All but two of the houses on the block behind Forestdale are gone. Instead of letting the space slowly fill up with trash and despair, Paul planted an orchard. In the summer peaches and pears and apples and plums grow on the trees. Vegetables of every make and model grow in the soil. Neighbors care for bees and collect honey in autumn. At one time it was used to exercise the horses that were stabled on the block—remember, this is in walking distance from downtown Detroit.

In the winter Paul floods the center of the horse track to make an ice rink. The growing area is situated in a great oval, about an acre, with space in the middle for the rink and a track running around the outside. The fruit trees ring the exterior of that, like an elongated bull's-eye. Paul's not sure how many of the actual lots he owns, but two at the far end are untouched save for a small path meandering through. Paul left these just as they were to show the contrast between what he had done and the wilderness it would have become. Some of the neighborhood kids erected a teepee back there and play their version of cops and robbers, standing on the enormous compost hill or flitting in and out among the farm implements Paul has collected, cabin-size combines, seeders, thrashing and harvesting machines, the hay baler.

Before the Harvest Party, Paul hides pumpkins he grows amid the foliage and each hayride pauses momentarily so the children can jump out and hunt for a pumpkin to take home with them. When they've each found one the ride continues through the community garden, which Molly cares for, and then past the house I was staying in.

The tractor snakes its way down the block and through backyards and alleys, passing the houses of ordinary people doing extraordinary yet simple things. These were folks who looked for community and an honest life and found it in Detroit: Adam the chef and his two children; Tim the Stanford graduate working in landscaping; Betty the generous and testy bartender and her on-again off-again boyfriend who shoots heroin but everyone likes anyway; Minnehaha, who grew up in the Belizean jungle with a white beauty queen mother and a Black Power father; Monk, a quiet lifelong resident and often the block's conscience; Paul's two grown sons and their growing families; Dan and Anne, a Polish couple who never left.

These aren't characters, remember, but real people. And maybe not the kind you think of when you think of Detroit, maybe not the kind you see on the news. Mothers who care for their children, people who work hard and only want their fair due, folks who care for one another in very real ways. Detroiters who aren't desperate or corrupt or criminals. Why don't we ever see these people representing Detroit?

It's a good question.

Children run the length of the block playing tag, riding skateboards, and the adults laugh, shout a greeting to an old friend, or eat venison stew or rabbit chili. The hay in the hay wagon is pokey and Paul has had a half dozen beers. I'm holding one, too, sitting next to Will, who has an unlit cigarette. The kids in the hay wagon are chanting, "Paul's too slow! Paul's too slow! Paul's too slow!" He revs the engine and the kids scream, knowing what's coming: the walls of the hay wagon bulge and I hold on to the railings as Will starts to holler his enjoyment.

Paul revs the engine again, this time for real, and we're off, careening around corners and jerking the wagon back and forth as the kids scream their joy and my beer slops out of the cup onto Will. We're thrust against one another in the packed wagon and everyone laughs and is happy, if only momentarily; the hay that Paul grew to feed the animals and my friends and neighbors feels powerful beneath my seat, my community helping one another and expressing joy in this place they said no one could love, a joy that cannot be bought. After another year of shit-kicking work in a community without consumers, I know I am home.

———

BAM! BAM! BAM! BAM! BAM! BAM!

I sat bolt upright out of bed from a deep sleep, gasping for air, my heart pounding. The gunshots sounded like a 9 mm from less than a block away. You always wonder when a stray one is going to rip through the house. The delight of the Harvest Party was through, and winter had set in.

There were gunshots almost daily near Forestdale at that time, and with police response at almost an hour, why call the cops? If you called them for every gunshot, you'd be calling them every day. The rounds would ring out like reminders to never forget that I could be seriously injured at any moment, that I could never get too comfortable. Fitfully I tried to get back to sleep.

A pleasant temperature inside the Forestdale house that winter, with the fire roaring, would be just under 50 degrees Fahrenheit. January in Michigan averages in the teens. I couldn't ever get the fire to burn overnight, and even during the day I could see my breath. My uniform that year was a Carhartt, wool hat, and insulated overalls, which I swore I would never wear because I find them hideous. The cold got the best of me. I would sleep in my coat and hat as well, and my father was worried I would asphyxiate under so many blankets.

One morning I woke up and the temperature in the house was especially savage. I could see my breath, and had to count down from ten to get out of bed. When I sat on my toilet, I saw an icicle the size of a carrot hanging from the sink faucet. I generally tried to keep the faucets dripping at night, as it's more difficult for running water to freeze, but it was getting too cold even for that and the pipes had frozen shut. I was showering down the street at Molly's and work on my new house had come to a halt on account of the cold.

I struggled to do anything, just to get out of bed. The stony cold, the hunger—the whole world fucking sucks, and you are just so small, only one person. And what the hell are you going to do, all by yourself and cold and hungry? You can't even take care of *you*. Now you're trying to get ahead a little bit, build a house? You can't even feed yourself properly.

But you get out of bed anyway. What else is there to do? You get up because you want to tell that motherfucker on TV he is a liar and a leech, along with anyone else who said you're crazy, who laughed at you and anyone like you. The anger can keep you going, but you have to suppress some of it and channel it into building something. Destroying things doesn't work anymore.

The cold created a frantic animal insanity. It's like being deep underwater, the pressure everywhere. Warming up wasn't as easy as jumping in a cold pool in the summer to cool down. Thawing out took a good hour and a half. And then you would become sleepy. Drinking helped a little, but was dangerous and expensive. The cold worms its way through your mind as if it were an apple. My pens would freeze. I would have to warm them up in a pot of water on the stove, careful to not let the tips slip under the surface and create an inky mess. It became a nightly ritual I called the "unthawing of the pens." My aunt came to visit that winter, and the dishes in my sink had frozen, plates and forks sticking out this way and that. She almost fainted.

On some of the coldest nights, my firewood running out, desperate, I attempted to burn some of the books I had collected during previous years for donating to prisons. Burning them never really worked (they create too much ash). I don't know if it's a sin to burn books to keep yourself warm when you're cold and hungry and out of firewood. I do know I had definitely thought it was, before I had to make that choice myself.

The more I was hungry and cold, the more I was aware there were hungry and cold people in the world. And it made me want to work harder. I thought it was important to experience what a large part of my new community was experiencing. I decided it would not defeat me, and I would use the cold, hunger, and physical pain to harden my body and will. I couldn't have done anything about it anyway, because I had nowhere to go and no money to get there.

I wasn't the only person without heat. Just on the block, Jake and Monk didn't have it either. I met dozens of people who have gone without: preachers, artists, the elderly. Heat is the biggest winter living expense, and it's the first thing to go. I've met more longtime

Detroiters who have gone without heat for at least one winter than haven't. The most common question I hear about a living situation is "Do you have heat in there?"

The local power and gas utility, DTE, is universally loathed. It's a for-profit company, and its rates keep going up. They do lots of "charity" in an attempt for people to say, "Well, look at all the good they do for the community." People don't need some ratty donated coats. They need fair prices on their heating bills.

The winter wasn't all bad, though. One Tuesday evening, about eight o'clock, I came home and thought a bottle of wine might take the edge off the chill. I've bought maybe three bottles of wine in my life, almost always sticking to the blue-collar staples of beer and whiskey. After buying it at a supermarket, I realized I didn't have a corkscrew, so I walked down the block, looking for someone outside, who I wouldn't disturb at dinner or family time or art making. Molly was stringing blue Christmas lights on her bushes, and offered to pop the cork.

Her house was always warm and full of animals. Between her and her roommate, Jennie, there were seven cats, two dogs, a couple of rabbits who lived in the garage, and chickens. The previous summer she had found two baby pheasants whose mother had been killed. They were too young to survive on their own, so Molly made an entire room in her house into a habitat for them, complete with sticks and grass and enough space to run freely until they were old enough for the wild. It was Molly's nature to care for things.

She was so fastidious, though, that her house never smelled of animals. The walls were painted vibrant orange or green, and were filled with art she had purchased in Detroit over the past twenty-five years: paintings of chickens, skulls, silver-painted guns, a 400-pound printing press someone had found in an abandoned school and given her, accidental Detroit ephemera that is daily growing in value. She had gone to art school, and as it turned out her skill was in curation.

She was the best hostess on the block, supremely generous, and an excellent carpenter.

In the center of her living room sat a wood-burning stove, and she had made a sitting cove behind it with a bench and lambswool pelt. As we chatted and I opened the bottle, she loaded the stove with wood. She would let me shower at her house, and left the front door open and unlocked so I could do so at my leisure. This is in East Detroit, remember. Most people have bars on their doors and windows.

The bathroom was tiled in colorful mosaic, work she had done herself. Usually she had candles lit, and a cat was most often curled up in the sink. Jennie had drawn faces on the toilet paper rolls over the toilet, and as I would shower she would sometimes sing and practice her guitar in the living room. I longed to ask her to play in the kitchen so I could hear her better, but was always too scared. I would take my time getting ready just to listen to her for a bit longer. Molly had insisted I use one of her towels, which she would launder for me, and it hung on a peg by the door next to hers and Jennie's.

When I got the wine open I offered her a glass. She asked me about work at the new French restaurant where she had just hired me, and at which she was the executive chef. She had been on vacation and was wondering how I was getting along.

Seven hours later I was dancing to ABBA in her living room with Jennie, who had returned from work to wine and whiskey bottles rolling about the floor. Four in the morning and Molly was splay legged on the rug, bouncing her head, looking at a record cover, schooling me on the '80s music I'd missed. That was the beauty of living on Forestdale. It was almost impossible to be lonely. No matter how hungry I was or how broke I was, someone would always feed me, invite me in, have a dance party on a Tuesday in the winter. It had snowed half a foot during our private party, pure white soft snow, the good thick kind, and all three of us decided to take a walk with the dogs on account of the beauty and wonder.

Outside was still and foggy. While we drank, the neighborhood kids had made what seemed like hundreds of tiny snowmen and placed them upon everything, on the hoods of cars, in front lawns, up in trees resting on branches. There were hundreds of all different sizes, perfect little three-ball snowmen with rocks for eyes and twigs for arms, none standing more than a couple of feet tall, the smallest the size of a tin can. Someone had built one on top of my mailbox, and when I opened it there was another inside. Each snowman smiled and glistened white in the silver darkness of a fresh Michigan snow and a full moon.

That winter I was the most broke, hungry, and cold I'd ever been, but no one on that block ever let me go without. They never let me forget I was part of something larger than myself, an organism made of many people, and that I would have the chance to pay it forward someday.

I thought we'd be left alone forever. It had been decades since anyone outside of Poletown cared for what happened inside it. I thought I might be able to live out the next couple in the stasis of the cyclical change of the seasons. Although I was cold now, it was to ensure I'd be warm in the future. Each year I'd be in a bit better position to live in comfort. Will had suspicions otherwise, and what he would tell me next was just the beginning of what was to come.

I stopped by his house late that winter to shiver by his fire for a change—he'd installed a woodstove in the kitchen. His furnace was working, but barely, and he didn't have the money to keep it much higher than 50. A new charter school had opened up just down the street, and they had been eyeing his house for expansion. They'd been sniffing around and making friendly with Will, but had so far not made any offers.

"So are you going to sell it if they ask?"

"Not if I don't have to."

"Dude, you could make so much money."

"That ain't what it's about. I could make money in a lot of ways," he said. "This is my paradise, this has been my dream for years. I don't want to move anywhere else, I don't want a—" he used air quotes—"nicer house. I like it right here."

"They'll eminent domain you out if you don't. You know what happened with the Poletown plant."

In the early '80s, the entire north half of the neighborhood was demolished to make way for a 362-acre auto plant, heavily subsidized by the city, state, and federal governments. More than 4,000 residents were deprived of their property by eminent domain. Fourteen hundred homes, several churches, and 140 businesses were razed to make way for the promise of three shifts of work a day. A Jewish cemetery is located inside the plant's grounds, as it was illegal to move it. If relatives wish to visit their ancestors, they can do so on two days a year.

Approximately 6,500 jobs were promised at the Detroit-Hamtramck Assembly Plant, as it's officially known, in exchange for demolishing half the neighborhood. At its peak employment, roughly 3,500 people worked there, less than the number of people kicked out of their homes to build it. It was the death rattle of American manufacturing, the last attempt at making cars in Detroit for anything more than lip service or sentiment.

Before that, in the '60s, Interstate 75 cut through the neighborhood. It was run straight through two of the most economically and culturally important black neighborhoods in the United States, Black Bottom and Paradise Valley, both of which bled into Poletown.

What was left was replaced with a model community, and the rest of the people moved to towering projects or the suburbs.

But even before that, the downfall of the neighborhood began in earnest. Poletown was bisected, north and south, by Interstate 94 in the '50s. This was the first inkling of what was to be called "urban renewal," a broad set of policies where large tracts of cities would be transformed by enormous public and private works projects. By 1962, more than 43,000 people had been displaced by urban renewal just in Detroit, 70 percent of them black.

Although these developments were genuinely thought at the time to be benevolent, there were, of course, winners and losers. The city, for example, was a giant loser. Those freeways allowed people to escape to the suburbs, pulling their economic might and taxes with them. Governments flush with postwar tax money were happy to build the infrastructure to accommodate them, while letting cities decay. It would start a long history of policy decisions that prioritized the suburbs over the city and ensured Michigan would have some of the wealthiest 'burbs in the nation surrounding one of its poorest cities. It was the start to building the most segregated metropolitan area in the United States, and would also have immeasurable consequences for individuals.

My grandparents were able to get some of the reclaimed lumber from a demolished house along the I-94 corridor when the government ran it through Detroit. They used the lumber to build their own home on virgin land along Lake Huron. As I write these very words, I'm sitting at my grandparents' kitchen table surrounded by a house originally framed with lumber from Detroit, perhaps Poletown.

My grandparents were both children of the Depression and worked hard. My grandfather built this house with his own hands. But this is how the past bleeds into the future. This is how, sixty years later, my family, myself, and people like us everywhere benefit from decisions made long before we were born. This house, this beautiful house that protects me from the elements as I write, warms me, keeps me safe, was made from the bones of someone else's misfortune. I'll never know exactly whose house this lumber came from or where their descendants are now. I hope they're doing all right and I hope they got a fair price for their home when the government came knocking and ordered them out.

I tried to prod Will some more about what he was thinking. He reloaded the stove and the teakettle on top began to whistle slowly. He refilled both of our glasses, each with cooling nettle tea, supposedly good for the liver. Was this just the beginning of some great change, or had it been happening for longer than I'd been alive, maybe forever?

"I don't want to think about it right now," he said.

The winter was coming to a close.

CHAPTER 4

Windows and Doors and Airplanes

Gratiot

I'd just shaved my beard off. It took me the length of side one of Bob Dylan's *Blood on the Tracks*. The beard had grown thick over the winter and I didn't have any clippers, only a razor. There was no mirror in the bathroom, so I did it standing at my dresser with water in a bread pan. I looked five years younger, but I liked it. When I woke up I couldn't see my breath and couldn't remember how long it was since that had happened.

I looked at myself shirtless in the mirror. I hadn't really seen myself naked in the longest time. Because of the cold, I would transition between the bath and clothes as fast as I could, never stopping to look. My body had become hard from the physical work and the chill. There was very little fat. I could see the strands in my muscles and pick out each one in my back. My face had become thin without the hair, and the shadows atop my cheekbones were dark. I needed a haircut. My stomach was smooth and hard. I could see purple veins running through my forearms, and the tops of my hands were spidered with them. I looked like a buck deer that had made it through the winter. And I had.

I needed a dog—something to protect me while I was in the house and the house when I wasn't. I didn't really want one, though. Owning a living creature would change the rhythms of my life, and tie me down. No more working all day then heading to the bar all night. I'd have to care for a being other than myself for the first time, and this worried me. I was barely caring for myself. But a dog was essential. I don't know anyone who has redone an abandoned house without a dog.

I went to the pound. I was looking for a puppy, something I could raise up to my lifestyle. My mother and I walked past cages of barking and miserable adult dogs to the puppy bin. There was only one left and he was stomping around in the middle of the room, playing with a splay-legged woman on the ground. He was black and tan with a white chest and had a little puppy snarl on his face, ripping up a frog toy. He puffed his chest and trotted over when he noticed us, the cutest little bastard mutt I'd ever seen, nine pounds of fuzz and teeth and tongue. His paws were way too big for him and he was clumsy but fearless. He was perfect.

"Hi, little buddy." I bent down to rub him, and he peed on my foot. The yellow stream became a puddle and I hollered for something to clean it up with. This obviously meant he was the one. I sighed.

I cleaned the spill and he rolled onto his back. His stomach was spotted black and white in patches like a milk cow.

"Oh, you have a fuzzy little cow belly," I said to him in baby talk. He bit my finger.

On the ride home, the little monster bit everything: my shirt, the car door, the seats, my chin, the seat belt; he squirmed and tried to grab the steering wheel. I settled on Gratiot (rhymes with "hatchet") for a name, from a main avenue running through the east side, just a couple of blocks from my house.

"Your name's going to be Gratiot and you're going to grow up big and strong and we're going to be best friends and play every day and I'll feed you crunchies and buy you toys and it might be cold for a little bit and I love you." I held his face and we looked into each other's eyes. He barfed on my shirt.

"Ugh! Gratiot. NO."

He burped happily.

That's when I realized the sentence I would be saying more than any other for the next two years was "Gratiot, NO."

He wriggled upside down on the floor in the Forestdale house as I inspected my beardless face in the mirror. He had the stuffing almost all chewed out of a Santa Claus toy he'd found in the pile outside.

"Gratiot, relax," I said, bringing the pan of water I'd used to shave back to the sink to dump it. The dog looked at me for a moment and went right back to what he was doing.

Something caught my eye out the window. Two of my neighbors were inside their house, sitting at the kitchen table with their chairs turned toward mine. They had cups of coffee and smiled and waved when I noticed them. They'd been watching my shave like a television show. It would be in the 50s that day, sunshine and blue skies, and I had a lot of work to do.

The first and most dangerous project was to attempt to seal my roof using an enormous blue tarp. I had done something similar to my Forestdale house with Norman, where we rigged some climbing rope around the chimney, so it was familiar, but my roof was much more challenging. The pitch on the Forestdale roof was standard, with standard valleys. Mine was a gambrel roof, completely unwalkable. The bump halfway up is called the hip, the tippy top the ridge. It looks like this:

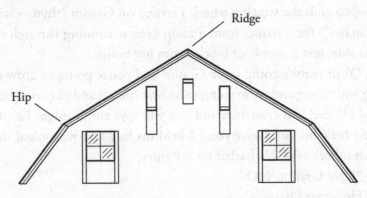

I enlisted Will because he was crazy enough to help on a roof project. We would have to float a ladder over the hip, throw the tarp over without getting it tangled, and nail it to both sides with strips of wood at the edge so it didn't rip. I borrowed a ladder and we went to work.

The side with the empty lots was no big deal. Will drove his truck next to the house and we placed the ladder in the bed. Will and I got up on the roof, he nimbly and I slowly, and got the tarp positioned.

Will unfurled a rope he kept in his truck and we tied one end to the tarp and another to a wrench, which we took turns attempting to throw over the ridge, laughing, and running when it would inevitably come crashing down on the wrong side. Finally, Will threw it over with a Herculean toss and we pulled the tarp behind it. He nailed the edge of the tarp in, frowning at me because I had convinced him, against his better judgment, to do it for me. I hate heights. I can deal with power tools, and snakes, and spiders, and small spaces, and clowns, and oceans, and loneliness, but I hate heights. You never know which phobia you're going to get. Now to nail the other side.

There was a slender alley between the abandoned house next door and mine, littered with the usual Detroit treasures, broken glass, rusting metal of indeterminate origin, filthy plastic, soggy lumber. Will and I tried placing the ladder in different ways, struggling with it, but it wouldn't fit. The angle was too steep, and the alley too narrow. By this time Will was doing his usual cursing.

"Sketchy handyman Will, always gotta help with the roof projects."

He heaved the ladder again, lost it, and it came crashing to the ground.

"God damn it!" he said, walking away muttering curses. "We can try to put it through the window next door."

"All right," I said skeptically. Obviously it was the only choice, but I certainly didn't want to get caught in that house with tools. I walked through the hole where the back door would have been. I heard water running downstairs and found the supply line had been cut behind the meter. Thousands of gallons a day were shooting onto the floor, creating a tiny lake, but the water seemed to be draining well. This was costing Detroit taxpayers hundreds of dollars a month, and it certainly wasn't the only abandoned house in which it was happening. I discovered years later the house kitty-corner to mine also had the water running in the same manner, and it had been on for more than a decade.

Upstairs, bullet holes pocked the walls. The inside was a bit like mine, with less trash, but broken plaster plagued the floor, and the running water made for a bright smell. The corpse of the house was pretty well stripped out, aside from some nice doorknobs, which I would go back and get later.

This used to be someone's home.

There was some glass still in the window we needed to get through, so I broke it with a hammer. Will lifted the ladder up to me in the house, over his head, and onto the roof. But the floor was vinyl tile and the ladder kept slipping. I asked Will what to do.

"Nail it to the floor."

He found some boards in the house, and after violently adjusting the ladder, he nailed a two-by-four to the floor as a backstop. He nailed another on top so the ladder wouldn't move up and slip. He looked at me. He held out a hammer.

"I'm not doing this one. It's your house."

I took a deep breath. "All right."

There's no courage without fear.

I put the hammer in my belt and grabbed some strips of wood, put some nails in my mouth. Will spotted the ladder as I climbed.

I ducked through the window and out over the alley, hoping the ladder wouldn't snap in half. I looked back at Will and wished I had broken out all of the glass in the frame. Some shards remained, looking like dinosaur teeth, and if I were to slip I would slide right through them, shredding my groin. If I fell, the nails in my mouth would likely get smashed through my throat. My leg might get caught between rungs as I tumbled, my body weight cracking it in half, likely never to walk again. Will had wandered away from the ladder, looking at something, and I yelled for him to get back to his post.

"You'll be fine. Just keep going. I'm hungry."

I made it over the hip, still carrying everything. I dismounted the ladder and stepped around it, leaning on the roof. I would have to wedge my foot between the ladder and the shingles, and extend myself completely to reach the tarp. I looked down in the alley. I wished I'd cleaned that, too. The shards of glass from the window gleamed like razors, along with some jagged and threatening pieces of wood, pipes sticking from the concrete, a board with nails in it like some caveman weapon. I began to hammer.

One. Two. Three. More nails. I worked my way across. Four. My fingernails tore at the shingles to stay aloft. The tar began to heat up, and I felt its dirty warmth on my cheek and through my jeans at the hip. I almost got comfortable and looked around a bit: four abandoned houses, two occupied. I saw a fence at the abandoned place two doors down, and what looked like a decent gate. I made a note of it for later. Across the street on the next block stood a large building, once a settlement house, now vacant. Vacant, vacant, vacant. Behind me, a building that looked occupied, but I wasn't sure, a squatted house and some more abandoned ones, and two abandoned schools, one a sprawling former high school named after Frederick Douglass, its towering windows gone, its floors filled with waste, the yard overgrown. I could see a piece of black theater curtain fluttering within one broken window.

A fear of heights isn't the fear of falling. It's the fear of jumping. Solid ground.

Back in the kitchen. No puncture wounds, no broken bones. I started moving the ladder down and shook off the adrenaline. "That's enough for today," I said.

Will had picked up what looked like a page torn from a magazine and was looking at it upside down. He peered at me over the top.

"You owe me."

"I'll buy you lunch."

———————

The next project was to brick up the holes in the basement. Scrappers had stolen most of the ducts, and had left large holes where the main trunks had passed through the foundation into the crawl space. A friend from college, an itinerant musician and activist, was in town that day and he helped me mix the mortar as I laid the brick. I'd never done any bricklaying, but thought it couldn't be that hard. This wall didn't need to hold any weight or be super straight, and it turned out decent. After, I helped my buddy design a multiple-person dragon costume for a protest he was getting ready for. We drew the plans right on the wall in my front hallway.

I had brightened the house up, too. The Kemps suggested two solutions from when they were doing their place. The first was to cut the top third off each board covering the windows. This piece could be hung and removed with just two screws, giving me some light without having to wrestle with the entire piece of ply. The other was to cut a hole about a foot square from the center of each board and seal the opening with Plexiglas, in effect a window in a window. These would let in enough light to work by, but wouldn't be breakable and would provide the same measure of security as the boards themselves, which wasn't a whole lot.

I needed to start thinking about the backyard, and yardwork was one of the things I felt I could get from the multitudes of acquaintances who'd said "If you ever need any help . . ." but had few real skills and liked the idea of helping more than the actual dirty work. It was the most labor-intensive of all the jobs. I figured most people had grown up mowing the lawn and understood the intrinsic pleasure of working outside.

Wild grapevine had taken over the yard, and had been creeping across everything, probably since I'd had my first kiss. It snaked its way up trees, killing them and tangling their branches, and down into the ground, anchoring itself along dozens of points in the trash-meshed soil. It hung from the telephone lines strung across the rear of my property, sagging them and creating an impassable curtain of vegetation. At its largest it was the thickness of a baseball bat, green and springy and living and tough.

Also populating the backyard were dozens of Ailanthus trees, or "ghetto palms" as we called them, the tree of heaven that Betty Smith so effectively used as a metaphor for tenacity in *A Tree Grows in Brooklyn.* They had become the bane of my existence. They're useless as trees, and ugly. They grow at an incredible rate, snaking into foundations and waste pipes, crumbling them, and are nearly impossible to kill. I did my best to clean the yard of them with my new chain saw, but they came back every year.

From years of falling leaves and dumping trash, the soil had turned to near compost. What was decomposable had decomposed, but the plastic and glass remained, threading itself throughout. It would all need to be dug and raked out, and sometimes the easiest thing was to just throw away the soil with it. Aside from heavy machinery, which I couldn't afford, there was really no good way to go about cleaning the yard, as each intertwisted layer required a different tactic and a different tool. Nine years later I am still digging other people's trash out of my backyard.

"I found the mother brain!" my buddy Nate said. He was working with me that day and seemed to have found the source of the grapevine, a gnarly stump buried in the ground. He was an unlikely candidate to live in Detroit at the time, from farm country in Michigan's thumb, and had grown up working on a milk ranch. He was likely one of only a handful of people living in the city who had voted for George Bush, but he truly was a great guy, six foot three, 275 pounds, and cheerful. He was studying historical preservation at the local university.

He chuckled as he pulled the strands from the tree, bending the branches with it. It didn't want to let go. "Come look at this!" he said.

I set the chain saw down still running and trotted over to where he was standing. He had picked up a clear glass bottle with a cork still in the top. He brushed the dirt off to reveal the name of a brand of whiskey I'd never heard of, and the word "medicine." He had a little pile of trinkets going, dirty action figures and tin boxes and beetle-looking pieces of auto parts.

"Sweet. You found it, you can have it."

"It might be from Prohibition, and worth some money." He gave the bottle a longing look. "Aw, I wouldn't take this from you. It came from your house. Where can I set it?"

"You sure?"

"It's all yours."

I placed it carefully in the truck and went back to the hot chain saw, still growling on the ground. It was the Cadillac of saws, a Swedish model, likely one of the safest on the market. Nevertheless, it was amazingly powerful, with a razor-sharp chain. It could cut through a waist-thick oak log in seconds, and I could only imagine what it could do to a person. The chain saw rivals only the table saw as the most dangerous of tools in the workshop.

I resumed cutting away at the brush in little spurts, clearing the fallen whips with my foot as I went. Something sounded wrong, a clinking. I backed off to listen, then revved the engine to clear the obstruction. I listened for a moment and revved again. The bar broke free from the saw body, throwing the chain and wrapping it around my leg. I felt the talons grip my jeans. It was over in a second, the air quiet with the stopped saw, me standing there hoping I still had a leg.

Nate called, "You okay?"

This time I was lucky. The chain break had stopped the rotation in a fraction of a second, slowing it enough to only kiss me. If it hadn't gone off, a trip to the ER would have been the least of my worries. It left a little half-ring of nicks in my jeans where the teeth had bitten in just enough to pull back the cotton in a testicle-crumpling warning. My first near injury, and I was going to wear that one like a badge of honor.

I hadn't tightened the bolts correctly when readjusting the tension on the chain, so the whole thing was my fault. I had forgotten the special adjustment tool at Forestdale and had stupidly tried to use a pocketknife and a pair of pliers to do the job of a wrench and a screwdriver. If I wasn't more careful the odds were I was going to seriously injure myself over the course of building this house.

"Are you okay?" Nate said again, rushing over.

I showed him the nicks in my pants. "Hey, cool," he said.

"I should probably stop for the day, and remember to bring the right tool."

"Well then, do you want to grab that door?"

I had told him earlier I'd been eyeing the front door on the abandoned house across the street. It was oak and had some nice dentil molding surrounding a window about the size of a pizza box, which was of course gone. The door had been painted in layers and layers of hideous colors, the latest being the purple of a cartoon dinosaur. I'd been avoiding it because I still didn't know what the neighbors would think. Sneaking into the house next to me to take some old doorknobs at dusk was one thing, taking the front door off a house in broad daylight was another.

Many neighbors had known the people who had lived in these houses, and still held on to an idea of what the neighborhood once was. I might not just be stealing the door off an abandoned house, I might be stealing the door off what was once Mr. Jackson's, where the baseball went through the picture window and, as a child, one of the neighbors had to mow the lawn all summer to replace it.

"I dunno, man."

"Ahh, it's fine. It's going to go to waste if you don't. They're going to tear that house down. Or it'll be taken by someone else. You're really protecting it," Nate said earnestly.

His argument seemed like the same one used to take mummies from the pyramids and justify them sitting in the British Museum alongside other antiquities removed for "protection" during colonialism. But this wasn't Egypt, this was Detroit, and this wasn't a pyramid, it was an abandoned house. What I was going to do would technically be stealing, but from whom? A memory? The people who had abandoned it, the governments that allowed it to fester? It wasn't going to Britain, just across the street, and was going to be used to eliminate abandonment at my place, not make more of it. If whoever lived there before cared enough about its memory, they could have burned it like photographs of an unfaithful lover. I was stealing a memory to make a new one.

I looked around and it didn't seem as though anyone was on the street, so Nate and I headed over and ripped the door from its hinges.

European season had come with the high summer. The artistic kids across the Atlantic had realized Detroit was cool before most Americans, and the city had long been a stop on the Euro art circuit. The Dutch in particular love Detroit. The fascination has something to do with the fall of European empires mirrored visually and rhetorically in the fall of American manufacturing hegemony, coupled with a distinct lust for urban planning. The logic goes that if the fall of empire can happen *in* America—Detroit was the proof—then it follows it might happen *to* America as well.

That year we had a group of four young German artists by way of Holland staying on the block, another small group of Dutch men, and a pretty architect from Italy.

The whole neighborhood was tearing the back off Jake's house as I walked over after my shift at work. More than a dozen neighbors smeared in black demolition dirt were holding tools or putting dark wood in garbage cans and little piles.

The Italian architect was sitting on Jake's lawn, too. She had dark, shaggy hair, a thin nose, and angular cheeks. When she spoke, her sentences were soft and sweet, like yogurt. She laughed easily, and was presently seated next to Will, teaching him to curse in Italian.

I introduced myself, and she said her name was Cecilia. Damn, I'd forgotten to wear my chain-saw pants.

The only other house on Jake's side of the block was right next to his, and owned by a concrete mason named Ian who had been in the neighborhood a long time. He was a nice-enough guy, but had a drug problem. He had recently been hanging out with some crack dealers, a couple of scabby-looking white guys. The neighbors all told him, "Hey, Ian, if you keep letting them stay at your house, they're going to kick you out of your own spot and you're never going to be able to live there again."

That's exactly what happened. When they threatened Jake one day brandishing a gun, he told them to go fuck themselves in the nicest way possible and went to the cops. Jake instinctually mistrusted the cops like most of the rest of us, but he was at a loss for what to do in this instance. The deals were happening at nearly fifteen-minute intervals, and he had been taking pictures of license plates and recording times, etc., all the things cops would need to shut the house down, but the direct threat to his life was the last straw. The cops told him, verbatim, "There's nothing we can do. Get a shotgun."

The neighbors figured they were going to have to do something before the virus spread. Jake asked one of the elders in the neighborhood to find out if the dealers were connected to any of the big gangs. We thought we might be able to come to some kind of peace, but they were just lone wolves. This meant higher-level discussions were out of the question, but it also meant we wouldn't be starting some kind of larger war by throwing them out. Some folks talked about burning the house down, but it was too close to Jake's for safety. There was also the notion of cutting down the giant tree in the front yard and dropping it onto the house, but that wouldn't crush it completely enough to make it unlivable. So we decided that making life uncomfortable for their customers would be the best option.

We took shifts watching the house from across the street. Cameras, noise, anything we could do to make the drug buyers know they were being watched. Tearing the back off Jake's was a show of solidarity and strength from the neighborhood. It needed to come off anyway, and Jake could have easily done it himself, but he wanted to let the dealers know he wasn't going to be intimidated, that this would keep happening, in force and right in front of them.

As Cecilia and I chatted, the neighborhood was beginning to finish up. The crew began to gather for pictures, and someone mentioned going to Belle Isle to get clean. I wasn't the only one without a shower, and we would often bathe in the river when it was warm enough. Cecilia asked what Belle Isle was.

"It's an island, but I don't think I'm going to be able to go. I have to work on my own house."

I had the door I'd stolen on sawhorses, ready to begin stripping it. The general rule was if I didn't get going on something for the house right after work and attempted to put it off till later, nothing would get done.

"Don't you want to show me Belle Isle?" Cecilia said.

Well, maybe I could take some time off from the house and work.

We rode together in the cab of my truck with a few others piled in the bed. She said she was from Rome, and smelled like she owned a shower. She'd just built herself a home in the Italian mountains, and was finishing up grad school. She was in Detroit for some transatlantic art project.

"I like this city, this Detroit," she said to me. "It is so"—she searched for the word—"so very real."

"It's all right," I said.

We poured out of the truck at the gravel parking lot about half a mile from the swimming hole. At the time the cops called it Patchouli Creek. Now they call it Hipster Beach.

I was first in the stream. Gratiot was off the leash and splashed in with the overserious determination of a puppy, except he was terrified once he touched the water. He wouldn't get in farther than his ankles, looking back to shore, mewling. Jake scrubbed himself with a bar of soap and was in up to his neck.

Matt, also from Forestdale, dived in headfirst. He had track marks up his arms, and was blind in one eye from metal scrapping. He had been using a torch on a tank he thought was empty but was filled with ammonia. When the gas exploded it knocked him off the scaffold. He was lucky the accident only took one eye. Now he swam to the far bank and hoisted himself from the water on a stone jutting above the stream like a diving board. At one time or another, he had made all the rock sculptures along the beach, large cairns, strange little mortarless monuments, and the diving board.

A couple of others got in quickly, including Eric and his girlfriend, Emily, who had also arrived from New York for an art residency. Together since high school, they had fallen in love with the city, stayed past the end of their residencies, and moved on to Forestdale. They were working on a project in one of the dozens of abandoned bakeries in Poletown, replacing the vanished pastries with cupcakes and pies made of concrete. They fit right in, and both would end up rehabbing homes in due time. Will stood wading to his knees, rolling cigarettes with Monk.

Cecilia was the only one not in the stream. She sat on the bank with her pants rolled to the shins, but wouldn't touch the water. I wanted to say something, but Matt was cuddling Gratiot in his arms, and carried the squirming dog into the water over his head.

"He just needs to understand he can swim," he said. I watched. Matt was part dog and I trusted him unquestioningly with anything canine.

Gently easing Gratiot into the water, he let go. After a second of sheer terror, Gratiot found he could float if he paddled, and made his way back to shore. Proud of himself and forgetting his former panic, his tongue lolled as he thrust his chest in defiance of his fear.

"Hey, Drew. Do you mind if I roll a cigarette?" Matt was drying his fingers off on a towel and holding my pack.

"Yeah, sure. Roll me one, too."

Emily was sculling on her back, splashing water at Eric, submerged to the neck. Cecilia sat on the bank looking lonely and pensive like the shy new girl in school, unsure of which lunch table to sit at. Jake was really scrubbing himself with the soap at this point.

"Come on in!" I called to Cecilia.

"I think I will just watch."

"Why? The water is perfect." I splashed some in her direction. "Come on. At least get your feet wet." I walked over to her, still in the water.

"Come on."

"It's the bobbles."

"The what?"

"The bobbles. You are not supposed to swim in water with the bobbles."

"The bubbles? What are you talking about?"

She didn't want to get into the water because it had some bubbles in it. Apparently in southern Europe, water that has bubbles is dirty.

"I've never heard of that. I've swum in this water my whole life," I said. "I grew up in this water and I'm fine. I'm healthy, I'm still here." I splashed some more in her direction, then some more onto my shoulders. "It seems kind of rude of you when we bring you all the way out here and show you this, but then you think it's dirty."

"But with all the factories, doesn't it get . . ." She gestured with her hand like beating eggs upside down but couldn't find the word.

"That's all downriver. It's all going the other way from us," I lied.

She sighed and rolled up her pant legs. She stepped in.

"You're not dead yet, are ya?"

She frowned and looked away.

"Look, we're right here." I pointed to Lake St. Clair on the tattoo of the Great Lakes I have on my left breast. Monte, the Chicano mural artist I'd met at the YES FARM standing under the painting of his unborn son, had done it for me at his kitchen table. His son, now two years old, watched while eating blueberries from a bowl one at a time. "Right here. Here's Lake Huron, where I grew up. The water runs this way and all the factories are down here."

She put her finger on the tattoo. She found Buffalo and Niagara Falls, the Upper Peninsula. She never got in the water past her knees.

———

My job was to frame two rear windows in the Queen Anne. I had traded someone on Forestdale an indeterminate amount of work for a couple of used windows, and they were slightly too big for the openings already there. I made new sills on a table saw my grandfather had given me, a saw with a good motor and a vintage cast-iron deck that had likely cut wood to make my grandparents' house from the houses that had been removed to make the freeway. Now it was back building the neighborhood it may have had helped to destroy. When masses of white people would move to Detroit a few years hence, many would openly wonder if this cyclical return was a genuine attempt to right the mistakes of the past, or if it was revenge for people whose parents or grandparents had left the city they once thought of as theirs and now wanted it back plus interest. I thought about Cecilia while I worked.

Reframing the window openings was far cheaper than purchasing new windows, but a hell of a lot more work. I would get the rest of the windows for my three rooms at an architectural salvage place in the city for anywhere between $15 and $50 apiece. I found a nice set of three casements, windows with a crank, with mullions, the grid often seen on colonial houses, for $100. One would go in the kitchen next to the door, the others side by side near where I planned to build the chimney in what would be the dining room. I found another long one, with three panels like a triptych, to go in the south wall of the kitchen, over the stove. Last, I scored a small one for the bathroom, less than a foot wide, for some natural light and to forgo having to install an exhaust fan.

For my job today, I had taken the plywood from the westward window openings in the living room and the afternoon sun was flowing into the dark house. I didn't really know what I was doing, so I framed the new openings a bit tight. Usually you frame them an inch or so larger than the window for warping and variance, and fill the empty space with insulation and cover the rest with trim. I had framed these to size and the windows didn't fit.

I really didn't want to redo it all. I would probably have to measure and cut and prime new sills, and the whole thing seemed like a mess. So I figured I could make this work. I was shirtless, perched inside the opening peeling large curls from the edges with a plane, widening the windows and thinking, merrily, about Cecilia. I decided I was going to ask her on a date, directly, something I had never done before. The pine curls fell on my naked shoulders and onto the front pockets of my jeans.

As I worked, I noticed there was an elderly woman on the back porch of the house behind mine watching me, and she interrupted my daydream. She had her hands folded over the top of a cane and sat on a bench as if she were feeding the birds in a park. It looked like she had been there for some time. When I noticed her she smiled and waved. I waved back.

I hopped off the sill and attempted to fit the window in again. It was close, but not perfect, and I thought I could force it without breaking the glass. This was a mistake. Nothing broke, but the framing cocked and warped the window just enough that the sills didn't sit quite right. I determined at the time that it was fine. Now, years later, every time I sit in front of that window in the winter and feel just enough cold air sneaking in to be noticeable, I'm reminded of my laziness that summer day. What would have taken me twice the work then will now take me quadruple.

I screwed in the window. One down. I put on my shirt and walked over to introduce myself to the woman on the bench.

She said her name was Mrs. Terry, and I told her what I was doing with the house. A rotund woman who had some trouble walking, she unleashed the most inviting cackle, like Little Richard at his pyrotechnic best. She had hard features that betrayed a softness that said she'd been a mother to more than just her own children.

She said she had worked as an elementary teacher in the Detroit public schools for thirty years, and her husband put in thirty at the Ford River Rouge Plant as a maintenance man. They had inhabited their house as long, and by this time owned it outright. They lived their own version of the American Dream in a crumbling America, but had no plans to move anywhere else.

Two of their sons lived with them, a sports coach and a cable installer. An adult son who was a Detroit police officer lived on the other side of town. She said I would meet them in time as well, and then told me to wait while she shambled back into the house. She brought me back a bottle of purple Gatorade.

I considered for a moment refusing it. I couldn't take from these people. Then I reconsidered. Who was I not to accept a gift?

"I know you be thirsty over there. I seen you working hard, boy. Yep." She nodded.

I opened the bottle and took a giant swig, the overflow running down my chin and staining my shirt.

"Thank you. I was thirsty."

The faint sound of blues music wafted in on the breeze from the west. I asked Mrs. Terry about it. She said it was a legendary blues jam and barbecue called John's Carpet House. It had gone on in the neighborhood for dozens of years. Originally it had been held in a house with carpeted walls, hence the name, but it had burned and now they held it outdoors in the lot.

"If I can get up out of this chair I'll take you sometime."

We listened to the smooth music for a bit, but it was interrupted by the jingle of an ice-cream truck, the incessant soundtrack to summer. They all play the same song, once a blackface minstrel standard. Mrs. Terry scoffed at the truck and waved her hand in a dismissive gesture.

"That house used to be beautiful, just beautiful," Mrs. Terry said, pointing back at my place. "That was the prettiest house in the neighborhood. It's a shame what they did to it."

"Well, I hope I can make it nice again."

"Take your time. Don't go too fast. Don't go too fast."

After finishing the windows, I decided to stop by the lumberyard to pick up some shipping pallets on my way back to Forestdale. The yard dealt primarily in roofing material, and as a result they'd put their extra pallets on the side of the road for free, some of them made from rough hardwood. I was making my fence from them, using the thin cross pieces as pickets, the sturdy longer sections for rails.

I'd bust them apart with a ripping chisel, a kind of sturdy, flat crowbar, breaking the nails, which were spiral, shot in with a nail gun, a bitch to remove without breaking the thin pickets. Sometimes I'd pay one of the kids on Forestdale a penny a nail to remove what was left, or just do it myself. I cut the tops into points with a chop saw my family had given me the previous Christmas. It was mindless work and I could daydream about whatever I liked, which was Cecilia.

The pickets were all different colors and sizes, some fat, some skinny, some tall or short, light and dark, and when I nailed them to the rails the effect was of looking at a musical staff. For what they had cost—the price of nails—they looked pretty good.

Grosse Pointe, our fabulously wealthy old-money neighbor to

the east, was getting ready to add to its own fence, one like that concrete wall of shame on 8 Mile. Already many of the smaller streets between Detroit and the Pointes were blocked off with obstructions that ran right across the road like little Berlin Walls, but this was on a far larger scale. They began by piling snow across Kercheval Avenue, a main artery and one of the largest roads connecting the two cities. That next spring, they added two sheds, to be used as a farmers market, completely blocking the road.

The thing was, both sheds only opened toward the Grosse Pointe side. Looking at the stalls from the Pointes, they're inviting and friendly. Looking from Detroit, we stare at the backs of two blank buildings and a physical barrier across a main road. Under pressure from Detroit the street was reopened, although the avenue was narrowed into something resembling a checkpoint.

This is the same Grosse Pointe famous for its "Point System." Before it was outlawed in the '60s, you needed to score a certain number of points to be able to purchase a house there, actually a collection of five municipalities. The realty association sent private investigators to judge applicants on things like "swarthiness," "accent," and "way of living," and whether your friends were "predominantly American." WASPs needed to score 50 points, Poles 55, Greeks and Italians 75, and Jews 85. Blacks, Latinos, and Asians were automatically disqualified, game over.

These agreements were called restrictive covenants, and they happened all over the place, not just in GP. Groups of real estate brokers, homeowners' associations, and builders would band together to ensure blacks could not buy homes in their neighborhoods and cities. This had the effect that, while whites were fleeing to the suburbs, even the most prosperous blacks could not. These sheds are just a part of what they've walled off, a sixth of the streets between the two cities now blocked, some with walls made of brick, iron spikes adorning the top.

They've outlawed restrictive covenants now, and it's tempting to say these metaphorical walls are all in the past. But they reverberate today. The average household income in Grosse Pointe Park is $111,974. Just across those walls in Detroit, it's $24,444. In 2015, nationally, the average white family holds twelve times the wealth of the average black family.

That inequality exists mostly because of racist housing practices like these restrictive covenants and redlining, which created the other wall. When blacks weren't allowed to purchase houses or were denied loans, they were also denied the prosperity, appreciation, and inheritance those houses provided to their white counterparts.

People aren't even shy about it. Our very own modern-day George Wallace of the north, L. Brooks Patterson, has called for more. In 2014, in an on-the-record interview with the *New Yorker*, he stated, "I made a prediction long ago, and it's come to pass. I said, 'What we're going to do is turn Detroit into an Indian reservation, where we herd all the Indians into the city, build a fence around it and throw in the blankets and corn.'"

The same article also noted when accused of racism by a black city council member, "Patterson publicly declared that he'd 'rather own a 1947 Buick than own' her."

As of 2016, he's the commissioner of Oakland County, our wealthy suburban neighbor to the north. He was first elected to the position in 1992. For more than twenty years a plurality of the people of Oakland County have believed he represents their views.

I was hoping my fence didn't have the same effect. I hated these walls and everything they represented. It seemed as though they were a literal rather than metaphorical line in the sand and whichever side one chose to live on was a declaration of allegiance. Right or wrong, I had even begun to hate the people who lived behind them, or at least not respect them. To live on the other side of something like that and turn your back seemed a cowardly choice.

The reality was, I didn't know anyone who lived on that side or why they chose to, only an impersonal history. My anger was directed toward phantoms, to ghosts of the past, still haunting the present.

Maybe good fences make good neighbors only if both sides care about keeping stone upon stone. I hoped I wasn't about to make one of those kinds of choices with Cecilia. I decided the next time I went back to my new house I would bring a socket set and take the red gate I'd seen from the roof. It would complete the fence.

———

"In Rome we have ruins right in our city. Are you jealous?" Cecilia said with a mischievous look that drew sweat from my palms. We sat at the point of Belle Isle where the prow of the island splits the river. I had asked her on that date. We had ridden our bikes to a jazz club downtown and after some drinks she had already begun to talk of overstaying her visa. We ended up kissing in the street in front of her house in the rain, my hat falling off into the rivulets of water moistening the road, water that had evaporated from the lake we now sat in front of. This was our second date. I asked her if she wanted to go on a picnic. She didn't know what that was but said yes.

"We have ruins, too."

"You do not have any ruins. In Rome you can just drive right up to them. To take a tour."

"We do, too. The train station's like a ruin. The Packard plant is like a ruin." The Michigan Central Station, abandoned since 1988 and eighteen stories high, was the most stately abandoned building in the city.

"But yours are not very old, only like fifty years. Ours are thousands of years old, they are ancient. You are jealous."

"I'm not jealous. Ours will be like that someday."

"But it is not the same. Tell me you are jealous."

She held my arm and stared at me from under her delicate brow. I could see the pink of her tongue tucked between her lips.

"We should go swimming," I suggested.

"You are jealous. I can see."

I stood to remove my clothing and smiled at her. She was almost a decade older than me. The danger of falling in love wasn't the age difference, it was the ocean between us.

We had been by the lake all afternoon, in a cove by the point of the island. Andy Kemp had shown me the spot. Every year when someone on Forestdale had a birthday, they would load scraps of broken tile, mortar, and grout into cars or cargo bikes and the birthday person would tile their age into the stones flirting with the water, the cool lake licking at their feet and the underside of the boulders. There were dozens down there, twelve-, fifteen-, thirty-year markers, varicolored and beautiful. We sat atop them.

"I'm going swimming. You can come with me or not."

"But what about the bobbles?" She looked at the water with her hands between her knees.

I sat again, covering myself, next to her. "The bubbles? Again? I've never, ever heard a thing about the damn bubbles. This water's clean."

"But what if we sink?"

"I was a lifeguard when I was in high school. I'll save you if you're drowning," I said. "It was a great job. I sat by the pool all day, memorized poems, bronzed."

"Bronzed?"

"Got tan in the sun."

"That is what my friends want to hear back home, the slang. I've got some shit," she said, testing the word in her mouth. It came out sounding more like "sheeet."

"You have to shit?"

"NOO!" She hit me and laughed. "My housemate asked if I wanted to smoke weed. Weed?"

I nodded.

"I said I didn't have any. He said, 'I've got some shit.' I've never heard of calling marijuana 'shit.' Yesterday he told me, 'I could use a drink.' " She laughed her husky laugh and gently touched me again.

"What's so funny about that?"

"I could use a drink. I've never heard like this before, I could use a drink. It is funny."

I shrugged. "I guess it's the language."

"How can you *use* a drink?" She stood up. "We will swim."

We stripped to our underclothes. She had on a gray camisole and underwear that made me wonder if she'd thought about me when putting it on that morning. I had packed my bathing suit in my backpack, but didn't feel right putting it on when she hadn't brought anything but what she was wearing. We waded in, but the water was tepid. She walked farther than I, over the smooth lake stones while I watched.

"It's getting kind of cold," I said.

"If we don't go now we will lose our chance."

She looked back at me from the waist-high water. All at once she dived in. It took her longer to surface than I had expected and for a moment I stood there worried. She came up thirty yards from shore, and all I saw was her head sticking above the water like a dog swims, hair flattened and glistening. I was impressed at how long she could swim underwater, especially water she suspected would damage her body. It was a bold move, one a girl makes. I wondered what she thought about during those few moments submerged, pressing against the chilly water with her hands and thighs.

I almost lost my shorts diving in after. I surfaced next to her, our bare legs entangled, treading in place. The water was cool and weightless, swift, bending around the point of the island. We were close enough to touch and I wanted to take hold of her there, warmth against the chill, but the water wasn't buoyant enough to hold us both.

"Do you like it?" I asked.

"I like it," she said.

"Are you jealous?"

"No!" she said, splashing me as she drifted off, floating on her back. I followed.

We floated with the current, happy to feel the water between our barely touching fingertips and bobbing waves. The lake was remarkably clean, fresh from Lake Huron by way of the St. Clair River. It's quieter than on the shore somehow, and even the crashing of the waves is diminished when you're in the water, as if the lake has pulled you aside to whisper a secret that needs silence to be true. We honored it, and only Cecilia's giggles broke the glacial pact. The current pulled us downstream, and we swam back to shore, walking again over the tiled birthdays.

"Can we sit in the grass and dry out?" she said as we climbed the bank.

I followed her up the slope, across the dirt path to where she lay arms outstretched in the tall grass in the sun. She had found a small purple flower, chicory, and felt it between her fingers without plucking it.

"People here think that's a weed," I said to her, smushing the grass down around us.

"I think it is beautiful."

"In New Orleans they put it in coffee." I lay down, shivering with the wet.

I put my arm around her, under her head. Abandoning her flower, she rested her face under my chin and we lay in the sun, not speaking, barely hidden in the grass. A couple sat holding each other on a bench down the shoreline, pointing to the water and gesturing. A middle-aged man walked by with a dog, not noticing us, or pretending not to.

"We should go back to our clothing," she said.

"Stay."

She sat up and wrapped her hands around her knees, letting her short brown hair drip across her bare legs, waiting. I watched her subtle movements, and noticed a beauty mark on her back, just under her right shoulder blade, visible above her damp gray shirt. For a moment I watched the muscles in her shoulders somersault as she stroked her legs with her fingertips. We would be leaving soon.

I sat up and wrapped my arms around my legs, too. She looked at me square and unashamedly, her head resting on her bent knees. I felt my stubble on my forearm as I looked at the lake and the couple sitting on the bench. Cecilia lay back down, silent and still, her chest barely moving with her breath.

It was time or not. I looked across the lake for a long while. I thought about my home and everything the Great Lakes mean to me. Of my ancestors who lived and died with the water's fortunes, bathed in it, picked our sad songs on worn-out guitars only for the lake to hear. We had lived with it as a constant companion ever since anyone could remember, like a good dog who never grows old. I thought about my great-uncles and my grandfathers who had tamed the lake in sailing ships, who ate the sweet flesh of perch plucked from her sandy bottom, about the beach where my parents and uncles and grandparents were married barefoot. I looked at it as if it were my last time, as a dying man might look at it, chin to the wind.

I turned and kissed her. We kissed long and hard and I was on her, first one leg then the other, my body on top of hers, one hand under her head, the other braced against the matted grass. We rocked with the waves licking at the shore, mimicking the motions of our love.

"Can we make love here?" she whispered. I kissed her neck.

"Right here? We're like three steps from the path."

She nibbled me on the shoulder. She said something about America, asking about our laws. "Will we get in trouble?"

The wind coming off the lake was cool. A burden had been lifted. I ran my hand under her shirt, my rough fingers along the smooth olive skin of her back. I gently pressed her against the ground and moved my hand around her body to her breast. She closed her eyes and arched her back and we were one.

A Fence Between
Me and the World

Neighbors baling hay

We walked back across the path to gather our things. In our place we left the grass matted like snow angels. We found our clothing and began the blissful hike to the bikes. I ran my fingers through the meadow, thinking of nothing.

We left Belle Isle as the sun was hanging low in the sky. I felt some kind of promise had been made, an international declaration of love, a peace. If I had to leave Detroit for a while, I would. I dunno, we'd figure it out somehow. Andy and Kinga accomplished it, right?

Back on the block the White Buffalos, the four visiting Dutch artists, were having a barbecue as Cecilia and I rode up, late. All of

Forestdale was piled on the lawn. Most of the food was gone and many of the older folks had started to drift off.

Cecilia and I momentarily parted ways, the brief absence creating anticipation, a secret pebble rolled between fingers in a jacket pocket. Some of the kids were practicing acrobatics and Garrett was in the middle of a handstand, watched closely by smiling children, laughing hysterically. I found a beer.

The Dutch girls had thrown a party so they could interview each person on Forestdale about how we had met, who we knew, and "how the block is connected." They had a giant list of questions. They wanted names, dates, and places. Big spools of butcher paper lay unrolled inside, and the women were mapping the relationships on the block as some kind of conceptual art project.

"We need to interview you, Drew!" shouted the large one who always seemed to be shouting.

"Ja, Drewbie. We must have you down and get your information. Everyone else has participated," said the one with the purple pants as she touched each of her fingertips together in turn and nodded.

"Yeah, sure, give me just—"

I felt a large hand on my shoulder. "Hey, bro, can I borrow your truck?" It was Monte, the neighbor who had tattooed me.

"Sure. What for?"

"The hay wagon's got a flat."

"I didn't know they were baling today."

"They're trying to finish up before it gets dark."

I told him I would get changed and be right back. He encouraged me to hurry.

"Do you need a pair of gloves?" he called after me as I opened my gate.

The hayfield's just a few blocks from Forestdale, a huge lot on which an old school once sat, long since demolished, about the size of four football fields. It's surrounded by abandoned houses, the ones that are still standing. Paul's been seeding the lot illegally for years with alfalfa to feed and bed the animals on the block, the pigs and chickens and goats. The rest of it went to the working farm he created at the school where he teaches.

When Monte and I pulled up, Jake's Honda pickup was almost full of hay. Monk was on top catching bales thrown by one of Paul's sons. I asked Monte to drive so I could heave the bales myself.

"I thought you wanted to junk that truck!" Paul yelled over the engine as he putted by on the tractor. He'd helped me fix it the week before when it had died. Lithe and sinewy, and familiar with mechanics to the point of grace, he had repaired it before I was finished feeling sorry for myself. Then he scurried away, off to the next project.

Paul's son climbed in the bed of my truck and stacked the bales we flung up by the baling wire. Andy and Kinga showed up on their bicycles, and Andy, lean and savage, climbed on the truck with it still moving to start catching. Kinga waved and smiled, then grabbed a bale and tossed it to her husband. I had my hands on one and threw it to Paul's son, who was almost knocked over catching the thing. He righted himself, looked at me cockeyed, then smiled. He stuffed the bale on the stack and I went back to get another.

That day I didn't wear gloves. I wanted to feel the prickly grass on the backs of my hands as I gripped the baling wire. I liked the feeling of my muscles working, my shoulders heaving the bricks, my legs on solid ground. I picked up a bale and disturbed a brown field mouse who hopped away. I almost tripped trying not to crush him with my boot.

The Kemps were wearing shirts Kinga had screen printed. Andy's was brown and depicted a lumberjack cutting down the incinerator. Kinga's was white and sleeveless; it pictured a rainbow-colored phoenix-pheasant rising over DETROIT. Her arms were white, hard and smooth like soap. The veins atop Andy's hands moved with his fingers.

Paul's son stood on top of the bales in my truck, stacking from my side, Andy on the other. He had his giant legs spread wide for balance, but even with a good toss, the truck still moved and the bales wiggled like Jell-O. The guys stacked them on top of the cab as we brought more, rising with the tide of the bales. It was twilight, and if you could ever see stars in Detroit they would just have begun to wake their sleepy twinkling eyes to the night. The burned-out houses had a shabby beauty silhouetted by the setting sun.

"No more," I said as the leaf springs began to sag and Andy teetered atop the load, taller than a city bus. We let the truck sit idle with the headlights on, and planned where to store the bales and what we should do next. Paul, kneeling on the seat of the tractor to get a better look, circled as ever, trying to get the last bits of hay before dark.

Community happens like falling in love. You can't plan it, or force it, or dissect it like a frog. You can't try to make it happen. It just does, like falling for someone. Sure, a relationship takes work to keep going, but your heart wants what it wants and so do your neighbors'. We stood with our hands on our hips and leaned against the warm hoods, joking and discussing the day's take.

Cecilia. I had forgotten about Cecilia. I had forgotten she had wanted to see this so very much. And who wouldn't? Baling hay in Detroit. I'd have to remember things like that from now on.

The door I'd shucked off the abandoned house had been sitting atop sawhorses on the Forestdale porch for weeks, taunting me. I'd been running around town showing Cecilia the sights and had been neglecting work on the Queen Anne; everything, for that matter. I hadn't talked to my parents in weeks. Cecilia was at some conference, and so today was the day. I pushed myself out of bed and stepped onto my porch to smoke a cigarette and start thinking about how to start on the door. The view stunned me, and I dropped the lit cigarette between the cracks in the deck and nearly started a fire.

The entire block was spiderwebbed in varicolored yarn, bright strands in dozens of colors connecting the houses and making a taut canopy across the street. I opened the gate and walked out into the road with my mouth open.

It must have taken hundreds of skeins of yarn in strands of oranges and greens and blues. The color seemed to flow everywhere, in some places becoming so dense as to provide shade in the morning sun. From my house alone dozens were tied to the porch and shot across the road or drifted around the corner, connected to the neighbors' houses, which in turn sported their own webs. It was magical, like a scene from Lewis Carroll. Someone must have worked through the night to make it happen.

A few of my neighbors stood in the street and some of the block kids were attempting to jump off porches and touch the strands. Another group of bigger children had found sticks long enough to strum across the yarn as they ran down the street to make a muted twang. I walked over to Garrett, holding a cup of coffee in his bathrobe on his porch.

"What is this?"

"It's the Dutch girls. Remember those slabs of butcher paper they made us draw all over? This is it. Some kind of map of the community."

I missed it on the night of the party, but I remembered filling out the list when I was drunk one evening. They had a map of the block, and questions like, "From whom did you find out about Forestdale? Who brought you here for the first time, who is your closest friend, who has helped you work on your house?" They made us use different colored markers for each question, and the yarn was the fruition. It was beautiful.

But the garbage trucks couldn't get through without being tangled in the web, so the entire block hauled their Dumpsters to the end of the street for the duration of the yarn incident. It was also strange that people were coming to the community and attempting to explain it to us. I can only imagine what the East Detroit neighbors thought, driving by and walking through. The sight was quite magical, though.

I went back to work on the door under this new canopy of brightness and candor.

I first needed to carefully pry up the trim holding what was left of the glass, tiny, mean-looking shards. I threw the Detroit Diamonds out and set the trim aside. I grabbed the Mister Blister heated paint-stripping tool I'd borrowed from a bar owner in Hamtramck for whom I'd been doing some construction work, and got to work bubbling the hideous paint and peeling it like chewing gum with a scraper. Stripping the paint was easy work, daydreaming work.

Hamtramck is an enclave city surrounded by Detroit and just north of Poletown. Once predominantly Polish, Hamtramck, they now say, is the most diverse two square miles in the United States outside of New York. Something like thirty languages are spoken in the public schools. It's the kind of place you can see a woman wearing a hijab chasing a basketball in front of a Yemeni restaurant, across the street from a Polish meat market, just a block away from the best Bangladeshi food this side of Dhaka, a stone's throw from an Albanian night club, while watching the mayor, a painter, dance the waltz at a Polish heritage festival.

A solid factory town, Hamtramck once had the most bars per capita in the country. You can still walk into taverns packed at 3:30 p.m., just after shift change. When Hamtown's main factory,

American Axle, left in 2012, it lost half its tax base. Yet, because of immigration, mostly by Arabs and Bangladeshis, the population has remained steady and the economy functioning, if limping. In 2016 it elected the first majority Muslim city council in the nation.

The Mister Blister was blistering beautifully and I had begun to strip the door naked, coats of paint representing years and tastes and residents. I'd gotten what was going to be my kitchen sink from the basement of the bar where I'd borrowed the paint stripper, a rebellious little place of loud, ugly punk rock.

The sink was cast iron and covered in white porcelain, a style that was old and fairly common, but this sink in particular was anything but. Built before the turn of the century, the building had always been a bar, and the basement room I was redoing had been a speakeasy during Prohibition. The sink was from around that time. In the late '60s and early '70s the bar—then named Lilly's—had become an important spot for the burgeoning proto-punk movement, both the legendary MC5 and Iggy Pop playing there regularly. I liked to think that some drunk night one of those original Detroit badasses had thrown up in the sink that was about to go into my kitchen.

Legend was that Fred "Sonic" Smith, the MC5's guitarist, had met Patti Smith, the Most Holy Godmother of Punk Rock, at the Coney Island downtown, where I'd taken Cecilia a few days before. Coney Islands—hot dogs with chili, onions, and mustard—are our regional delicacy, and when I mentioned to the kind woman chatting with us in line that Cecilia had never had one, she said, "You ain't never had no Coney Island," her eyes bugging out of her head.

Cecilia told me that when Fred Smith died, Patti spent an entire year in bed grieving for the man she loved. I wasn't sure if that was true, but Cecilia sure talked a lot about love—

"God damn it!" I'd burned my thumb on the damn Mister Blister. This was going to be a bad one. I ran it under cold water inside and returned to the porch to smoke and look over my work. Not bad, but the heat gun couldn't get into the molding, and I was going to have to use chemicals. As I smoked, Molly walked by, inspecting the strands of yarn, and shouted across the fence to quit working and come to the Hillbilly Yacht Club.

Every summer Sunday, the HYC was a party centered on the pool she made from hay bales. During the last week of baling, she asked us to dump a few dozen in her backyard, behind the chicken coop and next to the rabbit cages. With an idea borrowed from Paul, she was going to build a pool. I didn't see how this was possible, but I listened.

Toward the end of her life, Paul's wife, the mother of his children, developed a degenerative disease and didn't have much time. The doctor told them that swimming might ease her pain. But because of all of the budget cutbacks and the exodus from the city, there were very few public swimming pools. In what has got to be one of the most romantic gestures of all time, Paul used what he had and added to it his ingenuity to build her a pool in the backyard. He stacked bales in a rectangle, threw over a blue roofing tarp, created a frame with leftover two-by-fours, and filled it with water. It held. When all was said and done, the hay from the bales was used to nourish and protect the soil.

Molly's was built on the same principle, but in a circle. There was a ladder made from logs, and she had bought one of those floating chlorine cones and a filter that made a peeing noise. The price of admission to the Hillbilly Yacht Club was a fifth of liquor. (This rule, along with all the others, was rather laxly enforced.) The local brewers would bring plenty of beer and enough good cheer to last all day.

I quickly took her advice and moved from the half-stripped door to Molly's backyard. I ate some of the coq au vin she had made for the occasion while Garrett floated on an inner tube lazily holding a bottle of wine and singing a song I had a suspicion he was making up as he went along. He stopped only to take swigs from the bottle or burp. I sat next to Will on a creaky aluminum chair in a circle with some of the others who had just exited the pool and were toweling off.

The conversation had moved from the yarn gilding the block to the street artist Banksy. He had recently been to town, unable to resist the postindustrial pull of Detroit, and had painted a number of works. Some of them were immediately sandblasted, but there was one left, inside the Packard plant. It depicted a boy holding a paint can and brush, who appeared to have just scrawled "I remember when all this was trees" on the wall.

Some of the members of the gallery that had given me the lumber to board up my house had gone into the abandoned plant with gas-powered stone saws, sledgehammers, and a Bobcat and removed the whole chunk of wall, preserving it behind glass. They put it on display in the gallery. Some people, most prominently graffiti artists, thought this was sacrilege and were rather upset. Others liked the anarchic and preservationist spirit. I thought it was an interesting little act of performance art myself, and decided the whole conversation surrounding it was a silly little act of mental masturbation. The gallery promised not to sell it, to keep it always for the public to view. The conversation moved on, as did the participants, and I was alone with Will.

"The school made a bid on my house," Will said out of nowhere. The price, he said, was in the tens of thousands of dollars.

"What are you going to do?"

"I'm not sure I have a choice."

———

That summer the United States Social Forum, a sort of ideological precursor to Occupy Wall Street, was held for a week in Detroit. More than 20,000 people came into the city from around the world, slept in tents, went to classes and discussions, drank and partied, networked.

I didn't have much time to participate, but one of the events I couldn't get away from was a march staged by professional protest coordinators who had come in from California. They were marching in opposition to Detroit's trash incinerator. Generously, one of the neighbors had allowed them to use the YES FARM to stage the protest, and some of the organizers had come in early to set up home base and begin building the props, hundreds of spray-painted sunflower pickets, miniature incinerators, signs.

The protest would march down Detroit's main thoroughfare and past the incinerator, presumably raising holy hell and sticking it to the man—who would probably just hide until they left again.

There was an energy to town when the people started rolling in. The vibe wasn't unique, but this time it was bigger. Folks would come from all over with art and social projects and such, and inevitably they would ask for help. I came home from working on the house to find the doors of the YES FARM thrown open and music and white people with dreadlocks spilling out into the street. Cecilia was also working in the YES FARM in a separate room on one of her projects and I went in to say hello.

"Helllo, Dreeew."

"What's up? How's it coming?"

"It is good. I am almost finished."

"Good."

"Can you help me hang the sign tomorrow?" Her project involved some trading of business signs between Rome and Detroit, and she needed help screwing the sign to the building here.

"Sure. What's going on over there?"

"I do not know. A protest, I think."

I had gotten the majority of the fencing up and I had, in fact, taken the red gate from the abandoned house down the block. It worked well, even if it was a bit saggy. The fence would keep little Gratiot from escaping, and anything else from getting in. The fence meant protection, that I had divided up the land and staked my claim. That, like John Locke had written, by mixing my labor with the natural resources of the earth I had created ownership. With all these new people in town splayed out on the sidewalk, I was feeling a little protective of the city itself.

Cecilia and I went outside. Colorful kids spotted the sidewalk, spray-painting circles of cardboard and stapled them to wooden pickets, all of which had been bought at the local big-box store. One of the guys was busy painting sunflowers on the concrete. I looked at him for a minute as he worked. Eventually he noticed me and when he looked up he smiled.

"How you doing, brother?"

"Who told you it was okay to paint on the sidewalk?" I noticed the fence around the YES FARM had been done as well.

"Oh, it's okay, it's just art. Who doesn't like art?"

At some point I felt I had made a transition into a Detroiter, whether I was or not. Maybe I recognized a little too much of myself in these kids spilling into the city. Maybe I was trying to differentiate myself from these people who were going to leave, protect myself from getting too close, but I was rather cold and unhappy with the proceedings. Maybe I was worried they reminded me a bit too much about Cecilia, who would have to go home soon herself. Maybe I was worried I was making the same mistakes. Living in Detroit and being part of a relatively small group gave my life meaning, and I was just feeling the beginnings of losing it to an influx of people who may not have had the same values.

Nevertheless, it didn't seem like anyone saw the irony in cutting down real pine trees to make fake sunflowers. Or that a protest for clean air would use so much aerosol spray paint. I wondered what was going to happen to all this stuff once everyone left.

I asked Cecilia if she wanted to go to a bar to see a popular band with me that night, one Jennie, Molly's roommate, sang in.

She kissed me and said, "Of course."

The bar was an armpit and it was especially sweaty that night. A veteran's bar by day and a punk rock venue after, it was packed with the majority of the young, hip white kids in the city, only a handful at that time. The walls were black and crammed with all kinds of war paraphernalia, machine guns, helmets, medals. The crowd was turbulent, happy, and drunk. I was on my way.

I salmoned my way up to the bar and asked Cecilia what she wanted.

"I think beer."

"You want something nice, or shitty?"

"Something good."

"I want a shot. You want a shot?"

"A shot?"

"Yeah, liquor."

"I don't think I should mix them."

"Beer and whiskey? They go together like peanut butter and jelly."

"What is this peanut butter and jelly?"

An opening band wailed over the warm crowd. The drummer had his shirt off and was sweating, his fists reaching above his head to smack the skins of the drums.

"You've never had peanut butter and jelly?"

I ordered two beers and two shots. We walked outside and clinked our glasses to Detroit, downing the whiskey. She asked me about peanut butter again, clutching my forearm.

"It sounds too sweet for lunch. Maybe for breakfast."

"I'll make you one sometime."

We had a couple more drinks and the headliner started up inside. I could hear Jennie singing.

"Let's go inside and watch the band."

Jennie had a crazy look in her eye, and with every word she sang she shook her head and bared her teeth like a prizefighter who knows she'll win.

The crowd roiled. Pushing one another, slapping one another on the back, hugging. I was sweating, and momentarily lost Cecilia. A fat dude with his shirt off, who I didn't know, was really rocking out next to me, all sweat and hair and energy. He banged his head.

I got turned around and found Cecilia. I pulled her toward me with my forefinger hooked into the dip in her yellow shirt. The band was at full force, and the crowd undulated, completely under their spell. Jennie had taken off her guitar like she was revealing a gift, and I had my hands at the nape of Cecilia's neck, kissing her, tangled in her coarse shaggy hair, a sodden wreck.

My eyesight was a bit twisty from the alcohol, and the lights had tracers, and her arms wrapped around my waist and up to my neck.

"Do you want to get out of here?" I was drunk.

She grabbed my hand in reply. "Can we smoke a cigarette before getting on the bikes?" she asked.

The air outside was cool and the concrete cooler, as we sat against the cinder-block building.

"I need one of yours," she said, and I rolled it for her because I knew it would be faster than letting her do it.

I said something about folding love letters into paper airplanes and sailing them across the Atlantic.

We rode drunkenly back to my house and made love. I fell softly asleep.

———

"Wait, what did you just say?"

"Maybe I should go." I was lying with Cecilia in my bed that same night, having awoken just a few hours later. I reached over and clicked on the light.

"I always feel bad when this happens."

"What do you mean you feel bad? What do you mean always?"

"I have a life in Italy, a house, a boyfriend. We are engaged."

"You're engaged? Oh fucking Christ. What? I just— What? Why didn't you tell me?"

"Why didn't you ask?"

"Oh, fucking hell. Get out of my bed. Get out!"

She started crying and I thought I might throw up all that whiskey I'd had.

"What the hell, you couldn't have told me this, like, weeks ago? What the fuck."

"I will leave."

"No, don't leave. I, I don't want you to leave."

"I'm going to go." She got out of bed and started to root about for her clothing.

"Please, don't go. It's, like, two in the morning and you're on your bike. I'll drive you at least."

"I will be fine." She had gotten a pant leg on and was hopping around trying to swing the other in.

"This is fucked up, you know. How did you not tell me in, like, the month we've spent together? Why the hell did you wake me up to tell me this tonight? This couldn't have waited till morning? Fuck you."

She slapped me. I was momentarily stunned and she snatched her shirt from the floor. She turned and resumed angrily weeping.

"I am starting to fall in love with you."

"Well, yeah, me, too. But why now?"

"Because it is no longer play. Loving is dangerous."

"But, but. Ahhh! We can find a way to work it out. Wait, you're engaged?"

"You are so young."

I protested, and she cut me off.

"How old are you, twenty-three? You know nothing of love. You have no idea how hard this is. How do you think I feel? It is much more complicated than you make it out."

I drove her home in silence and woke up alone.

———

She sent me a text message the next day.

"Hello Drew . . . I wanted to say I am sorry about last night. I would still like to see your house. Will you invite me?"

I ignored the text most of the day and attempted to busy myself framing out the bathroom, which needed to be expanded. The room had originally held only a small sink and toilet, and I wanted to add a shower. The bathroom upstairs had one, but was out of the area I was going to heat for that winter. On the south wall of the room I had bricked up the window opening with glass blocks, which would be in the shower itself. I planned to tile the wall in mosaic—I figured I could get cheap or free ceramic tile, smash it up and arrange it, create something beautiful. I was going to tile the window in the shape of the sun, but I wasn't feeling so beautiful or sunny at the moment.

I had brought the scale drawings of the house I had made with my grandfather. I'd set a rock found in the yard and a pair of pliers on the edges to keep them from rolling up. They'd become dirty from bringing them here to work, but were still legible, although the crisp pencil lines were now smeared and fading. The plans my grandfather had gently walked me through at his kitchen table, the ones he wouldn't do for me, but made me learn myself, would dictate how big to frame out the toilet, the sink, the shower. I wished he could gently walk me through what to do with Cecilia, but the men in my family didn't discuss that kind of thing, just how to build houses.

I decided my grandpa was wrong about where to put the toilet and the sink, so I switched their places. Years later I would realize he was right all along, but it would be too late to switch them back. For now I felt good about making a decision on my own, one I thought smarter than the knowledge of those who came before me, those with more experience.

I did a half-assed job and was listless. How can you not tell someone you're engaged? Had I missed something, was I just that stupid and inexperienced? I replayed our conversations in my mind, looking for an inflection or an offhand comment I might have missed or willfully ignored. What should have been easy and fun on the house was turning into a drudge. Every few moments or so my internal monologue would swerve back to Cecilia, and each time a little inarticulate jolt would pass through my body as I remembered what had transpired and how stupid I'd been.

I was embarrassed for not thinking there might be a catch to all of this, that it wasn't me who was interesting or fascinating. It was Detroit. Cecilia just wanted someone to show her around. Of course, she wanted to nibble on this place, slum it for a bit and take off to where she came from, to this other man, who, I later learned, was fairly famous in Italy. It was Detroit that she wanted, not me. But what the hell? You can't help who you fall in love with, and I might as well try. The text was searing a hole in my pocket, and maybe, after all, she'd change that plane ticket and stay just a little longer.

I called and she picked up right away. I told her if she wanted to see the house, now was a good time. She agreed, and would head over.

When she arrived I grabbed her hand and helped her up onto the porch, as I still hadn't built any stairs. She left her bike unlocked resting against the house and stepped through the threshold ahead of me. The door, which was supposed to be hanging in the doorway, was still sitting on sawhorses on my porch, half-stripped. I was still screwing myself in and out past a piece of plywood.

"Well, this is it," I said, stepping in behind her.

"It is nice."

She lied. I led her through the kitchen and we didn't speak. I hadn't even accomplished half of what I had needed to before I was to move in. All the utilities still needed to be hooked up, and the sink from the bar stood forlornly on the unsteady stand I had quickly built for it. The floors were dark; the windows, still covered with plywood, were dark; my mood was dark. I'd spent so much time showing this woman around the city that I loved rather than working on this house that I needed to love, and it showed. I had framed one of the studs for the bathroom a bit out of plumb, and the whole place seemed shabby and inadequate.

Cecilia didn't say anything, and paced the floor, thinking. I smoked a cigarette, unsure of what to say or what I wanted to say, pugilistic sentences running jumbled through my mind all wanting to come out at the same time, but like the Three Stooges getting stuck in the doorway that was my stupid mouth. The late-evening sun was pouring into the west-facing windows I had framed out, the ones I had been working on at the moment I had decided I'd ask her on the first date. This house, once one of possibility, now seemed like a cell.

Cecilia grabbed my hand and kissed me there, in the sun. She led me back outside to the porch and we sat in the dying light. She had brought something, her computer, and pulled it from her bag.

"I will show you now, my house."

What followed next was heartbreaking. In the mountains and overlooking the ocean, the house was built from some of the finest materials in the world, exotic wood, glass, steel. She had designed it from the ground up, and her father, a wealthy man who owned a construction company, had built it for her. The house had just won a European architecture prize worth tens of thousands of euros. It was clean, new, well built, and sleek, everything mine wasn't. As we looked out over my vista, a jungled backyard filled with trash, empty lots, and two abandoned houses, one that was now being squatted by some junkies, I felt jealous. One of the photos showed her fiancé sitting in a room in Cecilia's house, and I wanted to be angry, I felt I should hate him, but I felt nothing.

Instead I felt ashamed of this house and this life I had chosen. I felt ashamed of the dirty plans I had made with my grandfather, and I felt ashamed of being ashamed of that. Where had my fighting spirit gone? Where was the "fuck you I don't care I live in *Detroit, motherfucker*, and I don't care what the rest of the world thinks, I'm badder and cooler than anyone else"? Her house seemed so nice and so exotic, and here I was in Detroit, a place everyone but me thought exotic.

What had I done? Why did I have to be the one to care about this place above all else? Why the fuck did I have to be the martyr? And now why did I have to be so self-pitying? Why did I have to be so poor, and why did I have to be left feeling sorry for myself while some other asshole fucked this woman I thought I was in love with? I didn't believe in God, so there wasn't some reward in the afterlife, just a dream that I might go up against the system and win, that by holding fast and not letting go I could make the world a bit better for others and live a comfortable life in the process. Well, right now I didn't feel like I was winning. Not by a long shot.

What could I do? If I'd left I would have been a coward. *I* would have called myself a coward. So there wasn't anything to do but pick up my plow and go back to work and attempt again to forge some meaning out of my meaningless existence, to convince myself that this struggle somehow mattered, that I wasn't some idiot speck of stardust floating in the cosmos. And if I could find that meaning, well, I could prove something to myself and others, that not only was a better world possible, a better world was happening, and we were making it ourselves out of the cinders of racism and consumerism and escape. If I failed—

Cecilia, already, was in the past. I was hoping I would find more in attempting to live a virtuous life than a pride in personal integrity, that one life, lived well, and with a little bit of luck, could be meaningful to others as well, could bend the direction of the great freight train of history toward justice and compassion and equality. I felt that if I just held on, to this place, to this city, to this vision of myself, that if I kept my grip firm the dream would always live, that it could be extinguished only if I gave up, if I left the city like so many others before me. When I first kissed Cecilia I had turned away not only from Detroit but from my history and my blood, for something I thought more interesting and sexy, a brand-new way of selling out. Even with the bonds of friends and relations and a home tying me here, there was really only one thing keeping me in this place, and that was my will. If my will was broken, so was the dream.

Cecilia had chosen the other guy, the other house, the other life, and I was going to have to find some other choice myself. Maybe by building this house I could make Detroit love me back. Work would be our vows. Cecilia snapped the computer shut.

"What do you think?"

"Well, obviously, it's beautiful."

"Are you jealous?"

"Yes. I am jealous."

My grandparents' sixtieth wedding anniversary was the very next day, June 24, 2010. I attended it instead of the rest of the social forum and the march with the sunflower pickets.

———

I made Cecilia her first peanut butter and jelly sandwich and drove her to the airport. She had finished her projects and it was time to go back to her Italian boyfriend, and her spectacular home. Wherever she was going it was likely to be clean and warm and not life-threatening.

On the day she was to leave, she asked first to see the famous Diego Rivera murals at the Detroit Institute of Arts, our world-class art museum built with auto money. We rode our bikes slowly through the early July heat, up to the imposing white marble building. The museum seemed a bit quiet, and when I tried the door, it was locked. I had forgotten the institute was closed that day of the week.

"Well, okay," Cecilia said. "It will have to wait until next time I am in Detroit."

I knew she was lying again. She'd never be back. I wouldn't get to see the murals that day, and her, likely never. But—

Jane, one of the founding members of the art gallery that had given me the wood to board up my house, was walking up the street. She wore a badge that said she worked at the museum.

I waved. I shouted, "Hey, Jane!" She stopped. "I didn't know you worked here."

"It's brand-new, and I love it."

I explained my predicament. She opened the door.

"Come on inside."

We would get a private tour. She led us through security and up the marble steps into the great hall, the floor decorated in mosaic, suits of armor, swords, and ornate muskets lining the vast corridor. Up ahead was Rivera Court, where the master himself had spent a summer convincing the world of the beauty of the working man along the walls of one of America's greatest museums. He worked just blocks from where mass manufacturing was born, when the middle class had been brought to life on five dollars a day, and where the struggle of building objects with one's hands became honorable and noble. He painted the workers larger than the king.

We stepped inside. Completed in 1933, the frescoes depict life inside Ford's auto factories and the endless nobility of man.

The twenty-seven panels portray advancements in science and technology, the fruits of the earth, the feminine and life-giving in relation to the masculine, hope, cooperation, and the totality of the human spirit, the interconnectedness of humankind, industry, and the soul.

Nowhere is the community spirit of Detroit, and everywhere like it, better portrayed than in what is likely the finest example of Mexican mural art in the United States. This is where generations of artists have come to dip into the well of inspiration, the church of creativity, the warm embrace of the imagination clasping hands with reality. I explain all this to Cecilia as we hold hands together alone in the empty museum.

I tell her: It took an outsider, a Mexican Communist, to show our heroism to ourselves. He showed us that what is inside us here is inside all of us, everywhere, man's legacy to the world. The figures are huge and all work together, different colors of men working and struggling and pushing toward one goal. Sand, rubber, and iron went in one end—and only but through the hands of man—a car came out the other.

This is Detroit's history, the heroism of the forge and crucible on display, a reminder of who we are as men and women and citizens of this planet. A gift to the city of Detroit, the fresco offers a choice: panels depicting poison gas and bombing planes mirror panels depicting vaccinations and aircraft of exploration.

They are not just offering us a choice of good or evil, forward or backward. They offer the choice between creativity and destruction. Rivera begs us to choose to create, to bring new life into this world, to make not just products but a brand-new heroic world of brother- and sisterhood, of nobility and honor. It could have been my grandfather or my father or anyone in my family depicted up there, and maybe yours.

He's asking all of us to do this. You. Create something every day. Despite what they may tell you, you artists, you mothers, you misfits of creativity, the world depends on what you can dream up. The ice caps aren't getting bigger. The bombs are still being produced. The cities never stopped being torn apart with inequality and suffering.

Practice. Practice creating that new world. Our very survival depends on what you can create. You. Not someone else.

You.

I took Cecilia to the airport that day and I would never see her again.

When I got home to Forestdale, Jake was loading protest junk into his truck from the YES FARM. The protesters from California had left all their stuff and split. In a bout of staggering irony we had no option but to put it in the incinerator. While they were off gallivanting to their next good deed far away from their mess, that shit went up into the air and into our lungs.

I was too tired to help right then, so I went inside my house, passing by the half-finished door I'd stolen still sitting on the sawhorses where I'd left it, and sat down in the shower and cried.

I called my father that evening to tell him I was sorry I hadn't talked to him in weeks. I told him something I'd never told him before, that I had been in love with someone, and I had just taken her to the airport, never to be seen again. I spilled my guts in one long, rambling sentence, telling him everything.

He was in transition, too. After twenty-one years of teaching farm kids to make auto parts and tools from steel and aluminum, he had been tapped to become the vice principal of the school where he'd spent his adult life. Where once he wore a blue shopcoat, now he was wearing suits. A tradesman since a teenager, he was making his way to management, climbing the ladder of the American Dream. When I stopped talking there was a pause.

He said he was sorry to hear it. My family spoke in the language of work and striving and hardness, and cute rich girls from Europe didn't exactly fit into that. He had worked hard for my family his entire life, and love and duty had always embraced each other as long as I'd known him.

The next question he asked was about the weather. Some things you just have to face alone.

But Will knew what was going down that day, and he called and told me to come over to his house. He had bought me some beer and a little bottle of whiskey. I lay flat on my back on the cool concrete outside his uncertain home as we talked and drank. I told him how stupid I felt, how young I felt. I was way behind on my house, and I'd wasted so much time. The social forum was done, everyone had left, and all there was to do was go back to work.

"For the people that come in and don't last, everybody's everything else is more important than what we have to do for ourselves," Will said. "People want to escape their reality for a while and snack on yours, but they don't want to buy the meal. Everyone needs help with their projects. Everyone wants to be shepherded around, and I bet a bunch of new people are going to move here because of that social forum. It's like church camp. People come on fire for God or whatever, then they're back fornicating the next week with their boyfriend. You lost this time, Drew, pretty hard. I know how it feels. You have a little bit of growing up to do."

I felt a bit like a whole city must feel losing half its population.

"People come to Detroit and places like it all the time." He snapped his fingers. "And then they leave. Once they get what they came for, Drew, poof. It's happened in the past, and it's going to happen in the future. You have to recognize that. You have to protect yourself. But . . ." He paused, and I turned my head to look at him. A cigarette burned between his fingers and he took a drag. "But you cannot harden your heart. You cannot close yourself off, you cannot shrivel the little ounce of good that brought you here, and has kept you here in the first place. And most of all, you cannot be the one who repeats it, who does it himself.

"We're all in this dirty old bathroom and the sink is clogged," Will said. "The faucet's running and the water's spilling out all over the floor. There's going to be lots of people running at you, trying to hand you a mop. Some of them will even be talking about love and lots will be talking about money. You got to remember to stick with what you were trying to do in the first place, which was fix the plumbing."

CHAPTER 6

Load-Bearing Walls

Carrying the beam that holds up my house

I smashed the beam with the sledgehammer and it didn't budge. I tried again, nothing.

Andy Kemp was yelling at me to get the jack. It was Labor Day and eight of my friends, my father, and a French Canadian film crew were inside my house as we were lifting the beam in place to hold up the roof. I had removed that load-bearing wall separating the kitchen and dining room, and had framed the opening for the new beam just a bit tight. Always a bit tight.

The beam was stuck as a dozen men held it above their heads. I scurried to get the jack from my truck to lift the ceiling so we could move the lumber into place.

I had found the beam a month earlier in a glass-recycling factory that had caved in a block away from my house. The building, which looked like it had been in the bombing of Dresden, was really just a pile of rubble—cinder blocks, bricks, trash. At one point it had been at least two stories high, yet now the only room that still stood above ground level was the bathroom, the white porcelain toilet broken and half gone.

What I was after were the laminated supports that once held the roof up. They were made from old-growth hard pine stacked atop one another and bolted through with steel rods. They measured more than twenty feet long and were thicker than a man's forearm. Each had a gentle curve, and I thought one would be a nice solution to an exposed-header problem—the beam would sit proud of the drywall on the ceiling and provide a nice focal point for the room, as well as a good story and a small piece of Detroit's history. I needed fourteen feet, cut out sixteen, and loaded it into my truck crossways with the springs creaking to drive back to my yard, the crew walking next to it like it was a precious treasure.

On the day we put it in, I rallied the troops on Forestdale, needing every hand I could get. Andy was hosting the film crew and agreed to come if they would be able to tag along as well. They were in town filming an art movie called *The End of Time*, and I said sure, as long as they agreed to help. I felt uncomfortable about this, but I needed the hands and Andy was invaluable. I found out later that one of the men holding the beam aloft was Peter Mettler, the director, fairly famous in some circles.

His crew was rolling as we lifted the beam and when it got stuck. As the men strained under the great weight of the beam the size of a tree trunk, I retrieved a jack and a 2x4 to push up the ceiling enough to slide the timber home.

"I can't hold out much longer."

When I got the jack in place the two-by was too long. The crew groaned. I found a circular saw and nipped off the end.

"We're going to lose it here, Drew."

Close enough. I cranked on the jack.

"I'm slipping here, my man."

The floor began to creak and I could see the ceiling rise by fractions of an inch.

"Drew. We can't hold this much longer."

"All right, there. Try it. Try it!"

I mounted the ladder with the sledge and hit the end as hard as I could.

"Yeah!" "Wooh!" "You got it!"

The beam moved a fraction of an inch. I hit it again. More cheers, it was moving. It was moving!

I hit the end again and finally it was set in place. My dad swung his hammer ferociously, pounding nails as long as his fingers to keep the beam tied in. It now holds up the entire house.

The Queen Anne was still a shell, its bones exposed, but it was starting to feel like mine. Built in 1903, its builder used horses to move the materials and lift the rafters, not cars and internal combustion. That I could simply drive to the hardware store in a matter of minutes, pick out whatever part I needed—almost certainly exactly the same as any other I could buy anywhere in America—was something of a miracle. When the house was built, boards were hewn with steam or water power and left rough, rafters were lifted with block and tackle by animals that ate and breathed. The builders very well may have had to clear the land of trees and stumps to build the foundation of bricks that had likely been made in a factory right in Detroit. I tried to imagine the men who had built it, working in white shirtsleeves and leather vests.

The house itself was once a living thing, too. The trees that made its skeleton and skin were once living organisms, growing and eating and reproducing in the forest. When the house falls back into the ground it will nurture the earth and will go back to being alive, too. In the grand scheme of things it appears nothing seems to ever really die.

Now more than ever, the house had become a constant presence in my life. I had screwed around too much that summer, but there would be nothing else but THE HOUSE for the next years of my budding adulthood. The first question people invariably asked was, "How's the house coming?" All of my money went into the house. All of my time not working to make that money would go into my house. All my thinking went into the house. All my energy went into the house. They say your possessions own you at some point, and if that's true, the house owned me, mind, body, and spirit.

Yet in a way the house didn't own me at all. The house *was* me. And I was it. I had put all of myself into this once-living building; it was my other, an extension of my body, my being, my soul. It wouldn't be that way if I'd just bought it new. I wasn't building a portfolio or an investment, I was building a shelter, a necessity of life, and by extension myself. It took everything I had, everything I learned, everything I knew, all the space in my brain and my muscles. It didn't own me any more than my body owned my mind. It's said that C. S. Lewis once wrote, "You don't have a soul. You are a soul. You have a body."

The value of the house is not just in dollars and cents, property value. The value is in shelter, warmth, a place to rest and feel safe and cook for my friends. It's in security, keeping me from the elements and danger, and always having a place to call home. It's in the knowledge I've gained, the hard muscles, the satisfaction of doing something right. My house isn't a commodity. All my work cannot be bought or resold; the hard muscles, the mental strength cannot be purchased. That dollar-and-cent value matters only when housing, shelter, is a commodity, when homes are meant to be discarded, the occupants moving on to bigger and better things. When a house is just something meant to be consumed.

———————

I had picked the day after the Harvest Party to move in. I needed to give myself a deadline or I would be able to justify pushing any date further back until I was wintering on Forestdale for another year. No matter what I had gotten done, or had not gotten done, I would sleep in my own house the night after the party and every night after that.

I was broke. It was looking like I wasn't going to have a furnace the next winter either, and I was going to be lucky if I had enough credit left to scrape together a water heater.

You might think a furnace would be more important than warm water, but that's not usually the case. The furnace takes longer to set up and the ducts are more difficult to route than plumbing—that only needs to go to the kitchen and bathroom. Cold air can be overcome in more ways than cold water. Every time you want to wash your hands, every time you want to take a shower, every time you need to wash dishes, clean out a cut, shave . . . even with a furnace it was cold anyway, as setting the thermostat to something civilized, like 55 degrees, in a house that was barely more than a construction site was unaffordable. Already being cold and sticking your hands in cold water each morning was a recipe for not only misery but sickness.

My dad and I started on the plumbing that weekend. I'd done some pipe fitting before but wasn't sure what to do about Detroit-specific problems like someone stealing your water meter and leaving nothing but a hacked-off pipe. On Farmer Paul's advice I got a compression fitting from Atlas Plumbing, down the street.

It was an old-school place, with a counter where men would

wait on you and knew what they were talking about, one of the last businesses in the neighborhood, a decade-long holdout when just about everything around them had gone to hell. They were real plumbers, and could help come up with solutions for any problem. Customers hung out in the shop, drinking coffee and shooting the shit with the employees.

Everyone around was willing to share their knowledge with an urchin like me. Along with other holdouts in the neighborhood, guys like these were the backbone of the city. They may have felt they needed to move themselves and their families to the suburbs for one reason or another, but never moved their business. They retained an institutional knowledge about the neighborhood and city that was invaluable. I looked forward to going in there and never got plumbing supplies anywhere else.

Other materials were a different story. I despised places like Walmart for what they had done to small businesses and downtowns across the country, and American manufacturing in general. That stuff is so cheap because it's made for cents an hour. But try as I could to shop local, I still bought things at the big-box hardware stores—the Walmarts of lumber—that had been putting local places and their knowledge out of business for years. It wasn't just good jobs that were lost—after the big guys came in and priced out the family places, many of those employees were forced to get jobs at their corporate competitors, often for a lower wage—also lost was the camaraderie, knowledge, and community that the old places fostered.

A lot of the time, too, those family places cared about the products they sold, not just in terms of quality but ethically. They were less likely to sell you a cheap Chinese piece of junk, not just because their name rested on it functioning properly, but because they intrinsically understood that their jobs and wages were tied with those of the guys in the factory in Wisconsin pumping out fittings. It was a losing proposition. We'd already lost most of the mining of the raw materials to the folks in South America and Africa now fighting the same fight we did in the '30s for a living wage. For one person to escape ethically unscathed from the additional cost in environmental degradation by these operations seemed impossible.

In our current world something like bottle recycling was, at best, an example of what we could hope to achieve. Throwing my can in the recycling bin or reusing some wood from an abandoned house was nothing compared with lumber companies clear-cutting rain forests or mining interests dumping millions of gallons of tainted waste into rivers. It would take wholesale societal awakening and change to interrupt this. Try as I might to be pure, I was complicit in the system. I was trying to be better but nevertheless made choices of expediency versus ethics.

When you turn on your faucet, or flush the toilet or take a shower, it is almost certain that that clean, fresh water is brought to you by materials manufactured or mined by someone in a bondage so great it would be illegal in America or Europe, by a process that is rapidly killing the very planet that we will leave for our children. We have slavery running through the walls of our homes and stitched into the fabric of our clothes. As a people we need to think about this.

The massive wealth inequality that this consumerist style of living creates might be all right if astronomical sums of money bought just the finer things in life. But it also buys political influence, the kind that encourages clear-cutting forests and demolishing houses instead of recycling wood, the kind that says American companies mining copper in foreign lands don't have to abide by the laws of labor or decency, that products like piping for a house can be made by near slaves and we should all look the other way because it's cheap. I was no better. I bought my plumbing from Atlas, but the plastic

PEX pipes I placed in my home were likely made by people making less than a dollar a day, the raw material for the fittings mined in a process scarring the earth.

Working with my father, I crimped these pipes together with brass fittings and copper rings. From the fitting at the lead pipe I split the line in two, one to go in a loop toward the hot water heater I hadn't yet purchased, the other to a manifold that would divide the water throughout the house, leaving space to add on the second bathroom, a hose bib for the garden, and a washing machine. At this time I was plumbing only the downstairs bathroom and the kitchen. We hung the pipes along the joists in the basement and shot them up through the floor to the sink I'd gotten from the bar, and up through the bathroom to service the shower and the toilet I had placed contrary to what my grandfather had suggested.

Because half of the bathroom was over a crawl space—the room was likely added on to the house during the advent of indoor plumbing—I threaded the pipes for the sink through the curb of the shower. They would be less likely to freeze going through the heated space of the house. I did, however, place the shower trap down there, unheated.

We connected valves to each stub-out upstairs, and from the valves stainless-steel supply lines to each of the faucets and the toilet. I had purchased what was just about the cheapest nickel-plated showerhead and manifold from Atlas and installed this in the shower basin, sweating a copper jumper between the two. Molly was coming by in a few days to pour a concrete shower pan, a job that would have cost hundreds of dollars but she was doing for free because "you're a friend." I wouldn't be able to test the shower until that was in, but I could see if water flowed from the rest.

"Do you want to check these fittings with the gauge again?" my father asked. He was casually checking some of the crimpings with a go/no-go gauge, a tool that measured the near-microscopic tolerances on things like machine parts and fittings such as these.

"Nah, I think we're fine. I'm pretty sure I got them all."

All that was left to do was test it. A plumber had lent me a water key, a long piece of rebar with a T-handle on one end and a fork at the other that fit the valve buried in my front yard leading to the street. I found the valve cover buried under sod, opened it with a wrench, and inserted the slender key. The water arrived at my house through a series of enormous pipes installed before my grandparents were born, much of it lead, now often switched to copper. This valve was the last and only thing holding back the massive water pressure from the municipal system. If something went wrong, if the valve was broken, the water line cut, I was screwed. If water didn't come out when I turned this handle, it was going to be a costly and time-consuming process. I called to my father standing inside to see if he was ready. This was it.

"Yep."

I turned the key. I could hear my father yell from inside.

"Hey! Hey! Shut it off! Shut it off!"

I turned it back, rushing into the house and leaving the key sticking out of the hole in the front yard. My father was soaking wet in the basement and glaring at me with a smile on his face, a specialty of his. We had forgotten to crimp one of the rings near the main line and the pressure had blown the pipe off, drenching my father, who was standing in front of it. As he wiped the water from his face with one hand, he held out the pair of crimpers with the other, looking at me as if to say, "Should have listened to your old man."

"Well, at least we know it works!" I said.

My dad shook my hand and congratulated me, his faux scowl breaking. "Andrew Man!" he roared, raising his hand for a high five and calling me by one of the nicknames he used when we worked together when I was a kid. "Okay. Let's take a look at these fittings and try this again, Buckwheat."

I recrimped the ring and checked the others. All good. For good measure, my dad closed the valve in the basement, nearest the main line, the one that could turn the whole house on and off from the inside. Now that we knew it worked, I'd be able to turn the water on at the street and from downstairs my dad could ease the valve open for any surprises.

I went outside and turned the key again, listening for my pops. All good. I went back inside and he called, "All ready?"—the signal to open the valve.

"All ready."

From upstairs I heard him squeak the spigot open and then a whooshing noise. Crystal-clean water from the Great Lakes rushed into the treatment plant, through miles of pipe beneath the streets of Detroit, into the spur traversing my front yard, then up through the manifold splitting it through the house. The water had made a journey of thousands of miles and years to be trapped in little plastic tubes running to my faucet. In principal it was a rather simple system—just cylinders to carry water around—but in practice it spanned the globe and the weather and thousands of years, from the copper miner in Peru, to the Roman aqueduct engineer, to the Chinese workers making plastic pipes, to the miracle of evaporation, climate change, and the Ice Age, to the cup I held in my hand as my father, smiling, watched me draw from my brand-new old kitchen sink the first water that had run through my house in a decade. I held the glass up to the light, then tipped it toward my father. I drank.

———

The back door was finished and all I needed was the glass. I had stripped everything down to the raw wood, and had recoated it in polyurethane, leaving a pleasant wheat color. I had made the door jamb new and the Kemps had given me a steel-barred security door I'd found in the garage behind the Forestdale house. Without some serious power tools or a skilled locksmith it was going to be nearly impossible to get through that door.

I had also created a small back porch, with a set of stairs. The porch was easy enough, but cutting the stringers for the stairs was difficult, as it involved some complicated math with a number of variables. This set of stairs was by no means intricate, but I wanted to do it right and have the treads sit directly on the stringers, not cheat and use ledge blocks. After failing to find a satisfactory lesson on the Internet, I called my grandfather, who walked me through the process, step by step over the phone, until I had a template I could work from. His lesson was sound and they worked beautifully, solid and without a squeak.

Just as soon as I purchased and installed the glass, the door could go in and the rear entrance would be almost normal. The house would start to feel more like a real dwelling and less like a construction zone. Someone on Forestdale suggested a glass shop in the suburbs. I still hated going to the 'burbs and went only when absolutely necessary.

Although Detroit is 83 percent black, the suburbs are about the inverse. We speak of only one great migration in the twentieth century, that of blacks leaving the Jim Crow South and sharecropping, to escape overt racism and lynching for factory jobs in the north. But really there were two, the second was whites moving to the suburbs to escape those same people looking for freedom. They were aided by all levels of government, subsidizing transportation, home loans, and infrastructure, making the building of the American suburban lifestyle likely the largest welfare project of the twentieth century.

Of course, I took the freeway to get the glass. Unbounded by any natural barriers, housing could expand west, south, and north as far as people could still commute into the city to work. Already having established itself as the motor capital of the world, we invested almost exclusively in freeways. They were great for getting people places, if you could afford a car, which 26 percent of Detroiters can't, but they also ensured that public transportation such as subways were the prerogative of other cities. There is almost no public transportation in Detroit aside from some dangerous and late buses that people avoid if possible. Metro Detroit has tried twenty-eight times to come up with a regional transit plan, but it's been stymied just as many by suburban politicians and residents who want things to remain exactly as they are.

I got off the freeway and followed my handwritten directions to the shop, a quaint little family place. The people inside were kind and genuinely wanted to help. There are those in Metro Detroit who have sworn off any and all dealings with the city, thinking nothing good can come of Detroit whatsoever, and there are those who have been caught up in the whirlwind of history, frustrated with how things turned out but at a loss for what to do, less Judas and more Pilate. The people who owned the glass shop were the latter. When I told them what I was doing with the $500 house I'd bought, like everyone else they laughed, and they ordered the glass for me at cost, the owner sighing and saying, "I don't need to make any money off this one."

It was people like these, when seen as individuals and not faceless masses of SUV-driving automatons, who would crack my self-righteous facade and instinctual disgust at the suburbs. It forced me to see that the reasons people left Detroit were maybe more complicated than I'd thought, and demonizing them wasn't as easy as I wanted it to be. Hell, I might have left myself, if my silly love affair with Cecilia had worked out.

Meanwhile, I was running against the clock. I installed the glass and then the door, but even with it in I had so many things to get through before I could even think about living there. The race was on. With the door began the fight against the cold, my weapons caulk and insulation and weather-stripping. I needed to install the metal chimney pipe I'd bought to get through the first year or two, organize what I'd left undone from the initial cleanup, and begin the entire process of installing electricity. This was all running me down. Work at the restaurant, work on the house, shower, sleep, repeat ad infinitum. Days were running into one another and I was developing permanent dark circles under my eyes. At twenty-four, my hair was beginning to silver.

Compounding this was that the city was changing, already. It seemed to happen gradually but perceptibly: people were interested in Detroit again, if just a trickle. One apple ain't a bushel, and it's sure not a truckload, but when you're starving it's noticeable. One of my best friends from college called, asking me to help find him a place in the city. He was from the suburbs, and lived there currently, one of the few people who hadn't moved out of the state after college. When I initially asked him why he didn't move to Detroit in the first place, he gave me one of the only honest answers I'd heard:

"Because I'm too much of a pussy," he said. He was now on the phone saying, "Well, you haven't been murdered yet."

Lots of experts began to move in temporarily as well. Kids with Ivy League educations would come stay a year or two, and the decisions they made would have an outsize impact in an undereducated city. Many would move on to bigger and better things and would not be around to see the consequences of those actions. It had begun to look as though people from outside Detroit were examining the city as if it were a child's chemistry set. We were now under a microscope.

The people who hadn't left were understandably wary. After a half century of urban renewal, debacles like the freeway and the Poletown plant that never really seemed to benefit Detroiters, people were skeptical when new, vast project ideas began to sprout; many, we were told, designed just for our benefit.

There were a lot of community meetings around that time, both on the block and citywide. The sense was that the reckoning had come, from all sides, and we had to make some principled decisions about our future. Businessmen and nonprofits started to visit us on Forestdale, looking for support. These meetings were held in the YES FARM.

One investor was a wealthy banker who wanted to turn the neighborhood into a farm, as if people like Paul who'd lived there for decades weren't working on that already. But he didn't want to support what was already going on, rather, to come in and start something with his name on it. In the end many figured he just wanted to piggyback on the down-home feeling of urban farming, and his project was a land grab. To get the okay from the city council he needed Paul driving the tractor behind his limousine.

The next guy who visited was a former addict running a drug rehabilitation clinic. He also wanted to turn the entire neighborhood into a nonprofit urban farm. Horses, pigs, vegetables, processing plants for jams and sausage, huge indoor hydroponics, and tanks of tilapia for fish farming. His ideas were enormous, although he had no money. He did have some city government and, soon, foundation support, though.

I was slightly more interested in the latter idea—he said he would be hiring residents from the neighborhood and citizens returning from prison—but the neighborhood seemed to hate it, maybe because some of the ideas had already been worked out with the previous guy and intentions had been articulated, but the reaction was immediate and swift, particularly from Farmer Paul.

As the debate droned on inside the YES FARM, Jake and I sat

on the front stoop and he told me a story, which he had experienced just a few days prior:

Paul and a small crew, which included Jake, had been working all day trimming trees, which was the power company's job. Workers for the for-profit showed up in the afternoon on an unrelated matter and told Paul he was in their way. Paul ignored them, and kept doing what he'd been doing all day. When they demanded Paul move, he became upset, put down his chain saw, and pointed at his chest.

"I'm the one who has been taking care of this neighborhood for twenty years. Me. You guys haven't been around. You've done nothing but watch this place deteriorate while raising our rates. Now you want me to stop doing what you guys should be doing anyway?"

The power company guy started to jaw at Paul and they squared up with each other. Paul put up his dukes. The electrician had his fists up, too. Jake was watching in horror, thinking he was going to have to back Paul up in a fistfight with the electric utility.

Just as they were about to come to blows Paul said something brilliant.

"You sure you want to lose your job over this?"

It defused the whole situation. Paul was never about to knock the guy out, but he couldn't punk out either. This was his 'hood and he was one of the few who took care of it. He gave the guy an out—his job—and brought it just to the brink to drive his point home. Everyone's honor remained intact. Paul and his crew went back to what they were doing.

I could see a bit of that Paul through the YES FARM door in this meeting. He was sitting in one of the pews nearly shaking with indignation, a righteous anger.

"What makes you think you can just come in here, never having farmed or grown anything, and take over what we've been doing for decades? I remember this with the fight over the Poletown plant.

They said it would be good for us, and what did it do but tear down the neighborhood. I remember . . ."

Everyone seemed to have these massive plans that required a ton of outside money. Nobody wanted to start small and scale up, prove themselves and their ideas to the neighborhood. They wanted to be the biggest, immediately.

And what would happen if they failed? We would be stuck with the mess, just like that incinerator protest junk. And this time not just the trash. What if, once they had gotten everything cleared, moved the people out of the way, and demolished their houses, their plans failed? What if they couldn't make farming profitable in the neighborhood? That would leave a nice open space for something large that might not be pleasant to live by or provide any jobs for the locals. Maybe a trucking depot or a waste facility. It had happened before.

That wasn't the end of the fight over the third round of urban renewal in Poletown. It would continue over the next seven years, and the man who had come to our meeting today would take his plea to the larger Poletown neighborhood and ultimately the city. The meetings at the YES FARM were but scale models for what was going on in Detroit at large, the first inklings of projects attempting to steer the city away from humane and transformational social change to opportunities to make money.

————————

The electricity was the last to go in the house because wiring was the most likely to get stolen and scrapped. Copper was one of the most valuable metals at the scrap yard, and I was worried someone would break in and rip the wires from the wall before they ever got used. I did need to get a head start, though. I figured I could add one run of outlets as long as I had fully installed, insulated, and Sheetrocked the walls so the scrappers would have to at least dig through that. I also needed to install the electrical box and main wiring so I could pass my inspection, a process that could take some time.

After some study, I put the electrical box in the basement with my friend from college who had just moved into the city. We snaked a baby-arm-thick main line from the box to a peckerhead outside, a hookup point for the power company. My buddy was a huge help, but it was a strange partnership. We had been best friends, and likely would be forever, but I had already changed quite a bit from college. He was working for one of the automotive consulting companies and making about eighty grand a year, right out of school. I had the feeling that if I had met him now I wouldn't have given him a second look, maybe despised him even. We're good-enough friends that I could tell him so, and he agreed. He disliked his job, too, and was working toward something else; what, he wasn't sure. He had taken the path expected of him and found it meaningless and empty.

What can I say? Even though for the moment he was a corporate shill, I loved the guy. We'd been through a lot together. This was also complicating my urban self-righteousness, but I had too much work to accomplish to fully parse it. My deadline was less than two weeks away and I needed all the help I could get. I was spending ten-, twelve-, fourteen-hour days banging on the house.

It was crucial that the utilities feeding the rooms above my initial three go in before I finished the walls downstairs. Both wiring and ducts had to be run before I put up drywall and enclosed everything. These appliances wouldn't be hooked up possibly for years, and spending the money and time running them while trying to get my three little rooms ready for the winter was an exercise in delayed gratification.

"Ah, shit!"

Water was spraying me in the face. It dripped down my shirt

and soaked my sweater. As I was cutting a duct into the floor of the bathroom with a saber saw, I had hit a pipe. The water was getting all over the drywall, which would now need to be cut out and redone. I rushed downstairs and turned the valve off.

"God damn it!" I clomped back upstairs to dry off and settle. There was a mop bucket in the hallway and I kicked it in frustration. I screamed, a deep primal bellow. Get it all out. One nice thing about not having neighbors is you can yell as much as you want without startling anyone. I screamed again for good measure. I was going mad. There was so much to do and I was so tired, and I was so broke and Things Just Needed to Fucking Work. I picked the bucket up and threw it down again.

"Settle down, Drew. Settle down," I told myself as I paced the hallway. I breathed, and went back downstairs to patch the pipe and get back to installing the duct.

After I had gotten home to Forestdale that night, my next-door neighbor came over and needed to talk. We took Gratiot on a walk in the Back 40. He still only weighed twenty pounds, and wore a little harness because he could slip out of a collar. He was to be neutered the next day and couldn't have any food until after the operation. He would be in the hospital overnight, so I wanted to give him a little bit of freedom before what was sure to be an awful experience.

My neighbor and I walked him on the leash until we all got to the 40, then let him run free as we walked in a circle, talking. He had just broken up with his girlfriend, who also lived on the block, and wanted to vent his pain.

"I don't know, I just don't know what to do." My neighbor did most of the talking as I listened. "I know the sound of her car. I can tell when she's leaving and coming—"

"Where's Gratiot?"

"What, the dog?"

"Gratiot!" I called. "Gratiot!" I'd had him for just a few months, and technically he shouldn't have been walking outside as he hadn't finished his course of parvovirus shots yet. I just didn't feel right keeping him cooped up. "Gratiot!" We rushed around the horse track, searched the garden beds and the underbrush, still no sign of him. I didn't care any longer about waking up the neighbors.

"Gratiot!"

I became more frantic. "Where do you think he went? Gratiot!" My heart raced. This was the first time I'd ever lost him. Horrible thoughts piled up in my head. What if someone stole him? What if they're going to use him as a bait dog? They told me at the pound that dogs like this are stolen and used as bait for dog fighting. I'd heard enough stories of people's neighbors carrying bloody pit bulls out of trap houses that I believed them. I could imagine him yelping, helpless, torn apart by savage mutts who had themselves been abused, making them mean and heartless, a circle of violence that encompassed those who had forced the dogs to fight in the first place. What about that guy pushing the shopping cart down the street? Maybe he took him. I'll kill that son of a bitch if I have to. "Gratiot!"

"Will you stay back here while I look for him on the street? Maybe he got out." My neighbor stayed in the garden calling for my dog. I felt a tiny bit how a mother must feel when temporarily missing her baby, a feeling I'd never experienced. I'd never cared for anything like I loved that dog.

I walked out of the alley into the street, increasingly frantic. "Gratiot!"

I still had his little leash in my hand.

"Gratiot!"

A purple car was headed the wrong way down Forestdale, a one-way street. It was going fast, too, so I eyeballed the driver, giving him the 'hood look, like, *What do you think you're doing?* The car turned in my direction and screeched to a halt just past me. It slammed into reverse and all of a sudden I was blinded.

"What kind of crack you smoke, motherfucker?"

I had four flashlights in my eyes and three guns, point-blank, in my face. I threw up my hands. I thought I was being robbed. Someone wearing black leather gloves grabbed me from behind in a bear hug and threw me on the hood of the car.

"I said what kind of crack do you smoke, white boy?"

He had his hand on my head, pushing it into the warm hood. I could feel his wedding ring on my skull. He kicked my legs apart and I could see one of the cops pointing his pistol at my face. He was wearing street clothes but had a badge dangling from one of those chains that look like they are attached to cheap lights in a basement. The car was unmarked. I don't remember if he was wearing a bulletproof vest or not, but he looked like a soldier, all straps and pockets. I guessed the other two were behind me. The cop holding me grabbed my balls, from behind.

"You have a job?"

"I'm a cook."

"Come on, all cooks smoke dope." He began to prod my clothes.

"You have any needles?" The cop holding my head down began to frisk me. He put everything on the hood of the car. He stood me back up straight and put his arms around my chest, feeling for weapons or whatever. One of the other officers grabbed my wallet and started going through it. "What are you doing in this neighborhood?"

I'd like to say I told him to fuck off, calmly explained that he was violating my Fourth Amendment right to due process and would not stand for this grave injustice. Or I had a girlfriend who was a lawyer for the ACLU and I would have their badge numbers. That I would put this all over the news and I would have their jobs or at least their apologies.

"I live here," I said meekly. I was shaking. You don't say those kinds of things when you have three guns pointed at you.

"What's your address?"

"Ah, I don't remember. I live right around the corner, over there." I couldn't even remember my address, let alone protest.

Another cop across the street had a black kid over the hood of another unmarked car. I guessed it probably wasn't his first time in a stop-and-frisk. This was way before anyone talked about it in New York. This was also just weeks after the police department killed an eleven-year-old girl, Aiyana Jones, coincidentally the niece of some of my new neighbors.*

I was aware of this as they held their guns to my face. If just one of those fingers slipped, or one of those guys got nervous, just one mistake, I would be lying in a pool of my own blood.

---

* The police who killed her were looking for a murder suspect and followed by an A&E camera crew shooting one of those cheap and exciting real-life cop shows. Aiyana was sleeping on the couch, and the police, dressed as would-be soldiers, threw a flash-bang grenade through the front window, burning the eleven-year-old girl. They didn't knock. And they had the wrong address.

Accounts differ as to what happened next, but as the police stormed into the house, Aiyana Jones was shot through the head and killed by a bullet fired from a police machine gun. The cops said her grandmother, in the confusion, grabbed the weapon and it went off. The grandmother vehemently denied ever being near the cop. Many people figured the police were jittery and careless, as an officer had been recently shot, and that a round was fired accidentally. (The police could later be seen off duty wearing shirts that read "Execute cop killers," their service pistols strapped around their thighs.) Some say the round was fired from outside the home, and struck her after passing through a wall.

We do know that an eleven-year-old girl lost her life in a military-style raid on her house, possibly one conducted for the benefit of the cameras. The police chief himself resigned shortly afterward, when his own pitch for a reality show was uncovered. I didn't know it then, but Aiyana was a relative of my neighbors and had she survived I would have likely watched her dance and eat and play and do kid things at one of the barbecues my neighbors held during the summer and insisted I attend. Instead, she never got to go to school, she never got to fall in love, she never got to be cool.

If I said anything wrong I would be lying in a pool of my own blood. If I made a sudden movement I would be lying in a pool of my own blood. They would claim I attacked them. There were no witnesses.

"You don't remember your own address, motherfucker."

"It's right over there."

"Do you have a job?"

"I told you I'm a chef."

"Oh, come on. All chefs smoke crack."

"Dude."

The cop's thick, hairy Popeye arms remained around my chest as the others looked through my stuff, my hands still in the air, rib cage heaving.

"Calm down, now. Calm down," the cop holding me said. "It's cool. Slow down."

They put my stuff back on the hood and the cop let me go. The one with my wallet saw my address on my ID and nodded at the guy with his arms around me.

"What are you doing out here tonight?"

"I'm looking for my dog. He's lost and just a puppy."

"What does he look like and what's his name?"

I told him, and he relayed the info to the other guys.

"We'll keep an eye out for him. We're looking for someone who's been doing some armed robberies around here. Do you know who that is? He's a black male."

First of all, I hardly fit that description. Second, they were just rolling around the neighborhood stopping every black male, and apparently anyone else they saw, in a process that felt like armed robbery itself. I knew who had been robbed: it was Jennie, Molly's roommate, coming home from a gig late one night. They had a gun and she screamed. A bunch of guys on the block had come outside to see what was going on and Norman got punched in the face and had to get stitches. One of the neighbor boys had his tennis shoes stolen on a separate occasion. They never found the guys who did it. This wasn't a particularly effective way of policing, to say the least.

"What? No," I replied.

The guns shot up once again. My neighbor was coming down the street, the weapons now pointed at him. He put his hands in the air and walked toward us.

"He's helping me look for the dog," I said.

They took his ID. I went off looking for Gratiot, muttering about how fucked up all this was.

As the cops got back in the car, the blond one with the crew cut who had just got done grabbing my junk said, "Have a nice night." They roared off.

"What the fuck, man, what the fuck?" My neighbor hadn't seen what had happened.

"I got to find fucking Gratiot." I walked back to my house still holding his tiny leash. I saw Emily and Eric sitting on the porch next door.

"Are you okay?" Emily asked. "What just happened?"

"Have you seen Gratiot?"

"Yeah, we saw him sniffing around your gate so we put him back inside. I gave him a bowl of food."

Consider for a moment. There are only three times I have ever had guns pointed at me point-blank. (I've been lucky.) Those three times have not been by "thugs" or "gangsters." All three have been by police officers. I knew, personally now, the mistrust of the police by people who live in places like East Detroit and Baltimore and Ferguson, how at worst they can act as just another gang themselves. Coupled with the hopelessness of rehabilitation in the American prison system, this is why I refuse to call the cops. That was just a little taste of what black and brown and red folks deal with every day.

————

The weather began to get cold again, both my goal and deadline inching closer. I *still* needed to have so much more done. Forever, more and more. Electricity, ducts, insulation, everything. I wasn't working on specific projects anymore, but whatever loose ends needed to be tied up, bouncing from one trade to another.

I got a cut that should have required stitches from a piece of sheet metal. My finger slipped, jamming my thumb into the end of some nice, sharp galvanized steel.

Sleeeept—

A clean slice.

I could see all the layers of skin right to the muscle. I superglued it, like a dog wound.

The neighborhood was scaring me, too. Shadowy dudes, maybe a dozen or so, played dice in the streets a few blocks south. The streetlights were gone and so were all the porch lights on the abandoned houses. I was working past dark out of need now, and finding out what the neighborhood was actually like after the sun set. The abandoned red house next to mine was empty and cold and terrifying. Anything could be happening behind those dark hollow eyes that were windows. Rats, crack, rape, murder. If it burned, mine would, too. I could see my breath again.

Wake up. Up and down the ladder. Back and forth between the house and Paul's garage for tools. Try to get the electrical up to spec before inspection. Finish the installation of the box and make sure I don't screw it up and kill myself. How many days do I have left?

Bolt the wires into the box. Screw in the wires before I have to do it when it's hooked up to the power. One false move and poof. I was exhausted. Fourteen-hour day. Thirteen-hour day. Fifteen-hour day. Windows, insulation, electricity, it was all the same, it blends together and in the end it's just work.

Move-in was in less than a week. I'd never been this broke and tired ever, and I hope it never happens again. My mind was cloudy. I could focus on one thing but not the big picture. What day is it again? Tuesday? I felt old and rusty, like my truck, surprised at what was holding me together. My credit card was maxed out. I didn't have a dollar to my name. Most of my words were curses, the only thing ready at the lips. I was hungry and cold, mentally, physically, and emotionally tired. So much needed to get done before I could live in the Queen Anne. Everything seemed like it was happening at once.

Get up. Work. Back to Forestdale for a shower. I finally—just before I was to move into my own house—had a shower. I turned it on to warm the water and went to wash my hands after using the toilet.

I recoiled involuntarily.

"Awww, shit."

There was a mouse in the sink, barely breathing. He was gray and almost cute. I checked the thermometer. Forty-four degrees. The mouse was wet from the slow drip of the faucet. I felt bad for him. He was just sitting there.

It grossed me out, too. Despite my empathy, rodents carry disease, something I couldn't afford. He didn't move when I got close to him, but didn't look physically sick or mangy. I could see his ribs moving with his little mouse breaths, quick, up and down.

I got in the shower without taking care of him right away. Maybe he would leave.

He really fucked up my shower. All I could think of was him, or her. I cut it short, put on my boots, jacket, and some leather gloves. I got a plastic bag, the grocery store kind.

He didn't even flinch when I picked him up. He had no fear. I looked into his little mouse face, his ribs still pumping in and out. He knew what was coming, as did I. I took no pleasure in it. When I put him in the bag I didn't even tie it.

As I killed him beneath my foot I heard his bones crunch. Even worse, I could feel the breaking of his tiny skeleton travel through the sole of my shoe, through to my feet, his bones breaking beneath mine. Although I thought it a mercy killing, I purposely extinguished the life of a living thing. I didn't even have the guts to check and make sure he was dead. I threw the bag in the Dumpster and let the lid fall with a hollow bang.

I wondered who I had become.

———

The Harvest Party was finally here, and I was as far along on the house as I was going to get. The winter was going to be rough again, but that wasn't anything that I hadn't dealt with before. The loneliness was new. I didn't have a whole community surrounding me, at least I didn't think I did. If I was in trouble I couldn't just yell and people would come running. At least I wasn't sure they would. I didn't really know.

I had moved in what little I could of inconsequential value, and came home to take a shower before the festivities. I returned some cans to the liquor store and was able to afford a six-pack so I had something to take to the party. People had started to gather at Paul's house, the lights had been strung, and savory smells drifted from kitchens.

More people started to show up. People no one knew. Jennie's band—at that time Jennie and the Sure Shots—was having its CD release at the YES FARM to coincide with the Harvest Party.

Somehow a notice made its way into the paper and all kinds of people came. Folks no one had ever met were wandering around Paul's house eating chili and asking, "Who lives here?" A microcosm of a coming Detroit. It seemed like the block's response was to get drunk. The hayrides were epic. People filled the street.

The main event that night was the show in the YES FARM. When they threw open the doors there were likely more people inside than had ever been before. Even the fire department showed up, mingled, and drank apple cider. Jake and I had walked down to the station earlier to invite them, and when we knocked on the door a burly man with a crew cut stuck his torso outside.

"What's on fire?"

They were jolly, and a lot of hand shaking and back slapping went on. Good guys. Jennie looked beautiful in a long white prairie dress and the band was as surprised as everyone else that so many people showed up. Jake became worried about the floor. In one place it was held up only by a single two-by-four.

When the music started everyone began whirling, an untamed rhythm, unbridled movement, a square dance on cocaine, the best of the country in the best of the city—pounding, undulating bodies an organism working as one, a hive of bees with the band as its queen. Someone was in the back banging the hard heels of his cowboy boots into the floor to the beat. Jake had to stop him, the floor beginning to crack. Sweat started to form on the brows of the musicians and they dug in harder, faster, feeling the instruments and coaxing all they had, their music pouring from the stage like the breaking of a dam. If the floor was going to cave in, it was going to happen tonight. The firefighters all left, running to a call, leaving half-drunk cups of apple cider. Emily and Eric left soon after them.

The music ran on. It seemed the band had an endless amount of songs and the crowd would have ridden along if they did. One man was doing a flatfoot dance right onstage, hollering call-backs to the people shouting encouragement in the crowd. I tried to get Gratiot to dance to the rhythm, but he didn't get it and seemed to be more interested in biting at my hands and eyeing the cupcake table.

Emily and Eric came back, shaken. They looked grave. The call the firefighters had run off to was the bakery where the two artists had set up their concrete cupcakes. We never found out why or how, but the bakery had burned to the ground.

CHAPTER 7

The Furnace

A freezing January day

"If someone has the audacity to come into your house," he told me, "they have the audacity to kill you. You have to protect yourself."

I had moved into my new home, as had a friend from work. I'd spent the first night alone, as I thought proper, but my buddy had gone through a wicked breakup with his girlfriend and desperately needed a place to stay. He showed up a few days later. This wasn't his first time living in Poletown and he'd never lived outside of Detroit. He was trying to make enough money to move to Arizona to stay with a brother who had just gotten out of prison and was now in college. I was inclined to listen to his advice about keeping myself safe in the city.

"I dunno, bud, I'm not sure I can shoot a person," I told him. We were both dead tired from working on the place all day, and sat on the floor drinking beers while the orange light from the woodstove danced across the floor of the nearly empty house.

"Then what are you going to do, take it? You aren't exactly the biggest guy on the block. You gonna fight some huge dude who grew up here, grew up fighting his whole life? You're selling woof tickets, man," he said, gently telling me I was bullshitting.

"Gratiot will be here. Like you said, he'll find his bark."

"What if someone poisons him? You know that, right? They poison dogs. When I was a kid someone killed the dog next door. He was a big, mean motherfucker. They put little springs and shavings of metal in pieces of meat and fed it to him. It cut him all up inside and he died. Then they broke into the owner's house."

"I would fuck someone up if they did anything to Gratiot."

"Now you're thinking right. How you going to help anyone else if you can't help yourself? You have to be safe. And you know the cops ain't coming. This is a decision you made, bro. Self-defense is part of self-sufficiency."

"You might be right."

"It's like a copy of Shakespeare's complete works. Every household should own a shotgun. You don't need to ever take it outside or anywhere else. You don't need to be proud of it. But if someone comes inside—" He shrugged. "If they have the audacity to come inside, they have the audacity to kill you. They have the audacity to rape your girlfriend and they have the audacity to leave you tied up in a corner to watch. I know you have a good heart but you can't be stupid."

"I'll think about it, but I'm too tired right now." I couldn't help but think about the mouse I had killed underfoot on my porch.

"You'd best make a decision quick, because now is the time people are going to be testing you. You're the new kid on the block—literally—they're going to try and find out what you're made of. And if you let them mistake your kindness for weakness, well, they may never stop testing you."

We slept fitfully, the orange shadows of the fire licking at the fear in my dreams. I was able to conquer the constant low-level terror in the daytime, forcing it from my mind by determination of will. But when I was asleep my subconscious ran wild, unbridled from rationality. I'd never had nightmares before, but now my dreams would often involve fire.

The house was pretty bleak: bare stud walls, no hot water, no electricity, no heat. It was all pretty grim. I put the couch in front of the woodstove, put my dishes in milk crates where the kitchen would be, and that was about all I had, aside from my tools.

I borrowed my father's camping gear, a sleeping bag, propane stove, and gas lantern. The previous winter my uncle had given me many of his tools, including a workbench. He was a hobby carousel horse carver, and was downsizing his house. Many of the tools were quite nice, but they also came with the random leftovers of a workshop active for decades: screws, nails, specialized hand tools, boxes of washers and nuts, bits of wire and string, odd files, sharpening stones, gauges, marking tools and measuring devices, an assortment of plumbing and electrical bits and instruments.

All of this was surprisingly helpful and represented years of collecting. It was a boon especially because I was so desperately broke. If I needed just a few trim nails, say, I wouldn't have to buy a whole box of them, I could fish some out from the multitude. I tried to set up what I had neatly, but left the workbench clean. I placed my mattress on top of that. I thought getting it off the floor would provide additional warmth and help protect me from any rodent surprises. I parked a small ladder next to the workbench to climb into bed. It was shaping up to be another brutal winter.

My wood supply was already dangerously low due to some locust that I thought would dry in time, but was still wet. I had some ash, the best for burning aside from oak, but not a whole lot, and a reasonable store of maple, which burns hot but quickly. I figured when I ran out I'd burn whatever I could—pallets, scrap, deadwood. I didn't have to worry too much about fouling the pipe—I was going to build a masonry chimney next summer. At least I would be able to sit by the fire again, although I wouldn't have friends just a house or two away to keep me warm or company. Much of the serendipity that was necessary for those kinds of interactions was gone, erased by the distance of a short drive. When I was out of sight I would also be out of mind, and I didn't know my new neighbors well enough yet.

Each time I drove between my house and Forestdale, where I was still charging batteries in the absence of electricity in the Queen Anne, I had seen a dog on a cruelly short leash tied to a fence. Each day the dog seemed to get bigger and meaner and more hyper. I felt bad for him. Maybe I was just imagining it or unfamiliar with it, but the neighborhood had an implacable feeling of menace those first months. Maybe it's that I was white and I was moving into a neighborhood that was largely black. Maybe it was real.

The neighbors were initially wary of me and I of them. The larger neighborhood was used to Forestdale and the kaleidoscopic people who lived there—once when I was coming out of the liquor store the next block over, someone tried to hustle me. His buddy told him to stop because "he's one of those white niggers over on Forestdale"—but this was different. The neighbors behind me, the Terrys, were friendly, but they weren't my friends yet. The other neighbors and I would eye each other from our respective porches, and I'd slip inside the house quickly and inconspicuously, escaping the chance that someone wouldn't like me, hate me, even. I felt like I had to prove myself to them.

I would tell myself driving back to my house that I would make an effort to get to know my neighbors at every chance. Or at least wave. On my braver days I would, halfheartedly, protecting myself in case they didn't wave back, pretending I was looking at something else. Sometimes they would wave, others . . . maybe they didn't see me.

In those first couple of months there was a guy who used to sit in a black car across the street from my house. He knew one of the neighbors, and I had begun to think he was employed by him, maybe to watch me. Or maybe watch over me. I don't know. But I had the strange sense that he was watching, making reports, even. I would wave at him sometimes. He would never wave back—and he saw me. We settled in together and I stopped waving, but I would always nod, and eventually he nodded, too. His presence started to peter out, and I've never seen him again, although he was a constant presence initially. The neighborhood was just as mysterious as when I'd first moved to Detroit from college.

Although Forestdale was within Poletown, and everyone was just about equally poor, people on Forestdale had options. They had college degrees and travel experiences and artistic ability and a sense of self-worth that had largely been encouraged—at least in its gestational period—by society at large. I had these things myself.

But by living in this new area of Poletown, I was stepping into an existing community I didn't know or necessarily understand. That was the scariest and most depressing part, a starting over of sorts, the fear of entering a room in which you know no one and having to make friends and fit in, by pain of arson, robbery, or death. People not liking me was one thing, but this time the stakes were high. With no one else to do it for them including the police, people had defended their neighborhood themselves for years, and rightly so. I imagined if I had made enough mistakes and really upset people they wouldn't hesitate to defend it from me, too. I felt naked and vulnerable.

The days were getting shorter and I only had so much light with which to work. I had called the power company the day I moved in, and they said they would be out within three weeks to turn on the power. Three weeks without lights. My body and life had begun to take on the rhythms of nature, sunlight and darkness, cold and warm. Minus the trappings of civilization, the seasons mattered again. Because I didn't have light I would live by sunrise and sunset. I was closer to nature now, closer to being an animal. I worked and worked and worked. I ate and slept and worked again. There was nothing else but work for me then.

Those first few weeks were a blur of sweat and blood and battery-powered fluorescent lighting. I tiled the shower basin with some cheap tile I'd been given, and hung plastic up over the walls. It looked like the room where the government had experimented on ET, but at least I would be able to get clean when I was able to afford a water heater, which needed to be soon. As much as I hated debt, I needed a shower more, if only to be able to get myself clean and make money.

My roommate was the rare soul whose vast and hard-won personal knowledge of the world hadn't beaten him down and made him cynical. He was hardworking and helped with the house. His brown-and-white pit bull, Jesse, would play with Gratiot in the backyard while we worked, nearly in silence. They'd wrestle and growl, Jesse teaching Gratiot how to be a dog while my roommate taught me how to get along in Poletown, gifting me little nuggets of knowledge.

Don't ever let anyone into your house you don't know.

Don't sleep with the security gate bolted in case there's a fire and you can't find your keys.

If you have knowledge share it, if you have power give it away, if you have opinions keep them to yourself.

He would organize and clean, and I would wire electricity. I wanted to get as many of the runs accomplished as possible before the power company came, so I wouldn't have to hook dozens into the box while it was live. I snaked wires through walls and down into the basement, stripped them, added outlets and switches, and hung lights while my roommate's battery radio played Motown.

"*Ain't no valley high enough,*" he sang into a broom handle like a microphone. He pointed at me. I didn't catch on.

"That's your line, bro."

"Oh, yeah. *Ain't no valley low enough,*" I sang to the pair of pliers I was holding.

"Together now!"

"*Ain't no river wide enough, to keep me from getting to you, babeeeeee.*"

When one of us was hungry, we would eat. When we were tired, we would sleep. And when I was just getting into a groove the power company called. They were going to hook me into the grid, attach me to the rest of the country through three braided aluminum wires, bring me back online with civilization, and, like Prometheus, steal coal from the ground to make light, this kind electric.

On top of the breaker box is a switch used to turn the system on and off, like Frankenstein awakening his monster. There's easily enough energy flowing through there—220 volts—to kill a buffalo. Electricity is silent and invisible, the one thing in your house that will slay you instantly. It also causes fires. The greatest risk comes not from the gas in your furnace or stove but from the electricity in your walls, wires heating up and igniting the timber locked behind drywall, sparks igniting dust clots, loose connections bringing ruin.

Instant death and fire were only two of the scenarios that I faced on the day I was to finally get on the grid with the rest of the country. The power company just hooked up the wires. They wouldn't be flipping that Frankenstein switch, I would have to do that.

A gruff suburban electrician who looked like he drank cheap six-packs in an aluminum lawn chair in the backyard hooked the wire from the pole in the alley to the peckerhead attached to my house. He had a mustache like a walrus and snickered at my home as he bolted the live wires to the service cable.

"You're either brave as hell," he said, looking down at me from the ladder and holding a wire that could potentially kill him, "or crazy as a loon."

At this point I didn't know either. The power in those wires he was bolting into my house had likely come from a mix of coal and nuclear, the latter from a plant just south of Detroit near Monroe, Michigan. It had once nearly blown up, serving as the narrative to the famous jazz song "We Almost Lost Detroit." I was hoping the house wouldn't go the same way. One of the nine Hopi prophecies of the end-times is that the country will become crisscrossed with a spiderweb. Maybe that was their way of describing the power grid.

When the electrician left, I put on rubber gloves, thinking they might offer some protection against the current, and told my room-mate to follow me downstairs. We stood in front of the box as if to dismantle a bomb. He held a flashlight and looked serious.

"All right, man," I told him. "If something happens, you're going to have to tackle me off of here because I'll get stuck by the current, but I'll probably be dead before you can get to me. It might blow up and kill us both."

He held the light and solemnly hunched himself to strike. I took a deep breath, blowing it out slowly through pursed lips.

"You ready?"

He nodded once.

I touched the switch quickly with my fingertip like I was testing a skillet.

Safe.

I put my index finger on the switch. I looked over at my roommate. He nodded.

Click.

It flipped.

Nothing.

I looked down at my chest and at my hands, then over at my buddy. He straightened up and took a deep breath. Everyone still alive. I didn't smell fire. Cautiously we walked upstairs.

"It's your house, you do the honors."

Watching the bulb on the ceiling, I flipped a switch.

Light.

We didn't say anything for a moment, looking at the shining bulb. Then my roommate burst into laughter. We ran around the house turning lights on and off in jubilation, one little victory against the darkness. He leaned back and stretched out his arms, pumping his legs in a happy dance, and I shuffled around the room twirling my hips to the silent music of success. It was the first time I'd really felt I was bringing something back to life, like performing CPR on a corpse that just took its first greedy gasp of air.

"VICTORY!!!!!!!!!!!!!!!" I shouted. "VICTORY!"

I strutted around like a cock, danced some more, sang with my friend. Now I could charge the batteries on my cordless power tools and use the corded ones. I could use a space heater if I was flush. I could take a leak without having to use a flashlight and I could work all night if I wanted to. But first, that night, that first glorious night, I slept with every light in the house on.

———

I took my roommate to the airport soon after and turned the heater on in the truck driving back. It was getting cold, pipe-freezing cold. It would be harder to keep the fire going around the clock. I would have to go back to work soon as well. There was no money. The gas gauge on my truck was broken, but I knew it was running on fumes. I walked back in the door to my house, my friend already in the air, and shut it behind me. It was when I heard the bolt click I knew I was truly alone.

The next morning I searched the newspaper at the liquor store kiosk, the bored attendant not caring if I was buying. There had been another shooting right up the street from my house. The gunmen tried to kill a pizza deliveryman for his cash and car. They shot him three times. Everyone on my block had been broken into but me. A friend had been abducted from a bar I frequented and sexually assaulted. Two more people who lived on Forestdale were robbed at gunpoint, one a brazen holdup as a half dozen people sat around a bonfire. A coworker was murdered in his home during a robbery.

I even had a collection of bullets I'd found, casings, the lead tips, entire unfired projectiles packed with gunpowder. Detroit is the kind of place where you just find bullets. In the sidewalk, embedded in roofs, lying in the street like they're no more than a twig from a tree.

The new police chief, James Craig, said that the good citizens of the city should arm themselves. He said he was scared to get gas at night in Detroit. He was nearly carjacked himself. When the police chief is scared, what are the rest of us supposed to do?

A crackhead stopped by and asked if I would take him to the scrap yard. I couldn't help but wonder if it was a setup. My neighbor to the north, Andi, said as much. She's a good woman whose house had just been broken into, the back door pried open while she was at work. She was an attendant at a supermarket meat counter six days a week, sometimes seven, a hard, honest job. I don't think she'd missed a day in about ten years. She didn't deserve to be stolen from.

The abandoned house next door was becoming more peering creature than clapboard structure. It seemed to watch me, silent and unmoving aside from the flicking of a tail, less feline than forked. That was now also my responsibility. When painful noises came moaning from the tortured structure, the dog and I, a framing hammer in hand, would be the ones to investigate. My heart would pound and breath quicken. Animal, man, the decay of neglect and time—most often I never found out what the noises were exactly, and the worry and wonder would follow me like a shadow.

Winter was miserable. The rain ruined everything. It was relatively warm, but the downside was the rain would not end. I could watch it plink, plink, plink into the jars and glasses, but there were never enough. When I would get one situated juuuuust right, the drip would travel slightly and I'd have to move the bucket again, and again, and again. New leaks would sprout. Gratiot seemed unperturbed about the whole thing and was in the corner fighting one small stream, trying to catch it against the floor with his paws, splashing. A drop hit him on the butt as he was trying to bite another, and he turned around with a little snarl, trying to find it. I was too tired to try to stop him from getting wet.

As I ran around trying to catch the leaks I sang to myself a Beatles song in an attempt to keep my spirits up.

"Fixing a hole where the rain gets in, to keep my mind from wanderingggggg."

I was singing more out of lonely desperation than joy. I had no idea where I was going to get the money for the roof. It was going to be cheaper to hire it done than try to do it myself. I had torn off and replaced plenty, the last on my former house on Forestdale, but with the gambrel, this one was senseless. It had taken us two weeks to get the roof on Forestdale, and that was relatively easy. A professional crew could have gotten it done in just two days. My roof was the only thing I wouldn't do with my own hands, and I justified it because the roof was the only thing that would cost more by doing it myself.

I'd just gotten bids, though, and the lowest was just under $7,000. That's more money than I'd ever seen at one time.

Now almost Christmas, the rain turned to snow. The pipes froze, both the shower trap in the crawl space and the sink supplies running against the outside wall. Out of necessity this would be the project for the day, and I called into work sick. If I didn't take care of this now the pipes would burst. I couldn't weld them back together in the cold, and if I couldn't fix this I'd be out of a shower till the spring and consequently out of a job. I built a fire and set it to roaring, and began warming a pot of water on my new kitchen stove, which my father and I had just run a gas pipe to.

Earlier that winter I had managed to install a water heater, purchased on credit. I paid Matt, the junkie from Forestdale, a couple of bucks to grab some lengths of black pipe from an abandoned house the next time he was looking for treasures. He delivered a tight little bundle wrapped in extension cord. I didn't have time to think about the ethics of outsourcing the stealing of abandoned materials. Too tired. Gotta keep going.

Soon after my dad had brought up a bucket of loose fittings, and we set to work connecting them to service the new water heater, the stove, and what would one day be the furnace.

"You can't keep living like this, Andrew Man. You're going to get sick," my father said, adding dope to the thread of a long piece of black pipe. The physical work was a respite from his new suit-and-tie job and the squabbles of small-time politics in small-town America that went with it. That work was never finished and everyone was never happy all at once. With the pipes they would join and seal or not. The never-ending politics, mirroring those going on in America at large, were chewing him up, even though he would never admit it, proud tradesman in a suit that he was.

"I know, I know," I said. "But what do you want me to do about it? There's just no money. This was the world you left to me."

"Get off that high horse. You did this to yourself."

Because of the thermal mass of the earth, it was warmer in the basement than upstairs, but still miserable. While my father and I worked on the plumbing, my mother cleaned the kitchen in her winter coat. They had bought me braces for this? People with less fortitude and grace would have abandoned me.

When I went upstairs for a coupling my mother repeated what my father had said, "You can't live like this anymore, Andrew."

She scrubbed at the new stove, a white Detroit Jewel from the '30s. My former roommate had left a bike I didn't need, and I traded it to someone on Forestdale for the gleaming white piece of cast iron. It was beautiful, without question the best-looking thing in my house. It had a small oven on the right-hand side, drawers on the other, a flat white-steel workspace on top. None of it was plastic. It was made before "planned obsolescence"—coincidentally invented right here in Detroit—and built to last. When my father and I had finished the gas lines and the utility had turned the main on, it was the first thing I lit, the glowing blue flame a point of hope on the lowest, coldest rung of hell.

I was thinking of what my parents had said a month before as the stove boiled the pot. I couldn't live like this anymore. I poured the roiling water into the shower but it didn't break the clog. There were already two inches of liquid in the pan from the shower I'd taken that morning, discovering the obstruction in the process. I'd only made things worse. If this water froze, too, it might crack the pan and I'd have a real problem.

I tried table salt. I poured all I had into the drain and poked at the clog with a straightened coat hanger. This didn't seem to be doing any good either. I called Will, who generously lent me his orange hair dryer, and I abandoned the shower trap to work on the sink pipes. Maybe the salt just needs some time. *I have to keep going. Gotta keep going.*

The hot air coming from the dryer felt good. I was wearing my insulated overalls in the house, outside the house, everywhere. The city didn't plow the streets in Poletown, and cars without four-wheel drive had gotten stuck, like in quicksand. I'd helped dig out at least four in front of my place over the last two days, but it snowed again and a handful were simply abandoned in the middle of the streets, their owners waiting for a thaw or a cousin with a truck that could pull them out.

After I worked the supply lines over with the hair dryer the ice finally broke. First slowly then all at once. Yes. One down. It didn't seem to do any damage.

From my bathroom window I could see a neighbor behind the Terrys' shoveling snow in front of the light-industrial building he lived in. I walked over to introduce myself and asked if I could borrow some rock salt. He was a white guy, about fifty, a tree climber and excavator. His business card said, "Down in a hole or up in a tree, I'm there when you need me." After some rummaging in his building he came back with a half-full bag. I barely knew him but he gave me the salt for free, and wished me luck.

I poured the salt down the drain and poked it again with the clothes hanger. I waited awhile, heated up more water on the stove, poured it down, too. Still not working.

I put on all the warm clothing I had and crawled headfirst into the crawl space. A rat scurried out. I almost threw up. I yelled at Gratiot to get it but he ran in the opposite direction.

I worked the exposed pipe with the hair dryer, staying under until I couldn't handle the filthy, cramped space any longer, and pulled myself out, gasping for air. I checked on the water on the stove. It was boiling. I poured it in the basin, scalding myself, and stirred the water around, attempting to raise the temperature. I poured in more salt. I repeated the process.

I repeated the process.

I repeated the process.

I repeated the process.

I was about to give up. One more time in the crawl space with the hair dryer.

Magically, the clog came loose, with a sound like *chunk*. The water drained. I grabbed some loose scraps of insulation and wrapped them around the trap, hoping this would hold out until spring.

I crawled on top of my workbench and tried to take a depression nap. It was too cold to really rest. I wasn't even particularly tired, but I didn't know what else to do. The anxiety, hunger, cold, and fear were endless.

I couldn't sleep. I had to get up every once in a while to make sure the fire didn't go out and freeze the pipes again.

For the first time in my life I got down on my knees and prayed.

I didn't believe in God and had no faith. At one point I was a stone-cold atheist. But I could no longer go on without any belief in something larger and smarter than me. This may make me a coward in some people's eyes. But I didn't have any other place to turn. The atheists weren't offering any alternatives for hope when I was cold and tired and alone. From the vantage of my dreadful, freezing house it seemed like modern atheism was born of excess rather than principle. They say there aren't any atheists in foxholes, and there aren't many who are hungry and scared and begging for release trying to make it alone through the first winter in an abandoned house in Detroit.

Maybe, I thought, if we were going to rebuild this broken city, we could build a new faith, too, a new religion out of the old ones. This house was showing me that anything could be repaired. We didn't need to throw everything out, just keep the good parts and toss the bad ones, retain the bits about loving your brothers and sisters and banish the rubbish about unclean women and hating gays, the parts that seemed to condone slavery and the genocide of the American Indians. Even Thomas Jefferson had cut apart his Bible, and some pope a thousand years ago had decided what was to be included anyway. Why not do it again? Like everything else, it, too, needed to be repaired, rebuilt, and reimagined.

On my knees, on the floor of that filthy, disheveled house, I was no longer too proud to ask for help, even if it was from a god I wasn't sure existed. But I had to believe in something.

———

My father called soon after. The only thing keeping me from spiraling into complete misery and suicide was that I still had so much work to do. There was always something to distract my idle time, always a way to wear myself out so I slept through the night dreamlessly tired.

"I talked with your grandmother and we're going to buy you a furnace for Christmas."

"Pardon me?"

My initial reaction was to protest—it seemed like cheating. I thought accepting something like that might constitute some kind of unfair use of my advantages over others. Not everyone has a kind and generous family, and the furnace cost about $850, not including ducts and accoutrements. My father had anticipated my reluctance.

"We already bought it. We won't let you live like this any longer."

Truthfully, I was relieved. The cold seeping into my bones and between my joints was more painful than bruised pride. I accepted the offer.

My dad came up between Christmas and New Year with my brother-in-law and we put the furnace in the basement, running the silver ducts from the plenum to four registers cut in the floor of my kitchen and bathroom, with two in the living area. The furnace was a forced-air high-efficiency model, sized for my house, and looked businesslike. I had wanted to use radiators, as heated air would dry out the house, as well as blow dirt around. But I wasn't in a spot to be choosy.

Turning the furnace on for the first time was nothing like the night-and-day elation of flipping the switch on the electricity or seeing the beam go up. I could only afford to keep the house at 50 degrees, which wasn't much better than I was living anyway, just enough to keep me from having to unfreeze the pipes. Warming my house any higher was throwing out money that I didn't have.

But my gloom was also born of the furnace having been purchased *for* me. I hadn't worked for the money to buy it like the sink or windows, hadn't studied for months how to do it myself like the electricity, hadn't stretched my cunning or bravery like taking the beam from the collapsed building. It was just a furnace, not a metaphor or connection to a larger ideal. I was thankful for my family, certainly, but the furnace was more of a product of defeat than a success. It was just a blue heater sitting in the basement and not a revelation.

————

The time had finally come for Will to move out of the house he loved and was forced to sell. The school had given him a date. But since he was poor, there wasn't the money for sentimentality. We were taking everything we could, cannibalizing the structure that was due to be torn down. I stood on top of a ladder with a circular saw, cutting off clapboard. It was snowing lightly.

"People are probably wondering what the hell I'm doing over here," Will said, as I cut the siding off his house.

"It's always kind of been like that, huh?"

Inside was sad-looking and bare. Things were strewn on the floor and his hard work had been undone. The art, the trinkets, and the wind-up music box with the broken note were gone. The house, once pulsing with life, was dead. It was now just a thing, a couple of boards nailed together.

Will was busy unscrewing cast-iron heating grates from the ceiling. All the birdhouses he had made were gone. The couch he sat on with his dog, Meatballs, was gone. All the instruments, the radio, gone. He was taking everything, the window weights, flooring, two-by-fours, sinks, light fixtures, scrapping out his own house.

"So this is it."

He looked down at me from the ladder.

"Yep."

We drove the chicken coop and piano to my old house on Forestdale, where Will was moving temporarily. He was trying to purchase a new place in the same yearly auction at which I'd purchased mine. He had found a house near Forestdale and it was in much better shape than his previous one, at least when he had started, but there was no junk forest behind it, no railroad trench in which to walk endlessly.

I asked him to call me when they tore down the house, and he demurred. I figured he wanted to be alone.

I knew this could happen to me, too, as did all of my neighbors. If someone rich enough or the corrupt city or state government wanted the land badly enough, they could find ways to push us out. If the land couldn't be had through attrition there were means to get people to leave. They had done it for an auto factory and a freeway. Why not a shopping mall?

The rich men always called it progress, but it was their progress. It never seemed to benefit anyone except them. Building my house and my community had given my life meaning. Shopping malls didn't.

Will came over one afternoon a few weeks later. He had caught the demolition crew just as they had begun to knock it down, and was there with his camera. He had taken pictures as fast as he could, and had made a kind of digital flipbook. We sat on my couch and he showed me.

On the screen his house was recognizable enough, shot from straight ahead. The dirty backhoe loomed on the right side. Someone from the left squirted the house with a firehose to keep down the dust. The backhoe hit the roof first. It had a great jaw, and after creating the first violent hole it began to chew at the house, knocking, churning, biting, grabbing. A raccoon scurried out, just as it had at my place when I was boarding it up. The backhoe, narrowly missing the animal, spat pieces of Will's dream out onto the ground, tearing away at a fantasy that was real, if just for a moment.

Will held the button on the flipbook and his house slowly became a pile of rubble. The great jaw on the backhoe became a fist, and smashed its bones into tiny pieces, boom, boom, boom, crushing it into nothing.

"This is the part where they pound it into the ground," Will said.

There's always something lost in the name of progress. In this case it was one man's home, a little dream. The danger is that in our relentless chase of progress we're erasing ideas and ways of living that we can never get back. Ideas and ways of living we may need to heal our earth and our ailing society. It's never the rich who have their homes torn down. The question to ask yourself is "By what—and whose—measure do we gauge progress?"

"This is the part where they pound it into the ground," Will repeated, holding the button on the screen. His home was now a pile of rubble and the photographs ended.

———

I made my kitchen counters out of century-old maple floors, rock hard and pried from an abandoned soda pop factory by a neighbor. I plucked my kitchen cabinets from a school that was being demolished. Aside from the cabinets, made from old-growth oak, strewn about the school were beakers and other science equipment, books splayed open like dead birds, desks, marble slabs dividing bathroom stalls, granite tables, chalkboards that still contained notes. It looked like some catastrophic event had stricken the nation, nuclear war perhaps, and the teachers and students had fled at a moment's notice. They say the functional illiteracy rate in Detroit is nearly 50 percent.

As I wandered around the school in my overalls, the backhoe was already pushing the other end of the building into the ground. I was able to scavenge at all because a friend had made a deal with the demolition company. We had one day to get out everything we could.

The school had been built just after the turn of the century. Walking through its quiet shadowed halls, I pried trim off the walls and unscrewed hooks from closets. Suburban flight had also left Detroit with dismal, almost criminal public schools. The Detroit metro area has some of the most school districts per capita in the nation, not to mention some of the most racially segregated schools, and one result was fewer students in Detroit and less money for them. We'd reinvented the school bus wheel over and over in the metro area—along with administration, infrastructure, and, significantly, busing costs.

An often overlooked turning point in the educational and democratic history of the United States occurred in Detroit in 1971. The local courts ruled that the schools in the metro area as a whole were unlawfully segregated for the same reasons blacks and others were kept from the suburbs. More than two-thirds of the students in the Detroit public schools at the time were black, the opposite of the surrounding 'burbs.

A district judge ruled that busing of students across *district* lines was to take place to reduce segregation. Students residing in Detroit would be able to attend the well-funded schools in Oakland County, for example, and an increase in suburban students in Detroit would help ensure the fruits of the public wealth that left the city in the second great migration would be distributed evenly, at least in school.

A crusade against the decision was made by white suburban parents. The campaign included arson, violence, and terror, the KKK notably bombing ten school buses rather than have them transport integrated students.

This decision was reversed by the U.S. Supreme Court in *Milliken v. Bradley* in 1974. The justification was that segregation wasn't a *stated* policy of the school districts—although the court found that the schools were, in fact, segregated. Because this segregation wasn't explicit, they ruled, it therefore wasn't deliberate. They ruled that school systems and district lines could not be responsible for school segregation, and busing was outlawed. This had an effect not only in Detroit, but around the country.

The schools in America today are more segregated than when Martin Luther King, Jr., was murdered. Detroit's schools are now often considered the worst in the nation. At the beginning of the '60s they were often said to be the best. Separate has always meant unequal.

It also apparently meant that beautiful buildings like this got pushed into the ground, too. I stopped at the leaded glass on the stairway to look across the courtyard and watch the cruel yellow arm of the backhoe eat into the school and place tens of thousands of dollars, just in oak and marble, into a Dumpster.

The same bitter principle was at work all over the city. Somehow blight was always blamed on Detroiters rather than those who had quite literally abandoned the city, leaving a mess.

The three cabinets in my kitchen were just about all the physical memory of what was once a school that had educated thousands.

Despite it all, my life would get better, in a concrete way, each day.

I was on my way to building the world I wanted to live in, one made largely from pieces cast off as junk. I added rescued cabinets, my dishes stayed cleaner. I added a secondhand window, I got more sunlight. I painted a wall, hung a photo, and the house became cheerier.

That first winter was cold and miserable, but it, too, served a purpose. It reminded me that every nail I struck was a strike for me—not for a bank, not for a landlord. Every screw I drove was for my own purpose, not to make investors rich with usury. Every bolt tightened was bringing closer the edges of the world I had imagined for myself. Everything I created would stay in my own orbit, satellites of the world in which I wished to live.

What I learned that first winter was that my goal wasn't to build a house. It was to transform *myself* by building a house. Houses could be torn down, memories and ideas couldn't. It wasn't always pretty, but it was under way. What living in Detroit had taught me was that the goal wasn't to build a new city. It was to transform ourselves by building a new city.

It also taught me I needed a gun. My father picked it up for me at a massive hunting store near my childhood home, a 12-gauge Mossberg 500 pump-action shotgun with interchangeable barrels, both cold black steel atop a walnut stock. It had been built for a single, sole purpose: killing things. In a way it was beautiful, and that beauty arose from its savageness. I spent a firm, rainy afternoon building a special shelf for it in my bedroom closet so I could grab it at a moment's notice. It would remain loaded, the ka-chink of the racking mechanism all that remained between innocence and death with the squeeze of a brass trigger. I keep it loaded with four rounds of double-aught buckshot followed by a single lead slug as big around as a nickel. I considered loading it with salt instead of lead, but I knew if I ever had to remove it from its shelf it was all or nothing.

Hopefully I wouldn't have to.

CHAPTER 8

A Chimney to the Sky

Friendships grow alongside vegetables in Detroit gardens

S pring had returned as it always does, the bright, generous whirling
of the sun and the rain playing a symphony on the green things
of the earth. The slate-gray skies of winter had been banished, and
the sounds of the birds and insects were back with the month of May.
After another winter nearly without heat, the first yellow-warm day
had the effect on the mind that taking a shower after a long time in
the woods has on the body. It was time to do my own encouraging
of the green things of the earth and plant a garden. I loaded my
hoe and rake into the red wheelbarrow and stepped outside into
the neighborhood.

197

My big project for the summer was the chimney. It was also time to meet the neighbors, but I was feeling less sure about that. Part of the reason the winter had been so tough was because I was still trying to find my place in everything. Constitutionally shy, I needed to force myself to meet the people who lived around me, to not slip in and out of my house. I needed to slowly and respectfully add my voice to the chorus of what was an already functioning community. I figured my best bet was with a garden.

I had started the soil the year before from leaves I had collected, spent brewing grains from the bar I frequented, and compost from Forestdale. I had piled it in square layers like lasagna in the center of my lots and bordered the bed with logs I had accumulated clearing my backyard. Out in the open I felt self-conscious in front of my new neighbors, unprotected by the walls of my house.

I grabbed the hoe and began turning the soil, a white guy in the middle of Detroit with my feet in the dirt, breaking up big loamy chunks that had compressed like diamonds over the winter. I hoed until my back and arms had beaded with sweat and the muscles felt loose and warm. I folded my hands over the handle in repose and saw Mrs. Terry, the neighbor from behind me, beckoning. I also saw a thunderstorm brewing.

I walked over to chat with Mrs. Terry for a moment, and she casually invited me to a Mother's Day party they would be throwing in their yard. I kept an eye on the storm. I figured she was just being friendly and didn't really want me to show up, but I said something affirmative. I could see the front pushing against the clear blue of the day, the sky divided in two.

I thanked her, feeling a bit better about my place in the neighborhood, but told her I needed to get the crops in before it rained. I had seen the news earlier but only just remembered this had been in the forecast, the bounty of the day encouraging my forgetting. The thunder was here whether I liked it or not, and I was going to have to work fast if I wanted to get everything in the ground. I wasn't sure I would. I waved goodbye to Mrs. Terry and went back to hoeing with increased vigor.

I worked quickly. Gardens had become the metaphor for what Detroit could be; the cold steel, captured explosions, and CO_2 of automobiles were the past whether we liked it or not. Gardens represented life: growing, spreading, healing, vegetables and fruit working in harmony, a community in the dirt but never dirty. At least it represented what I wanted the new Detroit to be. The wooden handle of the hoe, smoothed by years of work, felt easy in my hands, like I might beat the storm.

Like so much else, the U.S. food system has failed Detroit spectacularly. Much of the city is considered a "food desert," where access to fresh fruits and vegetables is nearly nonexistent due to transportation and economic challenges. It's no secret that poverty and extra weight overlap in complicated ways. Detroit is often the most obese city in the nation from year to year. A neighbor I recognized drove by. I waved. He gave me a nod.

When the row had been hoed, I dropped to my knees with an open package of mustard green seeds. The storm was growing closer. I drilled holes in the soil with my forefinger for the fetal greens, measuring the spacing with a yardstick.

Urban gardens are great for teaching people about food and cooking. In urban areas people are largely divorced from how food is produced, and a growing culture of ecological husbandry and knowledge not only helps people make better choices but also make better use of their choices. Knowledge about growing food leads to knowledge about cooking food, which leads to knowledge about personal health.

Drill the holes, drop in the seeds, move the stick. Don't go too fast or you'll mess up.

But gardens in Detroit didn't just begin as a healthy alternative to the junk sold at liquor stores. It was a way to meet your neighbors, brighten the neighborhood, and reclaim abandoned land for the community. Gardens in Detroit grew relationships alongside vegetables. This was the point, and this was why I was outside with my knees in the dirt. Getting outside leads to meeting the neighbors, which leads to community groups, which leads to safer streets and cleaner lots, which leads to self-sufficiency and healthy communities. As Grace Lee Boggs once wrote, "Building community is to the collective as spiritual practice is to the individual."

I moved on to carefully dislodging purple cabbages from the plastic cups in which they'd spent the first part of their lives. I buried them in the soil, patting each root structure, with faith that they would grow.

Detroit has the space, infrastructure, and knowledge to grow much of the food we need for the city, inside the city itself. Keep Growing Detroit, the nonprofit that supplied me with these transplants, has estimated there are already at least twenty thousand urban farmers and gardeners in the city. There are an estimated forty square miles of vacant land in Detroit, enough to fit San Francisco inside just what's been abandoned. Michael Hamm of Michigan State University calculated Detroit could grow three-quarters of its vegetables and more than half its fruit right here.

Stick in a plant, cover it with soil. There is little in an acorn to suggest it will become an oak tree.

What would it do to Detroit if, instead of subsidizing casinos and sports stadiums, we used that money to plant thousands of fruit trees around the city free for anyone to eat from?

Stick in a plant, cover it with soil.

What if they used that money to subsidize the building of windmills, solar panels, and geothermal heat and installed it in the city itself?

Stick in a plant, cover it with soil.

If instead of demolishing houses outright they surgically dismantled them using the materials to build more housing stock?

Stick in a plant, cover it with soil.

Both the temperature and the atmospheric pressure had dropped and I could feel the electricity in the air. The dog began to sniff, his hackles like a porcupine. The wind picking up, blowing his fur in beautiful whorls, propelling the neighborhood trash like tumbleweeds. I was so lost in the approaching storm and the work that I also lost my fear and self-consciousness in the neighborhood. I uncovered an earthworm and used a precious few moments before the rain to study it.

Urban farming and ideas like this begin to remove Detroit and cities like it from dependence on the global oil system and reliance on nonrenewable resources. Biking tomatoes down the street uses a whole lot less gasoline than trucking them in from Mexico.

I began planting peas.

This makes gardens dangerous. They are the zygote of an idea that can spread and grow and multiply into a worldview. They can take us from "theirs" to "ours." They can take us from an abandoned plot of land owned by a bank to a garden owned in community. From a foreclosed home to housing for the needy. From city blocks left for dead to communities without consumers.

Gardens are dangerous to those sixty-two men who control the natural resources of our planet and own half the world. They rely on our dependence. Gardens are dangerous to the politicians who support them. They also rely on our dependence. Gardens are dangerous to the idea that consumption and stasis are the only ways to live.

The last to go in was the squash. I gently placed them in the dirt, careful not to break their delicate tendrils. The storm was upon us.

Gardens are dangerous because urban farms and gardens are but one example, and like a mathematical theorem we can apply the principle of self-sufficiency to the other necessities of life: geothermal heat, electricity from the wind and sun, mass transit.

The first drum of thunder. The rain had begun. It was wetting my T-shirt and the dog began to howl. Six more plants to get in the ground. Maybe I'd make it.

Reclaiming abandoned lots leads to reclaiming abandoned homes, leads to reclaiming abandoned community, leads to reclaiming our abandoned souls and agency. Any act of self-sufficiency in concert with community is an act of rebellion.

Five more plants.

Our planet is going to *die* if we cannot find a way to live differently and solve climate change.

Four more plants.

Capitalism is based on limitless growth in a finite world.

Three more plants.

Nature's currency is life and is cyclical.

Two more plants.

The two will eventually become incompatible, and we are beginning to see the result with climate change.

One more plant.

I started with a garden.

No more plants.

No more plants.

I was soaking wet and the dog was rolling in the newly forming mud. It was pouring, the crack of thunder right behind me. I loaded my tools in the wheelbarrow and headed back to the front porch. Gratiot leaped up out of the rain. He shook the water from his glistening coat and I sat with him cross-legged under the eaves and watched the tempest. It was one of those great midwestern boomers that make it understandable why so many in the middle of America believe in an angry and powerful god. Lightning pounded the sky and the thunder opened it and the water dripping onto the porch from the gutterless roof crept ever closer to my feet. I was unafraid and unashamed. If we were going to do this, we would have to get to know our neighbors.

———

The chimney needed to be done before the roof, which was still leaking onto everything and destroying my house. It seemed to be getting worse, too, the rain flirting with the drywall I'd optimistically hung. If the two were to meet, the whole thing would have to be done over again. But I wasn't about to cut a hole in a brand-new roof, so the chimney was going to happen now.

I had read all the books at the library about chimney building and Jake had finished his last summer, so I had some kind of idea about how it was going to go. But aside from some crude bricking on the foundation, I hadn't done any masonry work. If it was built improperly it would topple over. As it would run through what would be my bedroom, it might topple over onto me. Through my research I had found pictures of fallen chimneys, and the damage was gruesome. Not to mention this would be carrying hot smoke and ash away from my tinder-dry wooden house. If I screwed up I had only myself to blame.

Will helped me frame out the openings. The chimney would sit on the slab in the basement, travel up through the living room, through my bedroom upstairs, and out through the roof a full seven feet so it would reach high enough for a good draft and code clearance. Will and I had to remove some joists and reframe a bit of the floor to get it where we wanted, but generally we got pretty lucky, as you sometimes do. In all it would be 35 feet tall, have approximately 840 bricks, and weigh at least two and a half tons. I was going to have to lift all of that.

In the areas where it wouldn't be visible—the basement and

through my bedroom, which would be drywalled—I would use chimney blocks for speed. The square blocks are made from the same material as cinder blocks, with a hole in the middle to fit the liner. The liner consists of two-foot-tall terra-cotta sections that get mortared together inside the chimney, creating a double wall like in a thermos.

The rest would be brick. They came from a building in the neighborhood that had mysteriously exploded, the pile spewing across the road like vomit creeps across a subway aisle. The building had been at least two stories at one point, but the explosion or whatever it was had made the road impassable. Although they had a Dumpster and maybe some bricks were making their way inside, nobody ever seemed to be working on removing them and the pile in the road never seemed to get any smaller. Nobody seemed to care. Even the electric company. On closer inspection the power was on in the center of where the building would have been, and there was some kind of wire sparking deep within that nobody had bothered to turn off.

I only took bricks that were on public property. I figured they were part mine, they'd been there long enough, and I couldn't get through the damn street. So I loaded my truck until the back springs sagged. As they still had pieces of mortar stuck to them they would need to be cleaned.

I awoke on Mother's Day to James Brown singing "It's a Man's Man's Man's World," the strings soaring and Brown's careening voice wafting from the Terrys' behind me. They had a tent erected in the empty lots next to their place, and dozens of people milled about. It was a sunny day and I stopped for a moment to smile at the friends and family together, but didn't see either the mister or the missus, so headed off to Belle Isle with the dog. I didn't want to get in their way.

That next week as I was cleaning bricks, Mrs. Terry again sat on her back porch and called me over. We chatted about the neighborhood and then she looked me straight in the eye.

"Why didn't you come to the party the other day?"

I stammered some reply about not wanting to bother them at a family event. She seemed kind of angry, actually. It wasn't a disappointed kind of angry, just matter-of-fact.

"Well, you live here now, you're family."

That was all. I promised her I would be at the next one. She dismissed me, and I had a lot of time to clean bricks and wonder. Was I missing some social cues obvious to everyone else? Had the society I grew up in somehow poisoned me to mistrust genuine acts of kindness from neighbors? Maybe I was overthinking all this.

Now that the weather had warmed some, I was able to open the interior doors and brighten up the house. I had moved my sleeping quarters into one of the rooms upstairs. My bed was on the floor, there were holes in the plaster, and I had little else but the dresser I had been given, but it felt more civilized to be sleeping in a designated room with a door and not on top of the workbench. It also freed up some space to work in the heated rooms downstairs. In between working on the chimney I had moved to drywall as well.

Sheetrocking really isn't any fun. The wallboard needs to be hung flat, any gaps have to be packed with joint compound, the seams get taped and then covered with at least three coats of mud. At the end everything gets sanded, an awful and awkward process that gets drywall dust everywhere. When using standard drywall mud, as I was, the minimum time any one wall could be completed in was four days, due to drying time.

But once I finished this, including painting, it would mark the end of major construction in my three-room living space—aside from the chimney. There were still, of course, trim and switch covers and smaller things to take care of, but the big life-disrupting projects would be over.

My trowel was loaded with drywall mud when I heard a scream. I ran outside thinking someone was being robbed. A neighbor was in the road holding a tiny dog, terrified. Gratiot was tearing across the yard toward her.

Everyone was on their porch now. Gratiot must have jumped the fence to say hello to her dog, but she didn't know that. She thought he was going to rip her apart.

I leaped the fence myself and grabbed Gratiot by the scruff, apologizing profusely. The woman was nearly in tears as I dragged him back to the house. What a wonderful way to meet my neighbors. I yelled fire and brimstone at the dog inside, although I knew it wasn't really his fault.

Later that day I walked over to the neighbors' house with my hat in my hands. I apologized. That was the day I really met the woman and her husband. They graciously accepted and gave me a lecture, but no hard feelings. They could have refused to speak to me. Sometimes mistakes make good neighbors, too.

A few weeks later as I was applying primer, another neighbor, Mrs. Smith, had her house broken into. While she was at work as a nurse, someone had walked onto her porch in broad daylight and smashed her front window, gone inside, and stolen what little she had, mostly costume jewelry. I was home but didn't hear any of the commotion. By chance, while I was getting the mail as an excuse for a break, I saw some of the neighbors milling about in the road. Mrs. Smith, who I had seen before and recognized, but had never really talked to, looked upset. I went over to find out what was going on.

A tall man with a shaved head was attempting to fit a piece of plywood over the window. "They just smashed her in. I swear one day I'm a get one of those little niggers with my pistol," he muttered.

I offered my condolences and introduced myself. He said his name was King and he had seen me working on the house. He lived just a block to the south, and we would be able to see each other from our respective front porches. The sheet of plywood he was struggling with was too small, but he said it was the biggest he had. I took some measurements with his tape measure and told them I would be right back.

I had a piece, once used to board up my own house, lying in the yard. After cutting it to size I brought it over along with some caulk. Most important, I brought a bucket of white paint. Mrs. Smith's house was white and the piece of ply was kind of dirty, so I figured I'd give it a quick coat. She was a dignified lady.

I set and caulked the board, but something changed with the quick coat of paint. The anger in the small crowd seemed to subside somewhat and everyone calmed down. Mrs. Smith reached for my hand.

"Oh, I got paint on myself," I said, holding the can and the brush.

"That doesn't matter, child."

I gave her my hand, and she held it in both of hers. She looked me in the eye.

"Thank you."

"You're welcome."

Before I left, every single person in the yard said, in their own way, that my house was looking better all the time, and they would watch over it when I wasn't there, and for my safety when I was.

The paint was just an accident, a little bit of humanity between neighbors, not part of some plan. After then I never had to worry about whom I could wave to and who would wave back. I was still always extremely aware of my color, and I hadn't proved myself yet, if I ever would, but this was a new step in getting to know the people I would be living beside.

When my truck broke down, the guy who gave me the salt for my drain, Woods, lent me a hand. I was trying to change the brakes but it was proving difficult. I had read all I could about the job and jumped right in, as usual, but I was stuck. I needed a special tool, but didn't know it. As I stood there frustrated, Woods strolled over with a buddy and told me what the problem was without even bending over. He had the tool and lent it to me.

"Do I need to give you any money for that?"

"It only costs money if I have to get dirty," he said.

Another guy from down the street, Scott, spent the better part of a day helping me when I broke one of the lug nuts off and had to repack the wheel bearings. He drove me to the auto parts store, gave me some of his own bearing grease, and set the new lugs at his home shop. He sat next to me and coached me through the rest until I had finished.

Weren't these the people who I'd been told were all drug dealers and criminals, people too stupid to leave Detroit? Why were they living here? Hadn't all the good people moved out by now, the ones who could? Weren't all the people living in neighborhoods this damaged broken themselves? Maybe they were all just stuck here and couldn't escape.

Or was it that they didn't want to leave, and those things were misrepresentations at best, lies at worst? Maybe I had stepped into a real community, one tied together with memory and friendships, history, shared experience and relationships, something that could only be built from years and trust and mutual understanding.

I'd had some time to think about that furnace again, too. It now sat quiet in the basement, made temporarily unnecessary with sun gracing the windows. Accepting that gift from my family was a relief not just from the cold but from the traditional masculinity I'd clothed myself in, the role of the provider, the American ideal frontiersman, the Man Who Needs No Help. It was a relief to admit I couldn't do it all myself. I couldn't be both above the community and of it; receiving gracefully was just as important as giving generously. If I was to truly embody the universal ideal, not just the classic American mythical one, I'd have to wash the shame of receiving help from my countenance, and in doing so any final subconscious judgment of others who took it.

———

The street leading to my house was blocked off by fire trucks and police. The house that was kitty-corner from mine was gone, but the fire was still going. There was a great column of flames spewing from where the front porch used to be. It looked like the gas main had ignited and they were working to get it shut off. I wormed my way through the trucks and explained to an officer where I lived.

"If it wasn't already gone, I'd tell you to let that one burn," I said.

The cop laughed. "I understand."

The fire looked like a jet engine turned upward, the flame close to the gas pipe blue, the orange reaching two stories to where the top of the house used to be. I could feel the heat from my back porch, and I was vaguely worried about my windows cracking.

The house was being squatted by some of the local junkies, and they must have had an illegal gas hookup. We knew each other by sight but weren't particularly friendly. I knew they were using the squat as a shooting gallery, and I knew that the woman staying there was called Sawtooth Betty. Matt, the junkie from Forestdale, knew them and went there to cop occasionally. He put in a good word for me, let them know I was cool and wouldn't call the cops, but also to stay out of my way and I would stay out of theirs. These kinds of interactions were more important for safety than any gun or dog or policeman. Above all else, my relationship with the neighbors would keep me safe.

It's a strange thing to be glad a house burns down in your neighborhood, especially one you can see from your back door. I feel a bit guilty now that I know the former occupants better, can see them as individuals rather than just junkies, but the first feeling I had was to be pleased. That was one less drug house I had to pass on the way home.

I watched the firefighters work for fifteen minutes or so and got bored. You can only watch so much stuff burn. They didn't have it extinguished before I went to bed. The next morning the house was just a foundation and a tiny pile of ash. I wondered if the dog who lived there had made it out alive. Sawtooth Betty moved into another house just up the street.

Whatever was going to happen, I needed to keep building. The next morning I started the chimney at the bottom. Mix the mortar, place the flue pipe. Butter the lower chimney block, slip the block over the pipe without disturbing it. Tamp it. Level it, tamp it again until it's level. Repeat. The blocks get harder to lift as they get higher. Try not to bump the flue pipe or you'll have to start all over. Start all over. Get the ladder. Hurry, because the mortar is drying. Climb the ladder with the chimney block and teeter over the fledgling chimney. Don't touch the pipe. Make sure the chimney is going up straight. Measure from your marks and the ropes you've strung.

Shake your head at yourself because it's a little off. Swear to do better next time. Get another block. Place it at the level of your head while on the ladder. Move it just out of square to compensate for the last block you screwed up. But not too much. The flue pipe still has to fit inside. Get another block and climb the ladder. Feel each of the muscles in your back. Get a small hernia from the final block. Get worried a bit. Say fuck it and keep going, you have mortar drying. Think about yourself at fifty with a broken, worn-out body like your father and grandfather and his father before him. Wonder if you're going to go deaf from the power tools like they did, need hearing aids at forty. The block hovers just over the mortar bed.

Be too proud for hearing aids and don't notice when someone

yells four feet behind you. Set the block and level it. The four-foot won't fit this time because of the floor joists. Get the torpedo.

Lower the final block into place from the top, using a pincer grip. See your knuckles swelling. Don't let the block fall. Just so. That's enough for one day. Wait, you should set the next flue pipe with the little bit of mortar you have left. Smoke a cigarette on the porch. Your hands are going to hurt later. They will crack and maybe bleed. Go downstairs and look at your work. Not bad. It's not professional exactly, looks a little homemade, but it seems to be working. Not too bad. That's ten feet. You only have twenty-five more to go. Be proud of yourself, just for a second. You have mortar drying.

————

I had gotten a job teaching year-round in a juvenile prison and was still working at the French restaurant on weekends. All that plus working on the house was killing me, but I desperately needed the money. I had to get that roof on. I worked five days a week at the prison, the other two at the restaurant, and every night I was able, on the chimney or whatever other never-ending project was at hand.

I walked in from work one day to find the drywall on the kitchen ceiling—the drywall I had just installed, mudded, and painted—bubbling. I thought this was odd so I got up on a chair and poked it with a pencil. Water squirted out like it was an enormous pimple. This was bad.

I'd learned a trick from a friend who had dealt with the same issue. Still in my good work clothes, I climbed back onto the chair with a drill and a bit an inch in diameter. Wet drywall is just about the perfect food for mold. They love it. I drilled a dozen holes in the drywall I had just hung and finished perfectly. It was all going to have to be redone. I still didn't have the money for the roof.

I decided I needed a day off. I went to visit Farmer Paul at the school for pregnant and parenting mothers where he taught, Catherine Ferguson Academy. I wanted to see how he had done it so well over the years. I still had only gotten sips of the man, and wanted to know how he became who he was, why so many people sought him out for documentaries or chapters of books, what made him one of the most innovative educators in America. I now had the excuse to corner him and he happily obliged.

The school was just blocks from downtown. As I pulled up in my old Ford, I could see that the building was unassuming, if subtly ornate. Fittingly, it was the only Detroit public high school designed by a woman, and named after Catherine Ferguson, a free slave who made her life's work education. The facade looked relatively normal. What was in back was striking.

A horse and a cow grazed on a circular track. Chickens roamed free, and a pair of goats grazed in a pen next to a clutch of sheep. Dozens of cages held rabbits, one for each student. Ducks and turkeys and geese wallowed in a pond, which an aid was mucking out with a flat blade connected to a long pole. Pigs grunted in the mud. A two-story red barn, which the young women had built, held the farm tools and milking stands, and upstairs was the loft where Paul stored the hay we had baled.

Around the track, arrayed in a circle, lay vegetable gardens, one for each young mother. Beehives sat behind in the orchard. Paul had done all of this. Over twenty years he built up the farm with his students, teaching them to care for their own children by first caring for animals and plants. Nutrition, health, hard sciences, math, construction, and chemistry could all be, and were, taught on the farm. It's worth noting the graduation rate at CFA was always above 90 percent, sometimes 98 percent, enviable for any school. The national average for pregnant or parenting mothers is 40 percent.

The produce that the women and staff grew brought in a bit of money at the farmer's market, and the balance was taken home by the women. It used to be that the gardens supplied a healthy lunch as well as a sense of pride, but because of a new food service contract signed by the Detroit public schools' emergency manager, that was no longer allowed. Their little farm would cut into the profits of the food service company.

I walked in the front door and asked the security guard where Paul's room was. After gently teasing a student walking past about a C on a test, she pointed toward his room. I walked past the gymnasium full of toddler's toys to his class.

The lanky farmer was at the front wearing jeans and a Leatherman on his belt, holding a piece of paper and posing a riddle to the young women sitting at long black desks, some of them groaningly pregnant.

"A father and his son are involved in a car accident," he read, looking up to make sure his students were paying attention. "Both the boy and his father are horribly injured and are taken to the hospital. The boy's father dies on the way, but the boy survives. When he arrives at the hospital the surgeon says, 'I cannot operate on this boy because he is my son.' How can this be?"

I waved my hello and sat in the back. Paul's room was filled with beakers, tubes, and cabinets full of specimens and strange things in glass jars. There was a greenhouse attached to the room and a young woman was watering the fledgling plants the students had grown from seed in milk cartons saved from lunch. I tried to figure out the riddle but was stumped, as was everyone else in the room.

"Nobody?" Paul said. ""Nobody has a guess?"

"What's the answer, Mr. Weertz?" one of the girls called from the back.

"The surgeon was the boy's mother."

The class gasped and I kicked myself for being so stupid.

"We're not taught to think of women as doctors. I didn't get it the first time I heard it either. I just wanted you to be aware of that, and consider what it means."

After introducing me, Paul handed out copies of the *New York Times* and instructed the women to read an article from the science section and report back what they had learned. When this was finished they all read together from a science textbook, each woman in turn. Paul was at the head of the class the entire time, running back and forth, gesticulating, writing things on the board, doing different voices for the different kinds of cells. It was quite a performance. At one point a girl put her head down to sleep and he ran over and shook her gently.

"Come on," he said. "You can do it. Just a little bit more. We're almost there."

The woman obliged after sighing, and Paul was back at the front with his angular energy. Three of the young women were called out of class for dentist appointments with their children. Paul made them take their homework before leaving, and they thanked him in turn. He got back into the cells again, talking about mitochondria, and stopped midsentence.

He rushed to the back of the classroom. All the young women turned to see where he was going.

"Come on, ladies. Come here, gather 'round." He took one straggling woman gently by the shoulders and led her to the front of the pack. One of the chickens in the incubator was hatching. We watched together as new life emerged from the shell, slowly and painfully at first, then free.

Everyone needs a hero, and Paul Weertz is mine.

After lunch Paul had the women outside for carpentry class. The inside of the barn was lit with little canteen lights strung from an extension cord and tools hung in neat rows on the wall. The hay from the upper level was pungent, and as we entered, the aid mucking the duck pond was now milking a goat, also pungent.

Its head was yoked in a milking stand, a wooden contraption like the stocks at a Renaissance fair, and the aid sat on a stool pulling on its udders and squirting milk into a mason jar. She asked if anyone hadn't milked the goat yet, and one girl said she hadn't but didn't want to. After some encouragement from Farmer Paul and the other students, and with one of the older girls showing her how, the young woman with an enormous belly started milking the goat. When she was finished they passed the jar around for tasting. It was warm and goaty.

In one of the cruelest ironies the city of bad decisions doled out in recent memory, CFA would be shut down within a year, the state-appointed emergency manager saying it was too expensive. When the time finally came to close the school, a number of students, alumni, their children, and teachers were arrested in an act of civil disobedience when they refused to leave the building. It was awesome, in the truest sense of that word, to watch pregnant women herded into cop cars by riot police and see mothers hand their children to relatives before being handcuffed. They were all taken to jail because they wanted the chance for a good education. Think back to your high school. Would you have been willing to be locked in a cage to keep it running? At the time it was only one of four public schools in the nation for pregnant teens.

Because of the community outcry, Detroit Public Schools tried to save face by selling the property to a for-profit charter school. Paul lost the farm, and was transferred with all the other teachers to other schools. A semester away from retirement, he rode it out and never looked back. The school was shut down by the charter within three years and the farm lies fallow, the barn rotting and the animal pens eerily silent.

The world might not be so cynical if we had more men like Paul, but it's hard to blame people for not following in his path when twenty years of brilliance and hard work are flushed away by bureaucrats. Paul built the school he wanted to see, that Detroit and America needed, and then they smashed it into the ground.

Lesser men would have given up. I probably would have. After all the work I had put into my own house—not even a tenth of what Paul had accomplished just at this school—I understood in my bones how utterly amazing was his creation, made from sweat and ingenuity, and how heartbreaking it was to lose it.

I began to worry that all the work I was putting into my place might not be so permanent either. The city could kick me out for anything it wanted, too. I hadn't been getting permits—I figured I'd start pulling permits when the city started pulling its weight in the neighborhood. It was absurd to get building permits right next to an abandoned house in an area the government hadn't cared for in years. But if the city bureaucrats wanted my land badly enough they would use this and whatever else was at hand to take it.

Farmer Paul seemed all I wanted to be, a Renaissance man with wide knowledge of the world, a citizen statesman, a teacher, a scientist, a frontiersman, the living embodiment of the impossible American ideal. A man who could fix anything, who obeyed only the rules of his conscience and intellect, the twenty-first-century incarnation of the best of the Founding Fathers, the Benjamin Franklin of our age. Paul is a great man and they still took from him what he made.

That afternoon at the school, I asked him the question I'd been asking myself for years without finding a satisfactory answer. *What makes you different? Out of all the things you could have done with your life, why did you come to Detroit and build a home and a community and a farm for pregnant girls and a swimming pool out of hay bales?*

Why didn't you quit?

He didn't have an answer right away, but after some thought he told me, "It takes a long while. You kind of get these bits and pieces and they come together at the end. One foot in front of the other, one step at a time. One thing leads to another." He shrugged. "But you have to take the first step."

———

The day I set to finish the tower of bricks was a sunny one. I enlisted a neighbor, Monk, to mix the mortar and pass it to me in the attic in a bucket on a rope. I had cut the hole in the roof large enough so I could lean a ladder against the chimney as it rose above the ridge. Butter a brick, place it, tap it with the trowel to set it. Butter a brick, place it . . . I was about half done when Garrett called from New York. I was covered in filth from the attic, mortar, and sweat from my own body and the wicked heat of the uninsulated space. But I thought it was odd, him calling me from so far away, so I told Monk to hold the mortar and took the call.

Garrett was in Zuccotti Park at Occupy Wall Street. I could hear the crowd in the back shouting periodically. The police wouldn't allow any amplification, as a tactic to slow the participants, so the crowd was using "the people's mike": When whoever was speaking would say something, it would be repeated in unison by the crowd, so everyone could hear, a low-tech and brilliant solution.

Garrett explained that he had just stopped by to see what was going on, and what he saw was incredible. I sat down on my attic floor and looked at the chimney. I listened as he told me about the free libraries, the tent camp, the newspaper they'd made, *The Occupied Wall Street Journal*. He said he'd bring one home for me.

The occupiers had been maligned in the media for not having any demands and being a leaderless movement. The media didn't get the point. Those kids out there wanted one thing: a better, more fair and equal world. They understood all of the issues of our time—poverty, race, gender, the environment, everything—were all too interconnected to be tackled separately. They all needed to be dealt with at once, the solution holistic.

Those kids didn't have time to ask for the crumbs of the wealthy gathered around that golden calf, they were too busy making their reality themselves, right there in the park. As the revolutionaries in Cairo's Tahrir Square wrote in an open letter to their brothers and sisters occupying parks across America, "We are not protesting. Who is there to protest to?" They were building a new world for themselves, one that reflected their values. It may have been impermanent but it wasn't naïve. On the contrary, it was the next step.

People were moving past blind protest. Woodstock—not just a music concert but a miniature city that the hippies said helped prove we could live together in peace—lasted three days. Occupy lasted three months and maybe next time we'd get three years. For a few days, a few weeks, a few months, people saw that another way of life was possible. They lived it, if just for an instant.

I hung up the phone with Garrett after saying thank you, and called to Monk for more mortar.

———

Near the end of that first summer in my house I hit a stone with the lawn mower. It bent the driveshaft and ruined the motor, which was already patched up with a discarded license plate and a good number of spare parts. Mowing the lawn had come to be the bane of my existence. I kind of liked when the grass got long and quietly waved in the wind, but the neighbors didn't. If it weren't for them I would just let it go. But I had moved into their neighborhood, not they into mine, and I followed their customs.

I'd finished only half of the lawn. It looked like a feral child, and I needed to leave for an errand that would take a couple of hours. What to do? I still felt on probation with the neighbors, but didn't know them well enough to speak to them regularly, enough to explain the situation until I could get a new mower. It needed to be taken care of now.

My neighbor King was sitting on his porch smoking a cigarette, and I walked over and asked him if he knew anyone who would cut my grass for a few bucks. He mentioned a white guy living with Sawtooth Betty who would do it, but he hadn't seen him around. I thanked him and told him if he saw the guy to have him get in touch with me, and left for my errand.

When I had come back the grass was cut just as pretty as could be. Someone had even gotten out the weed whacker and done all the corners and up against the fence, under the tree. It was a professional deal. I got out of the truck and walked around in the cut grass, surprised. King saw me and walked over.

"Hey, King. Did you end up talking to that guy for me? You know how much I owe him?"

"Nah, man, I just went and did it. I see you helping people around here. It's no big deal, really."

"Well, how much do you want for it? I think I'll have to run to the ATM."

It also meant he had spent a few hours in my yard, visually vouching for me to the whole neighborhood. He hadn't just mowed my lawn, but had told everyone that I was okay by his presence. It was a long way from what had happened with the previous owner of my house.

King laughed at me. "Nah, man, you don't have to give me nothing."

I was about to protest, but was reminded of something that had happened earlier that winter. My mother had come up to eat lunch on her way to take care of my grandmother. She had parked in the driveway, which was really my yard, and her small car got stuck in the foot of snow on the ground. We rocked it back and forth, and I got out to push, but we were stuck. Before I could go back to get a shovel, a big, rusty scrapper truck stopped and two giant men wearing oil-spotted overalls stepped into the snow-packed road. The three of us pushed the car right out, just like it was a go-cart. I said thank you, and I appreciated it.

"It's no problem," the driver said, and turned back to his truck. My mother called from the window.

"Hey, wait a second, guys." She was digging in her purse. "Let me give you something."

"Oh, that's all right, ma'am. It's not a problem, it was our pleasure to help."

"No, no, wait," my mom called. She had a few dollar bills in her hand. "Here, this is for you."

"It's fine, really," they said. She wouldn't take no for an answer and got out of the car.

"Mom, they said they didn't want anything. It's cool, let's go."

She didn't listen to me and ran over to the truck window and made the driver take the money.

I was humiliated, and got back in the car, sinking low and hiding my face.

We began to drive in silence. "What were you doing back there?" I finally asked, fuming.

"If I want to pay them, I can."

"Mom. You just ruined their good deed. Who the hell are we? Just because they drive that truck doesn't mean they don't take pleasure in helping other people. It's not all about money, and I know you like to do things for others. It makes you feel good. You just took that away from them."

Standing in my freshly cut yard, I thanked King.

It's the kind of thing you don't see on TV about Detroit, little acts of kindness from people just like anyone else trying to live normal lives. It's all fires or hipster bike shops, but rarely the little unsexy moments that make a healthy community, the long meetings, little gardens and lots of space, mowing grass that isn't yours. It's baling hay.

It's having a terrible day and going to the post office only to have the lady behind the counter not take no for an answer until you accept the can of Coke, paid for with her own money, she hands you in hopes of brightening your afternoon.

It's going to the chicken-and-waffles restaurant and hearing a table of high-school-age girls singing in joy to a song on the radio, oblivious to anyone listening, and having the entire restaurant applaud at the song break.

It was King mowing my grass.

It was showing up to the Labor Day party at the Terrys' after missing the Mother's Day one. Tents were erected on the lawn and the cooking utensils fired up. The DJ brought his gear and his crates of funk and blues and soul. Children ran around shouting or dancing in a line. The girls would twirl with their fathers, their hair freshly braided and tied with new bulbous rubber bands that looked like candy. The mothers sat around eating from heaping plates of ribs and greens and macaroni and cheese, salad, more ribs drowning in sweet sauce, fried fish, bread, steaming meatballs, lasagna, iced tea. They sat gently scolding anyone's children running about, as fathers played football with their sons on the cut grass, and women clucked and ran around "fixing plates," always fixing plates, "Can I fix you a plate?" "Let me fix you a plate," "Sit down, son, I'll fix you a plate," as if the flatware were broken if it wasn't heaping with food.

I found Mrs. Terry and paid my respects.

"Hey, Drew! Come on over!" She gestured for me to give her a hug, and I did. She called into the kitchen from the porch. "Jessica! Fix Drew here a plate."

"Thank you."

"Oh, thank me nothing."

I sat with the old-timers while they passed a jug and told me stories about growing up in the South, about the time they had gotten lost in the forest and told the dog to go home and followed him back to safety, about the red dirt roads, the overflowing vegetation, the food. They spoke of leaving home and of work in the Detroit factories, how beautiful the city used to be, who lived in what houses, and the women who were stone-cold foxes in their day. Of a city that had allowed for an unprecedented amount of black wealth and homeownership, and the historical forces that stripped it all away.

At times like those they were loose and willing to drop all their knowledge and I was going to make sure I would pick it up. This wasn't a chance that most white kids got, to listen to black folks talk freely about racism in such a simple, matter-of-fact way, but also of the pleasure, the special bond of the South and travel and migration and moving away from home.

It was remarkable that my neighbors and the people of Detroit were so welcoming to the new white people like me entering the city. It was our parents and grandparents who left, and like the prodigal son, it was us who were now returning. And largely we were welcomed.

What living around black people for the last decade has taught me is less about what it means to be black and more about what it means to be white. That because my family was allowed to build wealth when others couldn't, they could afford to buy me that furnace. Or why urban renewal never came to my grandparents' neighborhood but they got the benefit of it, literally building their house from it. How my uncle was able to afford to give me his tools. This didn't mean they hadn't worked hard for it, because they had. It meant that now we must work hard to make sure the past never repeats itself, that we must stamp out any vestiges of it today, and that we pay that borrowed time back.

I realized there were downsides to being white. That all the wealth, all the moves to the suburbs, had separated us from one another, had torn our own communities apart. That by dividing white and black we had divided ourselves as well. That we had separated who we were from who we strove to be, that the difference between what we were now and who we thought we could be was greater than we could bear. That who we are today carries a great debt, the debt of history, and until it is repaid we will never be at peace. If we wanted to be, once and for all, *Americans*—not white Americans, not African Americans—we had to face the past and its impact on today.

In some ways I was envious of my neighbors. The unspoken bond they shared was something I felt I was missing, something I'd been searching for all along. Like a lot of people in my generation, I was searching for community. I had found my tribe. The colorful folks on Forestdale and everyone like them anywhere in the world would forever be *my people*, but if we were to finally create the beloved community we would be able to do so only when all the tribes became as one. Building the house itself—all the bricks lifted, the Sheetrock hung, the elements battled, the sore muscles and blood-soaked Band-Aids—was the easy part. This was the real work. This was the hard work.

The sons and daughters and granddaughters on the Terrys' lawn had moved from football to foot races, and the DJ had moved on to playing slower, sadder songs, the Nina Simones and the Curtis Mayfields. The old-timers ruminated, and the children began to get cranky with all the excitement and fun and sugar crash of too much soda on a great day. People began to say their goodbyes and pile into cars or vans as hugs and assurances of future commitments were passed around like a tray of cigars, and every last person was full up.

People are so afraid of one another. That party could have been anywhere, anywhere in the world, but it just happened to be in Detroit, the most segregated metro area in the United States. If we're going to make this work we cannot be afraid of one another.

"Can I fix you a plate?"

CHAPTER 9

A Knock on the Door

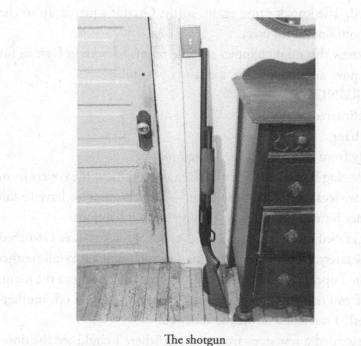

The shotgun

My dream of getting to sleep early was crushed by the infinite entertainment of the Internet. I had just purchased a smartphone for work, and with that one piece of plastic I had joined the 40 percent of Detroiters on the Internet. I hadn't had it in my home since I'd moved to the city.

I was sore from the day's work and turned off the light. I was disappointed I had wasted so much time on nothing. I still had a ton of things to get done in the morning. Gratiot thudded off the bed, frowning at me as I rearranged my legs. I floated into that liminal place between asleep and awake, the space of dreams. A soft knocking came from the front door, knuckles on hollow steel. I wasn't sure it was real. The knock came again, a bit louder this time.

I was awake now. The dog and I looked at each other, his ears cocked. The knock came again, softly. Gratiot squared up to the bedroom door. I sat erect.

I knew this might happen at some point. I'd been in Detroit for years now, and knew it was a distinct possibility.

CRUNCH.

Splintered wood.

A bang.

My front door was being kicked in.

The dog howled and snarled in a rage. I threw the covers from my bare legs and put on my boots—if I was going to have to kill another human being I wasn't going to do it barefoot.

I grabbed the shotgun from its special shelf, racked it, and switched off the safety. I'd never removed this gun and readied it to kill another person. I opened the bedroom door and the dog shot from the room.

"If you come in here I'm going to blow your head off, mother-fucker!" I screamed down the stairwell.

I stopped a few steps from the top where I could see the door. The dog tore at the steel, scratching, howling. I placed the butt of the gun against my bare chest and aimed it, right about where a man's torso would be. I yelled again and was silent, solid, and looking with one eye down the barrel, my trigger finger resting against the stock, my chest heaving. I said a little prayer and—

Deer are like ghosts. They often can sense your presence, your eyes on them before you even notice they're there. They can walk through a pile of dead leaves without making a sound. They're skittish, bounding off, gone in a second. It's the squirrels that won't shut up. They make more noise in the forest than anything else, chattering, gossiping, chasing one another. I'd been hunting whitetail deer with my father in the woods back where I had grown up each fall for years. We'd drive out to a property owned by a friend of his, load our weapons, and walk into the timber to kill graceful, peaceful mammals for their meat. I needed it desperately that year, the first I'd spent in my house without any heat.

The day was clear, and the wind coming from the west, the right direction to carry our scent out of the forest. We'd been unlucky that year, and hadn't seen anything. Hunting season was coming to a close and if I didn't get a deer it was going to mean a hungry winter. Even just one deer would feed me and a good portion of my family for months. We used everything. I would eat the organs, use the bones for boiling and stock, and I knew a woman back in Detroit, a hipster taxidermist, who would make a blanket or rug from the pelt.

The anemic sun was low in the gray sky. My father and I wanted to switch it up a bit and he pointed to a lone white birch tree at the edge of the forest, three hundred yards to the north. He said there was a stand just inside the tree line, set against an oak bigger around than a fat man.

I headed through the cornfield, the ground hard from frost. My father headed his way. The wind was low, so the day's sitting wouldn't be miserable. I entered the forest and it was dead quiet. I was a stranger, and all the animals whose territory I was entering watched me to see what I'd do.

The leaves crunched beneath my feet, and I found the stand. It was a good fifteen feet up in the tree. I placed my gun in the crook of a sapling and tested the ladder. It had been in the forest all winter, likely for many winters, and now it was part of the landscape like anything else. It belonged there. I climbed a couple of rungs and bounced. Seemed fine. I slung the gun over my shoulder and began to climb. I placed the stock under the seat and lifted myself free of the safety railing into the stand.

The ground was farther below than I wished. It was great for surprise, but if I fell asleep and fell out that would be it. I swallowed my fear. I needed the meat.

Once I got settled the forest began to wake up around me. The birds came back tittering and the squirrels resumed their spazzy dance. A path ran from around a bend down a slight decline and I had a good shot at whatever might come walking up. I sat as silently and unmoving as I could. Deer, like most animals, see movement, not shape. They couldn't see color either, and I was wearing blaze orange, as regulated by the state to prevent accidents.

I waited. Even though deer are silent, I couldn't help but look every time a squirrel made a racket with a jump in the leaves, or a fat little possum burrowed down into his hole. A hawk screamed and I could see her circling above looking for prey. The wind picked up and swayed the tree and the stand with it. I wondered why hawks made that scream, piercing the quiet, alerting all the animals to their presence.

I began to daydream. I liked the straight barrel of my gun against the crooked lines of the forest—nothing else was straight. The straightness said "made by man." The straightness was our advantage. The deer have a better sense of smell than humans, better hearing, and can run faster and live leaner. They require nothing but the bounty of the forest. Athletically and sensually, deer are superior to humans in almost every way. What we have is intelligence. It's what separates us. We have ideas. Sometimes those ideas become a gun, sometimes they become a house—

There they were. Two of them, does. Their fur was brown and their haunches sturdy, triangular white tails flitting in the breeze.

No matter how many times it happens, your heart always pounds, your adrenaline flows. You sit so quietly for hours, no stimulation aside from the show of the animals, and suddenly what you came to shoot is there and you're holding a gun. It taps into something ancient, primal, that man has not forgotten in all the years of fast food and TV and climate-controlled houses. The does were about the same size, one just a bit larger. Likely it was a mother and a grown fawn. Neither had spots, so it was legal for me to take either of them.

I clicked off the safety. Slowly, so they wouldn't hear. I moved it to my shoulder. The deer trotted down the path, stopped to sniff or nibble, and seemed to enjoy the sun behind them, the last few minutes of warmth on one of the last days of autumn. A mother and daughter on a stroll before bed just outside their home.

I hesitated. I needed the meat. I looked through the sight on my gun, the cruel, straight crosshairs trained on the chest of the larger deer. They were so peaceful. They do us no harm. I hesitated. I took my eye away from the glass and thought. Maybe I didn't have to do it. Maybe I was doing this only because it's what you're supposed to do. If you're a man you go out in the woods and you kill things.

I needed the meat. But did I really need the meat? Was there some other way I could get my food? This was natural, ancient, I reasoned. If I'm going to eat the flesh of animals I have to be willing to kill them myself, take upon my own soul killing something better than me so I can live in turn. I put my eye to the glass and again found her chest.

I hesitated again. I had been a vegetarian just a few years earlier. I pulled the trigger.

The roar of the gun cut through the forest, disturbing everything. I saw the orange flash of the muzzle. I saw the powder propelled from the barrel. I hit the deer. The shot knocked her off her feet. She was up running, gone, her fawn in tow. I watched them run until I lost them, and climbed out of the tree. I picked up the one spent shell from the forest floor.

Stupidly, I began running. I should have followed the blood trail, but I was too excited. I ran, stumbling and holding my gun in the direction the doe went. I lost my bearings and the deer. Had I in fact missed? Had I, worst-case scenario, wounded her and she was able to run off somewhere to die a slow, painful death? I might never find her, and I would have killed something living without even being able to honor it by nourishing myself from it. I stopped. I went back to look for a blood trail.

Sure enough, it was there. I followed the trail spotted on leaves, the grass, a smudge on a tree. I was lost in it, and I looked up. The fawn was staring at me standing next to her dead mother.

We locked eyes. For a moment we stood and contemplated each other.

She was in for a long, cold night. She would have to make it on her own now. All I could think of was the first twilight she would spend by herself and the jolt she would feel in the morning waking up alone, forced to remember what had happened. She bounded off. I forced it out of my mind.

When I came to the carcass, I poked the body with a stick to make sure she was dead. Then I got down on one knee and said a prayer. I thanked God, asked forgiveness, and prayed. I prayed hard for the other one, the one that had run off.

I went and got my father and we dragged the deer from the brush and gutted it, leaving the insides for the scavengers. I had made a perfect shot. Right through the heart.

"I'm going to blow your head off, motherfucker!" I screamed down the stairs again. The gun began to get heavy in my rigid arms, aimed at the door. "Whoever the fuck you are, you better get out of here or I'm going to kill you."

The dog was going insane with snarls, biting the door.

We existed like that for some time, me poised on the stairs, holding the same gun I had used to kill the doe, ready to pull the trigger; the dog in primal fury against the unknown; whoever was out there with their reasons and desperation: the perfect tableau of fear and rage and self-preservation, enveloped in the dark.

And then silence.

I gathered the courage to walk to the window and peeled back the bedsheet I used as a curtain. The side yard and streets were empty. I couldn't see out of the front of the house, because I had no windows, still plywood. I walked to the living room. I could see nothing. I checked the rest of the windows where I could, and the dog snorted, clawing. Nothing.

I was too scared to go outside. I didn't want to find anyone. I didn't call the police, I didn't want anything. Just whatever was out there to go away and never come back.

I sat on my couch, the cold steel and walnut of the gun on my bare legs, my hands shaking. I rolled a cigarette and lit it. I looked out the back window again. The house I'd bought for $500 was still not even half-finished.

There were gaps in the drywall, some walls uncovered. The kitchen needed to be cleaned. The floors were spattered with mud, out of joint, dim. Trim needed to be stripped, the room needed a coat of paint, the shower tiled, and on and on until I lost my mind or my body.

I knew that man outside wasn't my enemy. My enemy was the poverty that drove him to it. My enemy was the addiction stunting my community and the lack of help for it. My enemy was the desperation we've allowed to ferment within our brothers and sisters. My enemy—

Whether I liked it or not, whoever was out there was part of my community. And whether or not you like it he's part of yours, too. It seems like every week a new massacre is confirmed, reported on, and ultimately tolerated. Now we all live in Detroit.

It's very American to try to make a better world. It's even more American to do it with a gun. I know that ignorance comes from society and cruelty from pain. And I know fear comes from the same place. I had come to Detroit to help, to try to do good, and this seemed like the opposite. The danger, of course, was becoming a beast myself. The real danger was injuring my own humanity.

Had whoever was outside come in, I would have killed him. And if that deer in the forest could have defended herself, she probably would have tried to kill me, too.

CHAPTER 10

Progress Gallops

My kitchen, built from salvaged parts

Someone had started a neighborhood soccer league, and hundreds of young Detroiters were on the pitch at Belle Isle. It was the whitest group of people I had been in since moving to the city. I had joined the Poletown team with Will, Jake, and some others from Forestdale, our squad a motley crew in handmade uniforms next to teams with jerseys printed with local sponsors. The teams weren't exclusively white, of course, but it was undeniable that the vast majority of the participants hadn't grown up in the city. One could think all of young, white Detroit was on the pitch, a sea of white faces such as I hadn't seen since college.

The demographics of the city reflected this. Detroit proper gained 14,000 white residents between 2010 and 2014, its first uptick in sixty years. And the numbers were growing. The vast majority of the newcomers were like me: educated, relatively well off, and having the ear of the government and foundations. This new bloc of Detroiters had outsize political power. Whether we would use that to support and amplify the community ideals already present, or go the way of gentrification, remained to be seen.

We were looking for the opposite of the pain and alienation and social pathology we had grown up with, and didn't know if we would bring some of it with us, unintentionally or not.

One group crowd-funded a Kickstarter campaign, and received tens of thousands of dollars, mostly from out of town, for a larger-than-life-size bronze statue of Robocop to be displayed publicly. Some folks thought this was impertinent, considering the poverty of the city and a historical relationship with the police that was tenuous at best, a slap in the face and a flexing of power by a newly forming Detroit class that was educated and savvy with the Internet. Sixty percent of Detroiters lacked even basic access to the World Wide Web. A friend of mine once described the statue as a "litmus test" of what one thought of the direction of the city, a good indicator of when someone arrived in Detroit and from which class they came.

Meanwhile, new restaurants were opening daily and new art galleries were sprouting out of the cracks in our concrete. There was an undeniable buzz forming around the city, but it seemed most of the new business and media attention centered on a few neighborhoods near downtown, with the rest of Detroit left to burn as it always had.

Just as the city was closing the Catherine Ferguson Academy, the narrative of Detroit as the "comeback city" began to flower. Chrysler aired a commercial during the Super Bowl declaring its cars were "Imported from Detroit," playing upon the city's grit and determination to sell cars we barely made. I found it ironic that a commercial, the form of communication that teaches people they need products to be happy, vaulted Detroit into the American consciousness as something other than an apocalyptic hellhole.

Underscoring this shift was the fruition of dozens of community meetings held by the mayor and supported by foundations. The proposal they had come up with was called the Detroit Future City Plan. Many were immediately skeptical when the diagnosis mentioned race only in passing, given that the metro area is the most segregated and gentrification was knocking at the door. We became increasingly concerned when we learned that the plan called for some neighborhoods to be completely transformed, not into beautiful communities for the residents who already lived there but for such projects as water retention ponds and "green infrastructure." Some of the neighborhoods would be intentionally let go to seed, city services would be diminished or removed, and residents would be on their own.

This dynamic was playing out in Poletown through the developer who had come to Forestdale with plans for the giant urban farm. Supported by foundation money—gathered from some of the same institutions that had financed the Detroit Future City Plan—the developer had just purchased an industrial building in the neighborhood for fish farming and hydroponics. He was now petitioning the city to donate an enormous patch of land right up the street from my house, saying it would be the "largest urban farm in the U.S." Although the development wasn't yet at my doorstep, future plans for expansion would envelop my home.

Detroit's billionaires began to flex their greenback muscles, too.

There were rumors that Mike Ilitch, the owner of the Detroit Red Wings, Little Caesars, and the baseball team and stadium (the latter heavily subsidized by the city and state), was attempting to build a new hockey arena, partially with taxpayers' money.

Dan Gilbert, owner of Quicken Loans, Rock Financial, the Cleveland Cavaliers, and more than sixty skyscrapers downtown, went on a buying spree. He had made his money originating mortgages. Gilbert says he is so prosperous because he didn't sell junk during the collapse. It's difficult to tell for sure how much he contributed to Detroit's mortgage crisis, because Quicken is largely just an originator of mortgages, and the loans were almost immediately chopped up and sold in complex financial practices that can't easily be traced.

Quicken is being sued by the U.S. Justice Department for mortgage fraud. Gilbert just lost a labor lawsuit. One of his real estate companies also emptied a downtown building full of people, a longtime artists collective. Caught up in the wave of development, just across the street another high-rise, occupied by the elderly, was cleared by Broder and Sachse Real Estate. In a widely panned video discussing the new market-rate and fashionable apartment building, energetic white participants said, "This is our time."

Some of us began to wonder whose time it really was. The thing that made Detroit so special was that as we built the city once again, this time we had the opportunity to fix some of the mistakes of the past— racial segregation, power imbalance that came with wealth inequality, displacement as the city grew—and many began to wonder if this wasn't just a naïve dream, that Detroit would be built back as a mirror of the current America and the former Detroit. It wasn't just whites moving back to the city, segregation was moving back to Detroit as well.

The sickness of dissonance was upon me again. The ripping feeling I'd had when moving between tony Ann Arbor and the dirty streets of Detroit was back, and I no longer had to leave the city to experience it. Work at the prison and life in the neighborhood were old Detroit. The job at the restaurant and the soccer pitch were another. Again, I had my feet in both worlds and was attempting to make sense of it all.

At the moment, I still needed to get my roof on. Summer passed into fall. The mornings were once again cold, but tempered by a blur of work. Five days a week at the prison, two at the restaurant, repeat. Prison, restaurant, repeat.

I redoubled my efforts to get the roof on. I worked every single day, seven days a week, for months.

I took bottles back to the store. I'd eat rice and beans at home for lunch. My clothing became threadbare. I gave up beer, never went to the movies, rode my bike instead of taking the truck, waited until Thanksgiving to turn on the heat. Everything I could do to save money. I called the roofing contractor and he generously agreed to do the job in late winter at a cheaper rate than normal, to "keep his crew working" in the off-season.

I had a week off for midwinter break from teaching at the prison. Again I needed a deadline and this would be the time. In addition to having the money ready I needed to be able to work with the crew, taking care of things that could only be done in concert with the tear-off, such as repairing a vent pipe, adding a skylight from the salvage place, and getting as much wayward trash into the Dumpster as possible now that I could no longer take it to the incinerator without being charged. I turned down the temperature on the water heater. I left the restaurant last each weekend, working the longest shifts. I sold valuables, like the cap on my truck. I lined up small loans from my friends in case I wouldn't have enough.

Almost there, bank balance rising.

Work, sleep, eat. Work sleep eat. Worksleepeat. Worksleepeat.

Finally.

And then I found that my basement had flooded. The house had smelled funky for a few days, but I couldn't quite place it. One day after work I decided to check the basement, and it was ankle-deep in shitwater. I called my neighbor Woods, and he came over with a drain snake.

He explained that tree roots from my yard had grown into my sewer line, waste and water being the perfect plant food. Toilet tissue or something or other had then become caught in the tangle of roots and each time I'd flushed or taken a shower it had backflowed up the drains in the basement floor. I borrowed a pump and started getting some of the water into the yard, while Woods, teetering on chunks of two-by-four, rammed the snake through the main line, under the house and eight feet down in the yard. No drainage. We tried a different head. Nothing.

"So what am I going to have to do if we can't get this?" I asked him.

"You'll have to dig it up. I can do it, and I'll give you a good price because you're close," he said.

"How much will that cost?"

"Oh, a couple thousand dollars, probably."

Welp.

"Shit. Well, I have the money, but it was supposed to go to the roof."

Finally, Woods and I gave up. The clog just wouldn't break.

"You better take a look at these foundation walls, too, Drew," he said. "These are starting to bow pretty good. If you want, we can do this all in one sweep. If I dig out your main line I can get that foundation wall, too, for free."

Tired, I inspected the walls. They were all moving a bit, but the wall perpendicular to the electrical box was looking haggard. The mortar was crumbling and the bricks bowed a good three inches. I entertained the suggestion. I could take care of this now and start all over on the roof.

"Isn't there anything else we can try to get this water out of here and buy me some time?"

"You can sister up that wall with some headers and I can call up my buddy who has a bigger snake."

"Call the man."

Wait for the new guys. Carry the machine down. Pray the clog breaks.

Clunk.

The sound of water drained as I smoked on the basement stairs. Fifty dollars to Woods, seventy-five to the crew, and the roof was back on the funding list.

"You need to start thinking about that foundation, Drew. Soon," Woods said before he left.

—————

On a rainy February morning a Dumpster showed up, as well as a crew of Ukrainians. I had made it, the hard work paying off. In a week there would be no more drips, no more jars of rainwater, no more worry about ruined drywall.

Watching them work was beautiful. They were masters and operated together like a ballet troupe, scraping the roof clean of shingles and floating around the ridge as if it were nothing more than a playground. After removing the shingles they had to cover the old decking—strips of one-by called purlins—with plywood. When I saw them alternating horizontal and vertical pieces like a crocheted quilt, instead of butting them together at the corners, I knew they would do an excellent job and I was in skilled hands. I bought them lunch the first day because I remembered how generous it was when a homeowner bought me chicken while we were sanding floors.

All the upheaval was driving Gratiot wild. As I stepped onto the back porch, the little guy jumped up on the door to see out the window, throwing the deadbolt latch. I tried to coax him to undo it, but he just stood wagging his tail, as if mocking me. I didn't have a key hidden outside for fear that someone would find it, and had to borrow a hammer from one of the roofers. I climbed a ladder to the second story and bashed in the plywood covering one of the window openings that hadn't yet received its glass. While I was up there I noticed something.

On the next block over, in the old brick building once a "settlement house," but abandoned ever since I'd moved in, stood Farmer Paul. He was carrying a bundle of pipes through the back door. Once I got back inside, I grabbed my keys and headed over.

I knocked on the door and Paul answered in a dirty white work shirt and thick leather gloves.

"Oh, hey, Drew! How goes it!" He seemed excited to see me and removed one of the gloves to shake my hand. "I see they're coming along on that roof."

"They're doing a better job than I ever could. What's going on here, though?"

"The Boggs School, they're moving in."

"Ohhhh." I'd heard about this school from Paul earlier, and a few years back had even attended a few meetings. They were attempting to establish an institution based on the principles of Grace Lee Boggs, then still holding out a few blocks away. The school would pursue what they called "place-based education," teaching students to be good citizens as well as lifelong learners by using the assets and challenges within the community itself. Just taking an old unused building and fixing it up was a stunning first lesson. The founders of the school didn't need to kick anyone out to do it. I was happy they were coming to Poletown, but surprised.

"I thought the school was to be deeper east," I said.

"No, I think that lease fell through. You're going to be neighbors."

I was excited. These were good people.

"Well, I'm kinda booked now, but let me know when you need help. I'll be happy to pitch in."

Paul said he wouldn't hesitate, and I got back to taking five-gallon buckets of dirt from the basement and climbing the mountain of shingles in the Dumpster to be rid of it for good.

The Ukrainian crew worked fast. A job that would have taken my friends and me two or three weeks, at best, they accomplished in four days. Just like that, the roof was finished. They left my yard cleaner than when they started. As Will told me later, once a house has a new roof it's here to stay.

That year was the rainiest since the Civil War.

With the roof on I could really bang on the place, my eye on the foundation. I added gutters to slow the erosion. The wall next to the electrical box was bowing out like a fat man's stomach, and the others were groaning as well. It was looking like at least one wall would have to be replaced, but I was naïvely hoping that wasn't going to be the case. My dad and I blew a couple of holes in the brick above the ground line and added headers and posts beneath the joists to keep the house from sinking if the wall shifted, but I hoped adding gutters would buy me some time. I hung a plumb bob a sixteenth of an inch from the wall, so I could see if and how fast it was moving.

The saving started again. To add windows to the front I was going to buy them to size this time rather than attempt to frame them out. The windows in the front two parlors were mirror images of one another with some nice aesthetic balance, and I wanted to honor that at least in this portion of the house. This would be the facade to the world, the face of the place, so I wanted it to be somewhat uniform. I'd still install them myself, but decided I'd work on something less costly in the meantime.

The first thing I made was another woodshed so I could store two years' wood. I made the structure from pallets, the same kind I'd used to build my fence, some corrugated tin I'd found in the neighborhood for a roof, and the siding I had cut off Will's house, completing a kind of circle of reuse.

The shed ended up looking quite nice, if rustic, like a shack in Appalachia. I also needed a well-built honest-to-god shed to store the lawn mower and shovels and such. In addition, I needed to get the piles of material I'd saved from the initial cleanout outside, all the doors, trim, little pieces of wood and tile, pipes and tar paper. With this gone I could move my workshop into the parlor. Adding storage would begin to make this house less of a construction site and more of a home.

In the hours after work I studied a textbook of modern building my father had lying around, and designed a twelve-foot-square shed, a framed box with siding and a shingle roof. If I got stuck on the planning I could call up my grandfather and father for answers on roof pitch or the load capacity of two-by-six joists spaced at sixteen inches on center. Each payday, after siphoning off some of my income for future windows, I went to the lumberyard and bought a few two-by-fours, a couple sheets of plywood or siding, bundles of shingles, nails, and treated lumber. Like the Johnny Cash song, I got it one piece at a time.

My father came up one sunny weekend to help erect it. Everything was going well. I had constructed the foundation and decking before he arrived, cut and assembled the roof rafters, and the walls were coming along nicely, barn-raising style. My father and I knocked them together on the ground and lifted them up by hand, father and son on either end. We'd plumb the wall and move on to the next. We nailed the siding, framed the door opening, and got to sheeting the roof just as the sun was going down.

"So do you want to go to that Tigers game today?" my dad asked. I didn't, and he knew it. We'd been planning this project for some time, and ever my father's son, I wanted to finish this up and move the fencing around it. The dog couldn't be let out without supervision, and I wanted to be shut of this whole task. The baseball game could wait. There would be more.

"I don't know, Dad. I'd kind of like to stay and get this done."

"Are you sure? I've had these tickets for a while now. I don't want them to go to waste."

"Dad," I said, nailing in another sheet as he was cutting on the ground, "you told me when I was a kid, if it's worth doing, it's worth doing right, and you always finish what you start. I need to finish this."

"I'm going to the game whether you want to or not. I'll go by myself if I have to."

"Well, all right, then! You know how much work I have to do? Look at this place. I need your help. You have no idea how stressed out I am."

"Do you know what I deal with at work every day?" He pointed to himself. "You know how much bullshit I have to take? I need to have some fun once in a while, too."

He had recently been appointed the superintendent of the district he had been with for more than thirty years. He could be promoted no higher. He had climbed the ladder of the American dream, from working as a teenager pushing a broom in a machine shop, to a machinist himself, to teaching shop, to being head boss in the school district where he'd worked most of his adult life. He found it lonely and wanting at the top. It was making him sick, the petty indignities of a local politics as fractured and deaf as of those on the national scale.

"That ain't how you raised me. You taught me to work and work and work, and I've been working my life away on this place." I threw the hammer into the dirt and climbed down from the ladder. "You know how hard I've worked here? You know how much I've struggled—"

"Listen up, Andrew Man. I've been working my whole life to make your teeth straight, give you an education, and keep your ass out of trouble. Don't tell me about hard work."

I didn't have anything to say to that. He had taught me to work, and work I was going to do. I picked up the hammer and got back on the ladder. We worked together in silence.

When we finished the roof there was nothing left to say. He drove away as I dug the new holes for the fence.

I had made a mistake. I should have just gone to the ball game with him, instead of getting the work done and feeling like shit anyway. He was having just as hard a time as I was, working with what he had, doing what he thought was right. As with Cecilia, love and duty had once again come into conflict. Again I had made the wrong decision, although this time, it was the opposite one.

I worked on the shed until the sun went down.

———————

My grandfather had built me a complex set of stairs for the front porch consisting of two pieces that wrapped around a corner. My father and I still hadn't had a chance to patch things up in person, but there was another ball game, and as a show of good faith all three of us were going, grandfather, father, and son. I made sure I wasn't working. Soon after shingling the shed roof I drove up to my grandfather's to retrieve the stairs.

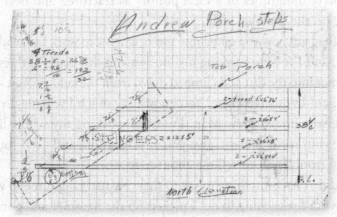

My grandfather's plans for the porch steps

Their beauty was in their functionality—built in two sections from two-by lumber from the big-box store, they were solid, staid, and functional. But behind the traditional construction was true complexity—these involved compound angles, intricate toe kicks, a setting that was less than square or plumb, and multiple other variables. I thanked my grandfather and asked him if he wanted me to pay him back for the lumber. He laughed.

"Of course not, bucko," he said. "I'm happy to do it." He went on to explain all the subtle deficiencies, pointing with the thumb he'd nicked on the table saw at the impurities that no one but he would ever notice and I would soon forget.

"I hope that's okay?" he asked earnestly.

It was my turn to laugh. "They're wonderful, Grandpa. I love them."

Both halves of the stairs wouldn't fit in my truck, so we decided he would follow me to the house, along with my father, to drop them off. This would be the first time he would see the place I'd spent the better part of my twenties working on. After helping me draft the plans, after giving me his table saw that cut the wood, after patiently answering questions and listening to stories of blood and sweat around the dinner table and over the phone, he would see the real thing. I wasn't sure I was ready for this.

He knew about the lack of heat. He knew about the condition of the neighborhood. He knew about the hunger, the toil, the exercise in monotony. He, of course, knew all this firsthand, gaining the knowledge for himself through his long life of building houses and struggle. But I wasn't sure he knew about my insecurity in wanting to please him, to be able to stand up as a man in front of all the men before me who had built the world around them.

He would inspect my work with the eye of someone who had been constructing dwellings for more than sixty years, and I was nervous. He seemed nonplussed. It was a simple equation, really: the stairs needed to get there and we both had the time.

We pulled into the yard and unloaded the steps with my dad. When we arrived, my grandfather seemed ill at ease in the neighborhood but didn't say anything. He had a jagged energy I'd never felt coming from him before. I could only assume what he thought about the city, as he'd never said much about it. My dad stayed quiet, probably wanting to see how I would handle this on my own. I asked my grandfather if he wanted to see the inside.

"Is my truck going to be okay here?" he said, scanning the surroundings uncertainly.

"Yeah, of course. Come this way."

I took him up the set of stairs I had made, in the back, the ones he had walked me through on the phone. These were beginner's stairs, nowhere near as complex as the ones he had created. On the third stair he stopped, my father watching. He bounced once, twice, to see if it had any give or squeak. He looked me in the eye and nodded; it was like kicking the tires on a new car. I opened the door I had made from the one I'd pulled from across the street, throwing the latch on the security bars I had bolted into the framing of my house. He stayed silent and thoughtful.

My response was to start talking, telling him every little hitch, the number of coats of poly I had put on the door, where I had gotten the beam to lift the house, each window I had encased, the shower, the cabinets, the pocket door, every little bit of trash I'd removed and how hard I worked to afford the roof. I told him about the bathroom I'd done the opposite way to what he'd suggested.

As with the stairs, I pointed out every little imperfection, each problem I wasn't able to get right or the places that just hadn't come together, the window that had been hung a bit too tight and let in a needle of air, the bathroom wall framing that was slightly out of plumb because I was thinking of Cecilia rather than focusing on what I should have been doing, all the little fragilities that nobody would ever notice but me.

I was rambling and stopped. I waited for him to say something. He slowly walked over to me and put his hand on my shoulder. I imagined lots of these interactions were happening across the city, all the kids who had moved to Detroit and places like it, the nervous parents and grandparents, their children and grandchildren dragging them into the twenty-first century over what they had created, and the reality of the new American dream we were about to inhabit.

"You did real good, Andrew Man," he said. "Real good. I'm proud of you."

His only suggestion was that the rear door should have opened the other way, against the refrigerator, to save space.

That afternoon, the Tigers beat the Yankees, 3–2.

All three of us drove back to my grandfather's house in his truck, leaving mine at home. After a couple glasses of Irish whiskey and a few games of euchre at the kitchen table, my grandfather went to bed in the house he had built for himself and my grandmother, and at one time my father. My dad and I stayed up a bit later and sat on the deck, overlooking the water, quiet, not talking much, but the lake said more than either of us could. The moon, casting its ghostly glow across the ripples like silk in the wind, and the heavy, churning body soaked up any feelings of ill will. We drank a couple more glasses of Irish washed down with cans of Budweiser, and stacked them on the burnished wood of the deck my grandfather had built.

———

The windows for the front had been purchased and were waiting in their shrink-wrap for my father to come and help install them. My bedroom upstairs was now finished and the second bathroom was on its way. That very day I had worked stripping the paint off the oak pocket door that hadn't been stolen. I was tired, but at least I didn't have to stare at unfinished projects in my new bedroom. The house was progressing nicely. I felt, if not exactly near completion, that this ship would hold water.

The only large task left was the foundation. The brick stomach had begun to push against the plumb bob and there was no question the wall was going to have to be dug out and redone. The job wouldn't cost much more than $500, but the labor was going to be intense. Woods had been forced to sell his tractor, so the digging was going to have to be done by hand, by me, with a shovel. I had about a year at most, and if the yard caved into the basement in the meantime the destruction might take the electrical box with it, likely burning down my house.

I left for work one morning as a film crew set up in the neighborhood. The state had enacted some incentives to draw the film and TV industries, and producers had begun capitalizing not just on the tax breaks but on the same grit and danger people in the neighborhood had been living with for years. Before I left, I stopped and asked one of the PAs what they were shooting, and it was a short-lived television show, a violent program of gore, corruption, and uncertain choices between good and bad.

The branding and repackaging of Detroit's grit was growing inescapable. T-shirts reading "Detroit" were ubiquitous. One of the most popular restaurants in the city, a chain newly built in Midtown, began selling what it called "crack fries." This was in a neighborhood that had previously been one of the hardest hit with the crack epidemic, a neighborhood that just years before had struggled, often to the death, with addiction. The newcomers to the city were making light of the agent that had destroyed so many lives. Some folks wondered aloud if they would be selling genocide bagels or Agent Orange juice.

In Poletown, some artists with no connection to the neighborhood or anyone in it had supposedly just received $30,000 from a foundation to tear down a house and build a brand-new one in its place. Things like that were becoming more common—just as mass tax evictions were starting. *The Atlantic* put the number as high as 60,000 properties, nearly one out of every five people in the city. That ugly cinder-block project house across the street from Will's old place was purchased by a young real estate developer and it was being rented out nightly, offering "the authentic Detroit experience."

I went back to my house for a last cup of tea before leaving that morning, and a white lady stopped outside and began walking around in my yard. I watched from my back porch, but I think she didn't see me, or didn't want to. Although this was odd, I didn't think much of it. Probably just some ruin-porn photographer or someone in the film crew. She didn't stop to speak with me, and I left.

My neighbor Andi called at lunch.

"You know there's a bunch of white people eating lunch in your yard, don't you?"

"Uh, no. I did not know that," I said. "They're filming some TV show in the neighborhood today, it's probably just them. It should be all right." My boss was looking over my shoulder, and I needed to get back to work. "How many of them are there?"

"I don't know," Andi said. "Mrs. Smith just called me, because she didn't have your number."

"I'm sure it's all right. I talked to one of the guys on the crew earlier today. They should be gone soon."

But the call itched at me all day, and I left work early.

When I got home the neighborhood was in upheaval. All the neighbors were on their porches, peering, and some from down the block were in the street. When I got up to my house I found fifteen students with easels stuck into my lawn, painting pictures of the house. I drove onto the grass and asked the first girl with a paintbrush what the hell she was doing. It had nothing to do with the film crew.

She explained she was in an art class at the university and her teacher had told her it was fine. Her painting of my house was rather complete. She seemed scared and upset, so I asked where the teacher was.

She pointed to a white woman sitting on my front porch, the one who had been walking around in my yard earlier. She had paint-spattered pants and was surrounded by students.

I walked over.

"What seems to be the problem here?" she asked me.

I was dumbfounded, and speechless for a minute.

"You're sitting on my porch, for one. Who told you you could be here, on my lawn? And sitting on my porch? I mean, what the hell?"

"We didn't know it was yours, we thought it would be fine."

"How did you think this was in any way acceptable?" I was livid. "How would you feel if I came to your house with fifteen dudes from the neighborhood and stood on your lawn with pencils and drew pictures of your house? Would that be okay? Is it because we live in the 'hood, you think it's all right to just set up shop on my lawn? You've obviously been here for a while. Those paintings are pretty far along."

"We didn't know someone lived in this house." She was becoming animated.

Two crowds were gathering, the group of students and another of my neighbors who had wandered over when they saw me. One of my neighbors put her hands on my shoulders to calm me down. I walked over to the others to ask what had happened that day. They were furious. I also wanted to make very sure they knew I hadn't invited these people onto my lawn.

They told me they had let the woman know, more than once,

this was my house, and they were trespassing. Nicely. They began trying to get hold of me when she was rude with them, talking about how she was a professor and they didn't know anything about art. This had gone on for much of the day.

I turned back to the teacher. As it turns out she was an artist who had received some success in Detroit years earlier and then left, like everyone else. She was back in town now that Detroit was fashionable.

"So my neighbors told you that you were trespassing, more than once, and you didn't listen to them. Why?"

"You're full of shit," she said, then began to insult me. "You don't know what you're talking about, you fool. You have no idea what we're doing here. We're trying to help you!"

The two groups of people, my neighbors and the students, started to yell at each other on my lawn, while the artist/teacher called me a liar and insulted my character, intelligence, and social class, while at the same time insisting she was just trying to "help." She said I should be grateful for her presence.

"Who asked you to help? Did anyone here? Don't you see how that's pretty patronizing?"

"Fine, we'll leave. We'll just pack up and leave."

One of my neighbors said something about the paintings they had made and wanted them destroyed. I knew I needed to regain my composure or everything was going to go to hell. I could tell them to leave and never come back, but really, what good would that do? I thought I might be able to act as a bridge between the two groups. This kind of thing was happening more often now, and would continue at a greater rate now that the city was changing and gentrification had begun its march toward a battle. This disconnect was playing out on my lawn in real time. I had to do something.

"All right, everyone." I held my hand up to the folks on my lawn.

"You guys have been here for hours. I'm going to go inside and get some water, and we're going to sit here and talk about this, all of us, why this isn't okay."

I figured a conversation might be a good teachable moment, and bring two segments of a new Detroit society together.

The teacher started in on me again, yelling as I walked into my house to get the drinks and calm Gratiot down; he had nearly chewed through one of the pieces of plywood on the windows trying to get at whoever was sitting on his porch. They had to have heard the dog.

I got back with the water and got some order.

"All right, so. Let's talk to each other. Please, can we state our names, first, at least?"

"This is bullshit," the teacher repeated. "I don't have to do this, you know I taught at Harvard? What we're doing here isn't ruin porn, we want to help you."

Ruin porn is like blackface in that if it were an isolated incident it would be little more than a tasteless curiosity. But like blackface there is a long history of ruin porn, and none of it has been good for the people who live among those ruins. This is what my neighbors were so upset about. This was an invasion, people who hadn't ever cared about this place, coming in only to take stuff away with the added insult that they were "helping."

"Hold on, nobody said anything about ruin porn—" I said, but everyone started speaking at the same time again.

I could see it wasn't going to work. People were too upset and set in their positions for any meaningful conversation. Every time I got started, the artist/teacher would begin insulting me, and talking about where she taught, and there was nothing I or my neighbors could explain to her about art. She reminded me, constantly, that she was helping us.

"We're helping" became the mantra of the capitalists, the billionaires, the ruling class that got us into this mess in the first place. The talk in the city became of "two Detroits." Almost all investment was happening in a few neighborhoods, and the usual characters were doing the "development," their benchmark of "progress" unchanged. One academic described the strategy for turning the city around as "trickle-down urbanism," mirroring the trickle-down economics of Ronald Reagan that had failed cities so disastrously. All the rest of Detroit was good for were pretty pictures of "Detroit Grit" to sell watches.

It was telling that the benchmark of "Detroit's Back!" was business—not how many of its citizens climbed out of poverty, or how racially tolerant and integrated we had become, or how well we knew our neighbors, but by the exchange of money. Like every other meaningful and radical subculture in the United States, Detroit and its ideas of transformational change were being commodified, represented by ruin-porn pictures, but not exclusive to the genera. And they were doing it with a smile and the sheen of "helping." When the transformation from people and ideas to money and objects was complete, those ideas—and the people—would lose their power.

I wanted to get all this across in that circle that afternoon, but I saw it was useless, a losing battle. The two groups just shouted at each other until order was completely out of my hands. Finally I said screw it, told everyone to go home, and went back into my house while the budding artists packed up their easels and art supplies and my neighbors slunk back to the homes they had owned for generations. Maybe this whole thing was impossible, the obvious inevitable.

One woman wearing a yellow bandana refused to leave, and sat on the sidewalk, which she was correct in saying was legal, and painted the abandoned house across the street. She was out there until sundown.

———

I retreated to where people understood. I sat with Will and Eric and Monk and some others around the firepit at Jake's, and we cooked meat over the open fire and potatoes wrapped in tinfoil within it. We called them family dinners, and they resembled hobo camps. We must have sat around that fire dozens of times over the years, discussing the best way to frame out a chimney, when to pay taxes, and how to get the electricity turned on in an abandoned house. They were unpretentious affairs, and helped us through the endless filth and work.

Eric the illustrator had just bought a house himself and was about to undergo the no-heat odyssey. Will was working along on his new place, which he was able to purchase at the auction. Jake was chugging along on his, no longer having to battle rogue crack dealers. When once we would have talked about construction, now it was one's place in a changing city, a change no one had imagined just years previously. A black U.S. president and a white mayor of Detroit? You would have been laughed out of any 2004 social gathering in the country.

There wasn't much to say. Progress was galloping.

As was Gratiot on our bike ride home from the bonfire. He loped along next to me on a thick chain I usually kept in my truck for pulling people out of the snow. I hadn't been able to find his leash that evening or even a carabiner to attach the chain to his collar, so it was affixed with a big brass lock, meaning I couldn't unhook him quickly.

Gratiot and I had made it a couple of blocks off Forestdale and I was feeling good, the dog falling into pace. A friend from work had given me a newly tuned-up bike to replace mine, which had been stolen, and it was humming along when four dogs came tearing out of the urban forest on each side of the road, snarling and spitting and furious. A whole pack of them was on the attack, and Gratiot and I were the prey.

I screamed at Gratiot to run and I dropped the chain.

I saw one of the dogs, a white-and-brown pit bull, out of the corner of my eye, his muscular shoulders pumping, running after us.

I kicked at him. Like an idiot, I was wearing sandals. Why did it have to be this night? Two more on the other side, mangy. Gratiot was keeping up.

I screamed at the pit bull and back at Gratiot.

"COME ON!"

I usually never traveled by foot or bike through the east side without armor: boots, a leather jacket, long pants, a knife or jack handle, a few rocks to defend myself. I stupidly didn't have anything that night, just the glass salting the streets and my bike. I pumped faster, the dogs behind me.

There was a three-lane road up ahead and I was thinking about making it across, looking for traffic. I screamed at Gratiot to go faster.

I made it across.

He did not.

He'd stopped, standing in the middle of the road facing off with the four dogs. He snarled and whipped the chain. The other dogs had grouped together like a pack of wolves, circling him. I was going to watch Gratiot get killed.

I had nothing to fight with. I looked around, no sticks, nothing to throw.

"Gratiot!"

I was unprepared and was going to watch my dog die because of it.

"Gratiot!"

Still no traffic. I dumped the bike and went in, visions of my forearms ripped apart by dog teeth. *I'm not going to let him die.*

I made myself as big as I could and stopped yelling for my dog, started yelling at the others.

"You best back the fuck up!" Gratiot was going to be hamstrung by the chain for the fight.

The brown-and-white pit bull was closest and barking at me now. I made it to the chain. I yanked on it, trying to get some slack so I could brain one of the dogs. The pit bull leaped, but it was a feint. The other dogs howled.

I dragged Gratiot across the road and the street dogs stayed on the other side.

They didn't pursue. When Gratiot and I made it a block away I got on the bike and we rode home, the injection of adrenaline draining slowly from my body. I could hear the street dogs bay in the distance.

When we entered the safety of my fence I sat on the porch and tried to wring the last of the sour adrenaline from my body. I grabbed Gratiot about the chest and dug my fingers into the fur of his shoulders. He licked my ear and squirmed. There was no question which Detroit we had chosen to live in, and I was doubting, after what I'd seen, that that choice could be undone. The only way out was through.

CHAPTER 11

The Years Roll By

Digging out the old foundation

Just after I got the roof on without incurring any debt, Detroit went bankrupt. Then it became unbankrupt.

It was funny, while we declared the largest municipal bankruptcy in U.S. history, there was an unmistakable feeling that money was pouring into the city. There seemed to be plenty of cash around, just none of it in the right place.

The rock-hard hard-on of all spurious subsidies screwing tax-payers was announced just a week after Detroit declared. The city and state gave hundreds of millions of dollars to the billionaire Mike Ilitch to build a new hockey arena. Detroit was so bankrupt it could find enough dough to give millions to someone who already had billions.

The rationale was, of course, employment. This was just a few years after the government granted the Marathon oil refinery, on the west side of Detroit, a $175 million tax break for providing the same silver bullet of progress: jobs.

It created fifteen.

That's more than $11.5 million per job.

And this after supporting a new jail, half-built downtown, nicknamed the "fail jail," which had been halted midway because of cost overruns. Numerous people involved with the project have been indicted and civil lawsuits abound. It was costing the county almost $1.2 million per month just in storage and interest fees.

To give you an idea of our priorities, Michigan spends more money on prisons than on higher education.

Aside from all the talk and increased attention from the national media, the bankruptcy didn't seem to change life all that much for the average Detroiter—unless you were on a pension. What did make things different was emergency financial management, a fancy way of saying state takeover of city government. Detroit's bankruptcy was shepherded through the courts by an emergency financial manager, appointed by Michigan's governor, Rick Snyder. In the last election Detroit voted more than 90 percent for the party opposite the governor's.

As with the other EFMs, Detroit's Kevin Orr had near dictatorial powers to make unilateral decisions, break union contracts, and—this is key—pension obligations. Every elected official in Detroit was stripped of their power, and Orr would be the sole individual deciding Detroit's governmental future. EFMs had already been appointed in almost every other majority-black city in the state, and when Detroit came under emergency management, more than half of the state's African Americans had been disenfranchised on the local level.

This is worth repeating. Half of the black people in Michigan had lost the right to vote for their local leaders. It was a stunning coup against democracy. The governor and legislature could determine a city was under "financial emergency" and install a bureaucrat answering not to the residents but to the party. It just so happened that nearly every single one of these cities was majority black. It also just so happened that the state owed Detroit millions in promised "revenue sharing" dollars that were never paid, distinctly contributing to the emergency.

To put this in the simplest terms, I, the person writing this book, had my democracy taken from me.

During the war against the Nazis, Detroit was nicknamed "The Arsenal of Democracy," on account of the auto factories that had been retooled to make the bombing planes and tanks that won the war against fascism. Now it was a cruel joke.

Citizens, of course, tried to fight it. When there began to be rumblings of an EFM in Detroit, the law granting the ability was recalled by a vote of the people, statewide. More than half of Michigan's voters thought this unconstitutional and unwarranted and struck it down.

The governor then rammed a new bill through the legislature with some marginal changes and attached a financial appropriations rider. This ensured voters of the state wouldn't be able to vote on the issue again, as our state constitution prohibits popular votes on laws with attached dollar figures.

The NAACP filed a lawsuit against the government, calling the new act an unconstitutional violation of voting rights. The suit was dismissed by the same judge who later presided over Detroit's bankruptcy.

This happened while I was paying property and income taxes to the very city I no longer had a say in as a voter. Losing my right to vote for who was to lead my city was a black mark on me as an individual, a free U.S. citizen. I will carry around for the rest of my life the fact that when I was a young man I had my right to vote removed, along with that of all my neighbors. Enough people thought I wasn't competent to make decisions that would affect me directly. I carry that as a shame not only on myself but on my country.

If you find this statement hysterical or overblown you might have to realize democracy just isn't that important to you. What if it was your right to vote?

The same political class that had brought "democracy" to Iraq had stripped it from Detroit. People in the city began to openly wonder if the folks who had white-flighted themselves now wanted the city back by any means necessary, including those less than democratic. Emergency management was also at the root of the poisoned water in Flint, Detroit's little brother to the north.

The era of the EFM in Detroit was when the water shutoffs and evictions started. In order to clean up the books at the Detroit Water and Sewerage Department for possible privatization, the city began shutting off water to tens of thousands of people during the summer of 2014. The move was condemned by the United Nations as a human rights violation, by groups such as the National Nurses Union as a public health issue, and by international clergy as a violation of basic decency.

Shutoff occurred without warning when a household was $150 overdue or two months late. Activists had been petitioning for an affordability plan for years, and the cost of the plan they came up with, just over $5 million, was about what the city paid a private company to perform the shutoffs.

The Nestlé Corporation siphons off 150 gallons of water per *minute* from the Great Lakes aquifers to serve their bottled water operation. Aside from a small permitting fee, they pay the residents of Michigan exactly zero dollars for the privilege to remove our natural resources held in common. In fact, the state gave them $13 million in tax breaks to locate the plant here. Conveniently, Nestlé's Michigan spokeswoman, Deborah Muchmore, is married to the governor's chief of staff, Dennis Muchmore. Could you imagine BP pumping the oil from beneath Saudi Arabia while paying nothing to the owners? Nestlé is now petitioning the state to increase their allowance to 400 gallons a minute, still, of course, for free.

Water was indiscriminately shut off to pregnant women, elderly people, and those with illnesses. Per Michigan's laws, children could not be raised in a structure lacking running water. If folks had their water shut off and couldn't find a place for their kids, the state would take them.

When all was done, more than 80,000 people had their water turned off, more than a tenth of the city. As reported by Joel Kurth of the *Detroit News*, DWSD cannot say how many of those people have had their water turned back on. The number of Detroiters still without water is likely in the tens of thousands.

While residential customers were getting shut off, Detroit refused to go after businesses that were past due. Places like Ford Field, where the Lions play, owed more than $50,000. The Chrysler group, which just received bailouts from the federal government, owed thousands. Amid all this, after having been shut off for years, the grand fountain on Belle Isle was turned back on—the park now leased to the state—the freely flowing water taunting those without it.

Water bills were also tied to property taxes, contributing to the eviction crisis. Detroit has some of the highest property tax rates in the nation. As people moved out, the solution to declining revenues was to raise taxes on the people who stayed. Coupled with being one of the poorest cities in the United States, this was disastrous. We were paying for nearly nonexistent services, yet paying the most for them. All those people who had left for the suburbs and were now paying taxes outside the city had left Detroit crippled.

After losing tens of thousands of homes to mortgage foreclosure, the crisis then reached the tax-foreclosure phase. *The Atlantic* estimated one-fifth of Detroit's population could lose their homes in this manner. That's more than 100,000 people, the population of Buffalo, New York. Imagine one in five people in your city losing their homes. It's a crisis of refugee proportions.

The foreclosures opened the door for speculation. After bleeding the city dry, people from the suburbs and all over the world began to buy up blocks of homes at rock-bottom prices and letting them sit, uncared for and dangerous. Michigan Radio has estimated that at least 20 percent of Detroit land is now owned by speculators. The vast majority of those structures rot.

Like the red abandoned house next to me, owned by an LLC. While whoever owned it waited for his payday, I kept boarding the place up every time it got broken into. I mowed the lawn once a week. I even put gutters on it to keep the rainfall from ruining my foundation. All of which were technically illegal. Anytime I stepped on the property or went into the house I could be arrested. If this notion seems silly, remember that Norman was taken to jail earlier in this story for doing just that.

Meanwhile, Detroit's march toward progress included the city's public schools, which have been under emergency management all but three years since 1999. In a gobsmacking bit of irony, the school district's debt under emergency management had ballooned, and DPS was out of money to pay teachers. The succession of emergency managers had failed even by their own standard, money. The debt increased. The curious thing was that nearly all that debt was owed to the state, as if they were trying to make the schools and the city financially unstable. When public institutions and commons are on the skids, it's much easier to privatize them and put more money in the pockets of your friends, and in some cases the corporations their wives helm.

During Detroit's orgy of "restructuring" there was apocalyptic talk about selling the prized public art in the Detroit Institute of Arts as bankruptcy payment, of chiseling out the same Detroit industry murals that Cecilia and I had stood before. They went so far as to have Christie's appraise the value of its major works.

This was just a ruse to scare the state's more liberal citizens into accepting a bargain. The governor's political bread was buttered by some of the major donors to the museum, including the DeVos clan, and there was no way, in an election year, he was going to sell the art they had donated. By holding an axe over the art it was easier to cut pensions when choices needed to be made.

And that they were. The pensioners got screwed, of course, but folks didn't really expect anything different. Pensioners took a reduction in their monthly checks, cost-of-living adjustments, and health care from what they were promised during their decades of work for the city. The average pensioner was making $19,000 a year. Keep in mind they just gave—not a tax break, a handout—more than $250 million to a billionaire to build a new hockey stadium.

Now tell me again who the welfare queens are?

The deal was part of a "grand bargain," struck among the city, the state, and private entities. The pensioners would take smaller cuts than originally proposed—another axe above a red herring—and none of the art would be sold. It was nearly a billion dollars in private and state money. Why there was that much cash available but not in the right place is a mystery.

Just four years before, the federal government bailed out Detroit's auto industry, to the tune of about $85 billion, similar to the plan they had constructed for the banks that were "too big to fail." Two of the Big Three filed for bankruptcy, and all three needed emergency loans. There was no bailout for the people of my city.

In the corporate media the bankruptcy had been discussed as "paving the way" for Detroit's "renaissance." And there was a renaissance of sorts, but thanks to research from the Wayne State graduate student Alex B. Hill, the revival was clearly less than equal.

In a widely covered paper entitled "Detroit: Black Problems, White Solutions," Hill confirmed a suspicion of many in the city. He calculated the racial makeup of a wide variety of start-ups, incubators, government organizations, universities, NGOs, and "who is accepted to [the] fellowships and the various programs and organizations working to revitalize Detroit." What he found is that in a city more than 80 percent black almost 70 percent of those leading the regeneration were white.

Is this how we run the "comeback city"?

In the words of Mikel Ellcessor, co-creator of NPR's *Radiolab*, Detroit's rebound is "an immoral, cosmetic sham."

Consider the political cronyism, the corporate theft, the poisoned water in Flint—and most especially—our loss of democracy, a dry run for the rest of the nation. Welcome to Detroit.

I dug out the foundation over a week in May with a shovel and mattocks, four and a half feet deep and eleven feet long through clay. There were parts of me that relished the work as I had digging that first hole at Will's for the pond, others that wondered if my labor was for naught. Over five trips I picked up the cinder blocks from the masonry yard in the neighborhood, the leaf springs in my old truck sagging like a tired mule. I set 110 forty-pound blocks in the basement and seventeen bags of mortar in the shed for when my family would come to lay them.

Garrett took a day off work to help me bust out the foundation with sledgehammers. He had just fixed his own recently purchased place on Forestdale with windows, electricity, insulation, and plumbing, and was moving in as soon as the drywall was complete. We carried the bricks out in milk crates, and stacked them in the yard.

On the Friday before Memorial Day, my father, uncle, and a cousin drove down early to lay the new block. My grandfather had become too frail to do much, and although he wanted to help and probably could have, my dad and the rest of us forced him to rest. While my uncle and I spread the mortar and leveled the block, my dad mixed and hauled with my cousin. We got the new wall laid in a day. It marked the end of the major construction, and barring anything unforeseen, everything else was cosmetic.

My grandfather did participate in his own way. He made me an heirloom toolbox, exactly the same as he had made for himself as a young man, and as he made for my father when he was about my age. The toolbox is oak, and my grandfather turned the brass knobs himself.

The rest of the house came a little at a time, but always progressing, my home stable and no longer the focus of my working and thinking life. It did what it was designed to do: keep the elements out, keep me safe and warm. In this I had succeeded.

What I had failed to keep out was uncertainty. With the changes in the city, both my neighbors and I now had to worry about being displaced, not just by fire or crime but by the billionaires. The bankruptcy marked the first shots in the battle for Detroit's soul. On one side stood the old methods of cold economics and scale, and on the other a grassroots movement of education, community, and compassion. We were going to have to pit our humanity against their money, and the fate of Detroit was now a microcosm of what was happening to the country at large. The building of my house was but one soldier, and I was determined to fight until the end.

I finished the rest of the windows and the second bathroom, and started one of the guest bedrooms. Little conveniences such as more kitchen cabinets or a new closet for the vacuum were revelations. The front porch came along, slowly, but I was finally able to sit on its sturdy haunches and wave at the neighbors walking by. I was a long way from no heat and keeping my dishes in a milk crate.

I even had time to begin to help others and pay back some of what I owed. I was happy to oblige when Paul asked for a hand with the plumbing on the Boggs School. Teachers, administrators, and parents ran around inside, painting rooms in bright colors, stocking the library, and making posters of revolutionary heroes like Rosa Parks and Cesar Chavez. As Paul and I worked they installed a new playground directly in view of my front porch and the stairs my grandfather had made. I was hoping I would be able to hear the children playing at recess, their innocent shouts and cries of joy a reminder of what I was fighting for. The building, abandoned for years, was now a school.

When Paul was ripped away from the Catherine Ferguson Academy, one of the first things he did was plow up another couple of lots on Forestdale and plant another orchard, just under a hundred fruit trees. Free of work requirements, he spent most of his time running around helping anyone he could, installing electricity, giving advice, using his Bobcat to cut a day's work down to an hour. He helped me with a plumbing project and refused any payment.

Will was all set up in his new house in the neighborhood, but plenty of people still couldn't understand that even though he had been paid to leave his paradise, that money wasn't what he'd wanted in the first place, and money can never buy what's important in life. He had a whole new set of problems now, a perennially flooding basement and a leaky roof being just two. The Dequindre Cut, where we once walked the dogs amid the grandeur of nature in the heart of the city, had now been turned into a jogging track. The animals and the dense foliage were gone. Who knows where the Oracle went or any of the other people living down there.

My friends from the YES FARM started going their own ways, yet we all remained part of the same community. Each of the three founding members had purchased houses in the neighborhood themselves. Jake got married, and Eric moved into his formerly abandoned house on the west side. Molly found a new chef's job and the Hillbilly Yacht Club appeared every summer. Monte, the artist who had given me the tattoo of the Great Lakes, had, with his wife, purchased their own house. Their son was now in middle school.

After the YES FARM, the apothecary building was turned into a bicycle repair and teaching shop by some neighbors and one of Paul's sons. They held clinics teaching the neighborhood kids how to repair their bikes, lending out tools and knowledge and expertise. Another young couple, straight-up urban farmers making their living growing things in Detroit dirt, was able to purchase the house next to Jake's, formerly the crack house. They moved in with their son, and another was born inside.

There were so many babies born on Forestdale! There was going to be a whole generation of kids who grew up in Detroit. More people were figuring out ways to make it in the city with children.

The Kemps continued to raise theirs, adding to their house and garden and love for one another. The first of their daughters was off to college, the University of Michigan, my alma mater. Andy would stop by my place on his bike after work and drop off seeds for the garden, or I'd stop by theirs and they'd feed me homemade burritos, kimchi, and more ground cherries.

Matt, the guy who had taught Gratiot to swim, died of a heroin overdose. His wake was in the true Detroit style, at one of his favorite bars in the Cass Corridor, packed with teary, drinking mourners.

I attended Grace Lee Boggs's hundredth birthday party, and just a few weeks later she died peacefully in her sleep. She had taught us to make the world we wanted to see in Detroit and had left us with a nice round century of knowledge to build upon.

They found a corpse in a house I can see from my back porch.

I can't remember the last time I heard gunshots in the night or saw a wild pack of dogs. Since that dark night my shotgun has remained on its shelf.

A young couple moved into the house kitty-corner from me and were making it their own. The young man proposed to his partner in an abandoned house nearby. He said that when his fiancé looked at the dump he wanted her to see not abandoned, dangerous garbage, but the spot in which he proposed, where they made their love forever. She said yes.

Another couple bought the abandoned house on the block just north of me, and homes were being snatched up like they were going out of style, which they were. Due to fire and occupation, there were almost no abandoned houses in the neighborhood and the days of the $500 house were coming to a close.

I would run into Zeno every now and again, and he seemed to be doing better than ever. I tried to track down the old hooker with the hole in her neck, but she was nowhere to be found. The art gallery that had given me the boards for my house and had taken the Banksy mural from the Packard plant sold the painting after promising not to, angering everyone.

Gratiot was still a brilliant fuzzy mess and alive, thank God, despite his bravery.

My dad retired from the school district with thirty-six years in public service. He built the first LEED Platinum certified primary school building in Michigan, which makes the district money—they farm enough electricity to sell it back to the power company, while teaching students about sustainable energy. My friend who helped me install the electricity quit his corporate job and opened a set of bars.

As for me, I wrote an article about the neighborhood, and my house, trying to attempt to explain some of the tensions in the city. I told a few of the stories that are included in this book. It was published by BuzzFeed, and as it happened, a lot of people read that story, almost two million. It seemed to touch a nerve, and the outpouring of support and connection from around the world was almost too much to bear. I spent happy weeks answering e-mails and questions, grateful that so many people had come to care about little old Poletown.

But my favorite letter involved Forestdale. I had mentioned that Paul was attempting to find a way to groom the ice rink in the Back 40, and I had found him one day with his clothing iron plugged into an extension cord, trying to iron the ice flat. That, of course, didn't work. People as far away as France and Canada sent me plans for homemade ice-grooming machines.

But someone called Paul with an offer of an honest-to-god Zamboni, the kind they use at professional hockey rinks. It was municipally owned and unused, and the price was about one-fiftieth of what it would have cost new, $500, the same as my house.

Paul thought about it for a while, and went back and forth on whether to pay it. Finally he decided against it, that the money could be better spent elsewhere. One of the new neighbors, Amos Kennedy, a famous printmaker, stepped in with a $500 check.

"It's for the community," he said.

Paul picked up the thousand-pound ice groomer with his tractor, and like the hay bales before, drove the Zamboni through the streets of Detroit to shocked and pleased looks.

I used to want to keep Detroit a secret, to not have it handled by too many for fear it might break. My thinking has changed. The city will transform whether we like it or not. The only question left is *how*. Understandably, those who have been at this a long time are worried about the new influx of money and attention to the city, in part because we're worried Detroit will lose some of its radical neighborliness, that people will be gentrified from their homes, the city will become an unaffordable dystopia ruled by numbers instead of beating hearts. It's as if Detroiters have been on strike—a strike for community, fair living conditions, and self-sufficiency—and the worry is new residents like me will act as strikebreakers.

We have to remember the fight isn't against our fellow workers. We're all products of the same society, and in our pursuit of justice we cannot forget compassion. The fight is against the corruption of the bosses, the politicians, the moneymen, those who perpetuate inequality, racism, and antidemocracy for their own gain. Those who are making the city into the image of a dollar sign, not the spirit of Detroit backed by Joe Louis's fist. We need a new measure of progress.

Scabs are only scabs if they cross the picket line. Many of the young people moving into Detroit and places like it are aching, desperate to join the union, a brotherhood and sisterhood of meaningful lives lived simply and in chorus with others. These skills are not innate and must be learned, as I had myself, building my house. When used effectively, privilege can work as leverage.

I wake up in the mornings in a room that once had holes in the wall, an empty space where a window should have been, and feces on the floor. While I once slept on my workbench, my bed is now soft (without being too soft), the walls smooth and white, and morning light pours in from the window I installed myself. The floor is clean enough now to rest my bare feet and look at the first thing I see every morning, a framed poster reading, "Whenever you feel like you're nearing the end of your rope, don't slide off. Tie a knot. Keep hanging. And remember, ain't nobody bad like you," the nightly refrain from Detroit's most beloved disc jockey, The Electrifying Mojo.

When I walk to my second bathroom and look at myself in

the mirror, I can remember it's here I once tied a climbing rope to escape on Devil's Night in case the house burned. The bathroom is now finished in brilliant white on white. In the mirror I see hair graying before its time, my tired eyes sitting atop shoulders and a chest muscled with work. My hands carry calluses and scars, the knuckles swollen, badges from a life fully lived.

As I walk down the unfinished stairs I walk by holes in the plaster from when the house was originally scrapped out. I've passed these imperfections a thousand times, but now I can see they contain new plumbing and electrical wires, both of which I earned little by little working crushing jobs and installed with my own hands. Each time I walk by I think about fixing them, sometime. I know anything can be fixed.

On my way to the kitchen I run my fingers against the new door I'd installed after someone tried to kick in the old one, the one I'd put in when I'd boarded up the house, the door at which I aimed a shotgun to kill someone.

I make breakfast on my stove that I supplied the gas to, next to countertops pulled from a soda factory, underneath a beam I stole from down the street and a dozen of my friends helped install. I listen to the radio while cooking my breakfast, and light from all the windows I bought for a couple bucks at a salvage place warms my bones. During the day I will tinker with this or repair that, sometimes doing my old work over again, better this time, following years of experience.

And when I sit on my porch in the evening, as the sun goes down casting a red ribbon dance over the city I love, my body aching from the day's work, I am happy to be alive and I am unafraid of what may come.

Even if it's simply sitting on the porch, watching the sunset and listening to the birds as the dog sniffs the waning summer air, I know that this is a victory. At least for myself I've built my own little world, and all the money on our decaying planet can't buy that. I live with decency, relative security and self-respect. But I can't truly have any of it until my neighbors do, too.

———

I had just finished what was likely to be the final mowing of my lawn before the winter came. Woods was sitting in his truck and called me over when the mower went quiet. He was in the driver's seat smoking.

"What's up?"

"Climb in here a second."

I sat on the passenger side and lit my own.

"Did you check the auction for that house next to you this year?" Woods asked.

"Yeah. It wasn't on there." Whoever owned the LLC had paid the taxes, or something more nefarious was going on, always a possibility in Detroit but it wasn't listed.

"Did you notice anything else?"

"No, not really."

"The Terrys' house is going to be up for auction."

"What, how?"

"I don't think the missus knows. The house is registered in the old man's name, and he hasn't been all there for a while." He tapped his temple. "The dementia. I doubt she has any idea they're behind."

"So did you tell them?"

"No, not yet. You know she doesn't have any money and you know she ain't no good at the Internet."

"When are you going to tell her?"

"I wanted to talk to you first. I have an idea. You have any money?"

"Some."

"I'll talk to her, but we might need to buy that house back. They've been great neighbors, and I would hate to lose them. I think we'll be able to get it back for five hundred, but we have to put a two-thousand-dollar deposit down to make any bids at all. I don't think anyone would bid on that house. We can split it fifty-fifty, and we can put it in her name, so she gets the bills."

I thought of all the barbecues I had been to at her place, all the times she'd offered encouragement, watched over me while I was working, and the first day I'd met her, when she'd given me, a stranger, a drink on a hot day.

"Oh, Jeezus," I sighed. "Yeah, I guess I would be able to do that. Just two hundred and fifty?" I lit another cigarette. "All right, sure. I can probably come up with that. You talk to her, though, and see what she has to say."

Me and a new foundation

CHAPTER 12

Someone Else's Home

Detroit has become home

Someone had placed a $500 bid on the house. I'd been watching the auction in the weeks leading up to the final countdown and couldn't believe it. I sat there looking at the computer for a moment. This was going to be much more complicated, and maybe way more expensive than I had hoped. I placed a bid of $600. I thought about that soldier at the auction where I bought my place, bidding for his family against the Greek with deep pockets. I wondered what had happened to him, if he had found a home after all.

I called Woods to let him know, and we decided not to tell Mrs. Terry. I made some calls to see if there was any way I could find out who the opposing bidder was, and explain to them the situation. There was nothing. Whereas before you could see, in real time, who was bidding on properties, just that year the county had stopped it. I guess some speculators were a bit nervous about all the attention they made buying up homes, including those of people who live in them and had owned them for more than thirty years.

I e-mailed everyone I knew and splashed social media with a plea that if anyone was, or knew who was, bidding on this particular house to contact me so I could explain.

No one knew. I did receive a huge outpouring of support from the Internet, though. People who I barely knew or didn't know at all offered to donate money. Volunteers from different states, and even different countries, offered to help in any way they could. The first Latina city council member in Detroit called me asking if she could help. Friends whom I hadn't spoken to in years phoned me, asking to donate or pitch in somehow. One gentleman in London, a graphic designer, made a flyer from what I had written and tailored it to Twitter. I'd never heard of him before and haven't since. He just sent it to me and asked for nothing. Unfortunately I didn't have any infrastructure to take donations and the bidding price hadn't moved. I was still the top bidder, and I was hoping it would hold out.

One of my former coworkers at the French restaurant had opened his own coffeehouse, and I went there to use the Internet and watch the end of the auction. I told Woods to be on standby near the phone while he was at work, in case something happened. There were thirty minutes left to closing, and if the price stayed the same, the Terrys' house would be safe. At fifteen minutes I thought we were home free. Surely whoever had placed the first bid recognized the house was occupied and the better angels of their nature had prevailed.

Ten minutes.

Five minutes.

A bid.

The war for our humanity is upon us. It is personified by our politicians, our interactions on the Internet, in tens of thousands of people
losing their homes in places like this, in the violence wracking our
country, the gun deaths once tolerated only in Detroit broadening
to suburban enclaves all over America. It's on the front page of every
newspaper in the country.

But it is not lost. Not yet. As spring approaches I have more wood
to cut for the fire, a garden to put to plant, and more friends to help
fix up their own homes. The water from an overtaxed sewer system
floods my basement and again I pump it out. The city installs more
streetlights and old habits die hard. Spring's cyclical rebirth is upon
us and the inevitable change of the season is at hand.

As before a summer thunderstorm, the air is heavy with the
coming transformation, the rain, the lightning, the release. Things
cannot stay this way for long. The souls of the people are angry,
they are hungry, uncertain of the future. The people are becoming
desperate, yearning for some kind of hope, any kind, a way out, a
way through. They know it in their bones, in the hunger in their
stomachs, the crumbling of the roofs over their heads. The fire is
lit and the pot will boil.

It is your sacred duty to find hope somewhere, anywhere, and keep
trying to make that world in which you wish to live. I don't succeed
at it every day. But I try, and know I must keep trying. The thing
is, there are a lot of people who feel just like you. You're not alone.

I find hope within the sanctuary of the walls of this house, nailed
into each and every board I placed myself, screwed into every light
switch, flowing out of each faucet. But it is bigger than that, and does
not reside only there. It's located in the hard muscles I've gleaned
from the lifting, in the keenness I've gained from the figuring, in
the confidence I've earned from the struggle, in the bonds I've made

with my neighbors through work and hard times and celebration. What I've gained, nobody can take away from me and money cannot buy. No fire or billionaire can crush it into the ground.

I haven't yet been able to build the world I want to live in outside the walls of my own house. But I've seen it. And *I'm* not alone. My neighborhood, this city, this country is *filled* with people who haven't been beaten. As you read this, Paul Weertz might be driving his tractor. Will might be playing his banjo in a circle of friends, singing and laughing and making merry in the face of destruction. The neighbors might be firing up the barbecue or the Kemps growing food in their garden, feeding some young searcher ground cherries and courage.

And I'm still here. I'm still fighting. I haven't given up, succumbed to cynicism, ironic detachment, or absurdism. The one thing I'm proud of is I haven't been beaten. Not yet. I've tried to stand up for what I believe and what I thought was right, and this city and this world have not broken my spirit.

Right at this moment I might be banging on this old house, cursing and sweating and bandaged, hoping I can make my corner of this earth a little kinder, a little warmer, and a little bit more cheery. I have no idea if I've made any difference at all. Maybe I've made things worse. But I tried. If it all blows up in my face and my house burns down, or I get kicked out, or I make a fool of myself in a myriad other ways, I know that I did the best I could with what I had. Our only failure can be trying nothing new. I haven't given up yet, and the game ain't over. I live free. I'm still here.

The sneaky bidder was trying to wait just until the end in hopes I wasn't watching and snake the Terrys' house out from us. I made a bid of $700 and called Woods. For each bid recorded in the last five minutes the clock would start over. He bid again. As did I.

"Hello."

"Hey, Woods, someone else is bidding on the property."

"No."

"Yep. We have to decide how much we're going to be able to spend."

"Who the hell would be bidding on an occupied house, I mean—"

"Woods, there's no time. He just placed another bid. It's at one thousand dollars right now. Should I bid again?"

"Yeah."

I clicked.

"We have to make a decision here, buddy. We going to go up to fifteen hundred, two thousand?"

"I don't know, fifteen hundred, I guess."

"It's climbing again."

We bid.

"It's at fifteen hundred right now, Woods, what should we do?"

"Go ahead and do it."

Seventeen hundred.

Eighteen hundred.

"I can go as high as two thousand, Drew, I don't think I can afford any more."

It's a funny thing, deciding, in U.S. dollars, how much good neighbors are worth. To put a price, a dollar amount, on how much someone's security, the only home in the world they have, costs. Do unto others, right? Love your neighbor, right?

Right?

Well, in dollars, how much do you love your neighbor?

"It's at two thousand, Woods. What do we do?"

"Do it."

"This is so fucking stressful, this is so fucked up." I clicked the button.

"He bid again. It's at nineteen hundred. Do we go up to twenty-five?"

"I don't know, Drew, I don't know where this money is going to come from. Go ahead and do it, I'll figure something out."

$2,000.

$2,100.

$2,200.

I never got the chance to find out for myself how much my neighbors were worth. As a great man once wrote, only those who fall over the edge truly know where to find it. Woods and I purchased the house for $2,300.

I ran back to the Terrys to tell them we had got it. Woods had told the missus we would be bidding on the house that day, and she was home waiting. The inside of her home, the one I momentarily owned, was cool and dark. Mrs. Terry played with a grandbaby in a diaper, her boys at work, but her brother was sitting with her, reading the family Bible. When I told her, she cried. She said she would find a way to pay me back, somehow. Later, I'd receive it, too, fifty, a hundred dollars at a time.

I ran back and forth to get all the paperwork right, and decided to put the house back in the Terrys' names. Everyone I had talked to beforehand told me to put my name on the deed until I got paid back, but I didn't want to hold someone else's house hostage. I had a thought, just a glimmer, to fill in my name on the deed. I could have, I would have been well within the law to do it. I had paid for it. But I put the house in Mrs. Terry's name, along with one of her sons. It was theirs. I owned it for about an hour.

Afterward someone remarked, "That's very George Bailey of you," referring to the film *It's a Wonderful Life*. That movie had a happy ending, right?

Right?

I was lucky. This was the first time in my life I had any savings and could have done something even remotely like that. Their house and security was paid from the advance for this book you hold in your hands.

Loaning them the money was a small act, just one house, and one family, and frankly it's not enough. The problem is systemic, not personal. I realize ending the book in this manner plays right into the white-savior narrative. But the struggle is not over, this isn't the end. Detroit is out there, places like this all over the world are out there. I have no tidy endings or easy solutions to offer you. We have to do what we can, and when you dedicate a life to attempting to expand the possible, anything can happen. I may have saved one house, and my neighbors and Detroit might have saved me, too. I know that's cliché, but it's true. What matters is we did it together, that we pull one another up out of the mud of fear and mistrust of our fellow man, together. If we work with one another we can win.

———

That very evening I was relaxing on my couch. My shoulders were sore from hunching over the computer all day, and the tension of the sale. A fire was going in the woodstove. Someone from Forestdale said he had been able to buy an abandoned house just up the street from me in the same auction. I was going to have a new neighbor. I heard a car horn once, then a couple of times.

Someone was really laying on it now. It was continuous, a good two minutes of horn. I considered getting up and telling whoever was doing it to cram it, but I figured it was just a kid and said forget it, I'll wait it out.

Woods called.

"What's on fire?"

"What?"

"Something's on fire. I just stepped outside and something's on fire, by you."

I put on my shoes and ran outside with Gratiot. I thought maybe a spark from my chimney had lit the abandoned house next door. I smelled smoke, and considered going back in for the extinguisher but decided against it.

I couldn't see any fire next door. I went into the alley. I could see black smoke, and thought it might be my neighbor Andi's place.

"What's up, Woods?" I could see him in the alley just ahead of me. We turned into the lot between Andi's and the abandoned house. The fire was on the northeast corner. A car was in flames. I heard it pop. Then a small explosion. I put my arm up to shield my face. The car was really going, the flames two stories high. If the fire department didn't get here fast it was going to take the house and maybe the one across the street with it.

I turned back to get the dog, who had followed me, into the yard. Two young men walked down the street and said something to me I couldn't hear. Gratiot jumped the fence again and I put him in the house, but for some reason I stopped and got the mail as the fire raged behind me. I called the fire department on my way inside and they told me they were en route. I laid the mail on the counter and looked at who it was from, strangely calm. Andi called and I told her I'd be over.

She was in her bathrobe as we watched from her porch. The neighbor from across the street, now Sawtooth Betty, was on hers, and she crossed the road to stand next to us. King came down, too, and gave me a cigarette. A crowd of teenagers watched it from the street, and one of them kept saying, "I just got out of jail." The fire department arrived and put it out. An arson investigator did not stop by.

When it was all over Andi returned inside and King went home. Sawtooth Betty asked me to give her a boost through her window because she'd forgotten her keys.

As she stood on a plastic chair, I laced my hands and gave her a leg up, and I held the window as she wiggled through. I put the chair back on the porch and went home. I decided it was a good night to check my smoke detectors.

When I woke up the next day the house still smelled like burned rubber. I pulled on my jeans and boots and got ready to hang the Sheetrock in my office. As I opened my windows to let in some fresh air, I heard a reassuring sound. Children were playing in the new playground of the Boggs School, their tiny golden voices echoing throughout the neighborhood like bells. I listened to them for a moment before I headed to work upstairs, something to behold and kept as a gift until it moved again, the great wandering of hope on the American frontier.

Can you hear it?

"I feel sorry for people who are not living in Detroit. Detroit gives a sense of epochs of civilization in a way that you don't get in a city like New York. It's obvious by looking at [Detroit] that what *was* doesn't work. People are always striving for size, to be a giant. And this is the symbol of how giants fall."

"People are aware that they cannot continue in the same old way but are immobilized because they cannot imagine an alternative. We need a vision that recognizes that we are at one of the great turning points in human history when the survival of our planet and the restoration of our humanity require a great sea change in our ecological, economic, political, and spiritual values."

"These are the times to grow our souls. Each of us is called upon to embrace the conviction that despite the powers and principalities bent on commodifying all our human relationships, we have the power within us to create the world anew."

"We are the leaders we've been looking for."

—Grace Lee Boggs, 1915–2015

Acknowledgments

This book would be nowhere near its final form without the kind, even, and often brilliant guidance of my editor, Colin Harrison. I thank him dearly for pushing me so hard. I also wish to thank my agents, Jenni Ferrari-Adler and Shaun Dolan, for their tireless work, enthusiasm, and encouragement. My most sincere gratitude to them for believing in a blue-collar kid from Michigan.

This book would not have been possible without Sandra Allen, both for taking a chance on this story in its infancy as a feature for *BuzzFeed*, and for profound edits along with Steve Kandell.

I would like to thank the many people who supplied art for this book, including Kehben Grier, Kinga Kemp, Garrett MacLean, Amy Philp, and Mike Williams. Thank you to Dan Cuddy, Sarah Goldberg, Kyle Kabel, Elisa Rivlin, and Paul Whitlatch at Scribner for making this happen.

Joel Peterson and Rebecca Mazzei have long been great patrons of the arts in Detroit and have generously extended that support to me in many ways. A very special thank-you is due them, my Detroit community, and everyone between these pages. I would particularly like to thank the Weertz family, especially Paul, and everyone else on Forestdale for feeding me, helping with the house, and caring for me as if I were family.

I would also like to thank everyone who has helped me along on this journey—book, house, and otherwise—Pat Ahrens, Andy and Sara Bailey, Mark Binelli, Ben Bunk, Eric Froh, Siobhan Gregory,

Sarah Hayosh, Nate Izydorek, Duryea Johnson, Chris Jones, Jerry Klein, Sam James Levine, Andrew Marok, Monté and Erin Martinez, Molly Motor, Steve Neavling, Chris Powers, Dave Roberts, Matt Temkin, Elaine Thompson, Mary Lee Thompson-Goldsmith, G. Richard Thompson, Char-Lene Wilkins, Mike Williams, James Woods, the 555, the Adrian Center for the Arts and Luke Barnett, Kevin Miller and Atlas Plumbing, the Thomas Philp family, the Terrys, Zach Massad and Randy Voss and the Motor City Brewing Works, and everyone else who got dirty or bought drinks on my behalf. It takes a village. Rest in peace, Matt Davis.

As this is my first, I would like to thank the teachers and mentors who grew me from nothing into a person who could even consider writing a book: Buzz Alexander, Charles Behling, Diane Cook, John Lowe, Oyamo, Jeffery T. Schultz, John Cox, and Chris George and everyone at the *Bakersfield Californian*. I very much appreciate your guidance and support when I was just beginning to think about writing professionally.

Readers of early drafts included Heidi Kaloustian, the Kemp family, Meg Lemieur, Karen Lewis, Mike Medow, Diana Nucera, Dave Torrone, and Mary Kate Varneau.

This story also drew on the work of scholars, activists, and storytellers including Grace Lee Boggs, Mark Binelli, Dan Georgakas and Marvin Surkin, Bill Wylie-Kellermann, Monica Lewis Patrick, and Thomas J. Sugrue. The Boggs quotes at the end of this book first appeared, respectively, in *American Revolutionary: The Evolution of Grace Lee Boggs*, documentary, 2013; as approved by Boggs in 2006 to Robert Shetterly for his painting series *Americans Who Tell the Truth*; from an article entitled "Seeds of Change" that Boggs wrote for *Bill Moyers Journal*, 2007; as told to the author and nearly everyone else Grace came in contact with.

And finally I would like to give immeasurable thanks to my

family, without whom neither my house nor this book or anything good in my life would be possible. A very special thank-you to my parents, Amy and James, in particular, and to my grand-parents, at whose kitchen table much of this book was written. I love you all.

Photo Credits

Photos courtesy of the author, except:
   Pages 1, 9, 67, 175, and 275 courtesy of Mike Williams
   Pages 95 and 123 courtesy of Garrett MacLean
   Page 147 courtesy of Amy Philp
   Page 273 courtesy of Kehben Grier

CPSIA information can be obtained
at www.ICGtesting.com
Printed in the USA
LVHW090058240822
726678LV00002B/150